GRIZZLY SEASONS

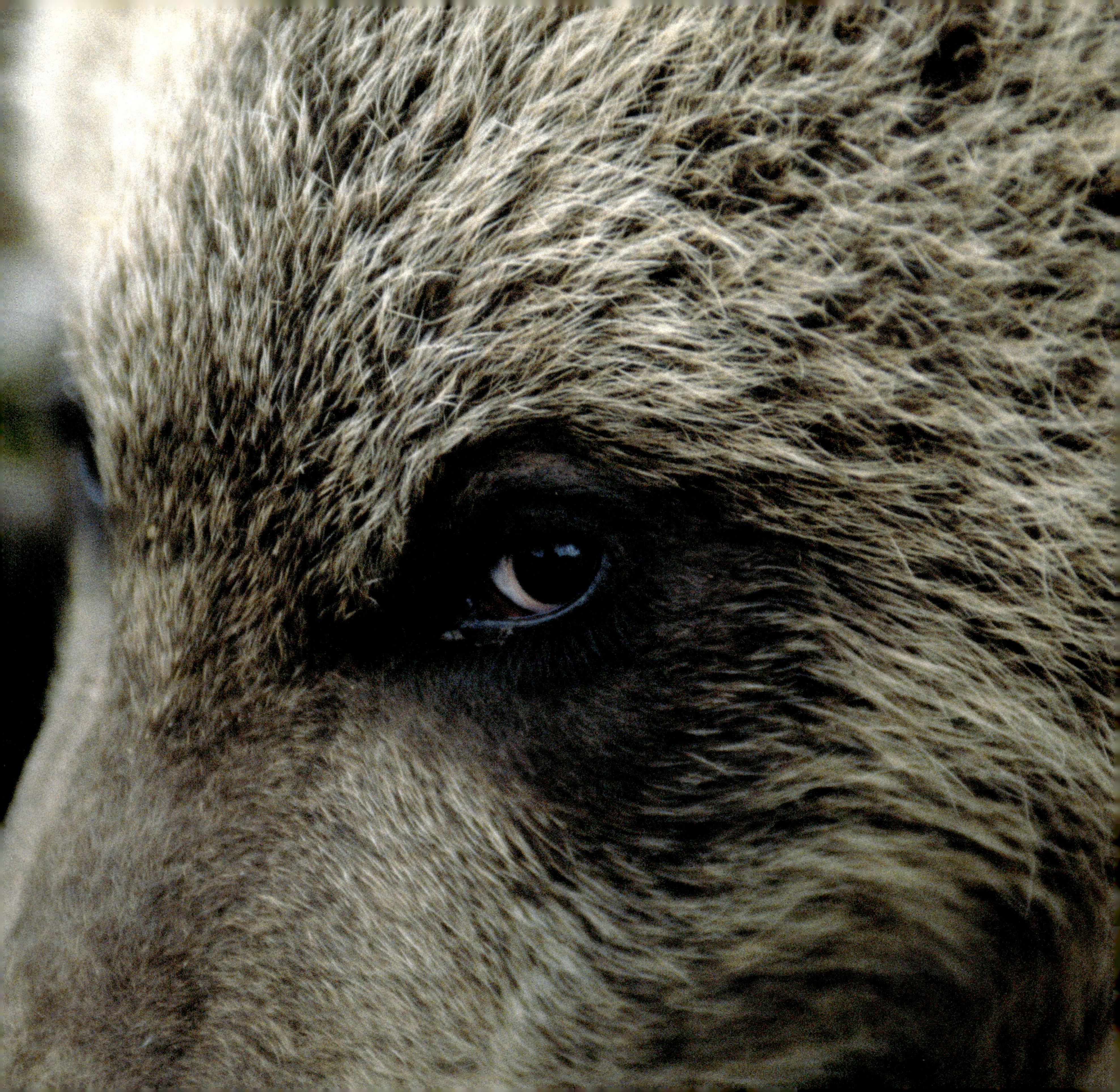

GRIZZLY SEASONS

Life with the Brown Bears of Kamchatka

CHARLIE RUSSELL
AND MAUREEN ENNS

RANDOM HOUSE CANADA

 Published in 2003 by Random House Canada, a division of Random House of Canada Limited, Toronto. Distributed in Canada by Random House of Canada Limited.

Random House Canada and colophon are trademarks.

www.randomhouse.ca

National Library of Canada Cataloguing in Publication

Russell, Charles

Grizzly seasons: life with the brown bears of Kamchatka / Charlie Russell and Maureen Enns.

ISBN 0-679-31221-8

1. Grizzly bear—Russia—Kamchatka Peninsula—Pictorial works.
2. Human-animal relationships. 3. Russell, Charles. 4. Enns, Maureen. I. Enns, Maureen II. Title.

QL737.C27R873 2003 599.784 C2003-900654-9

Jacket and text design: Daniel Cullen
Printed and bound in Belgium

10 9 8 7 6 5 4 3 2 1

Contents

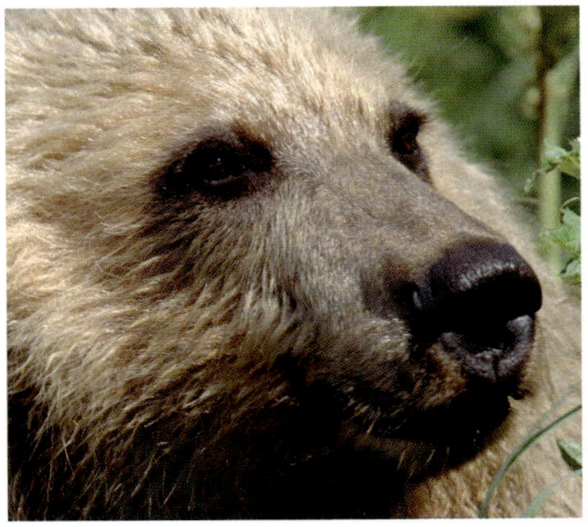

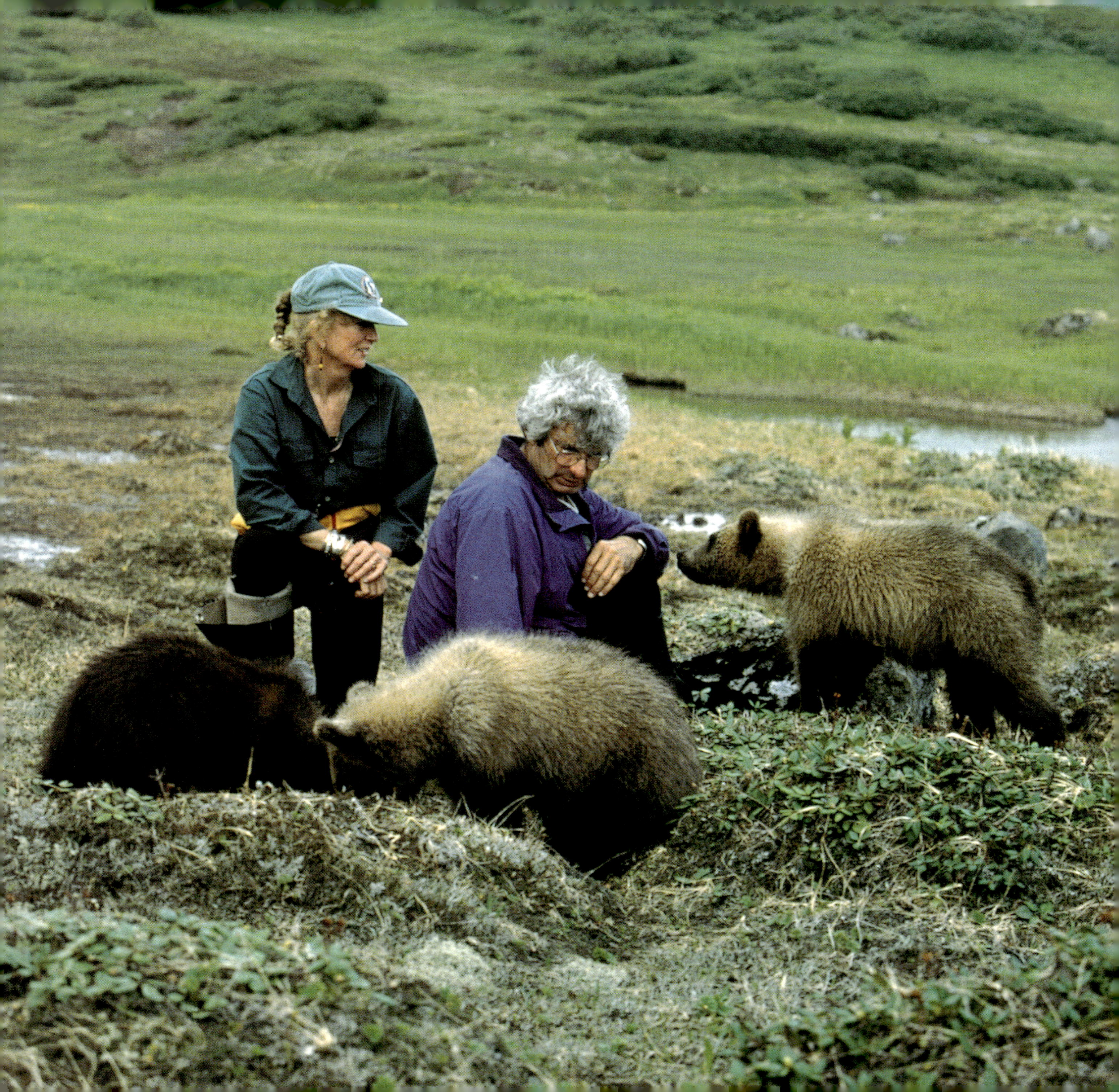

Introduction

I can't imagine a world without bears. For the past seven years my partner and I have been privileged enough to live for five months of the year in a remote wood-frame cabin we built in the South Kamchatka Sanctuary, Siberia. This varied and beautiful landscape is home to the world's densest concentration of brown bears, formidable creatures who travel well-worn paths through the tundra from their winter dens down to crystal-clear waters that will become rich with spawning salmon.

For myself, a naturalist and guide born on a ranch in Alberta, I've spent over forty years studying the nature of bears and our human reponses to them. I have had the great fortune to have been joined in this, my life's work, by Maureen Enns, an artist and photographer. Maureen's first feelings were similar to those of most people, who feel fear and apprehension in the face of these giant, mysterious animals. But luckily, Maureen is the kind of creative, curious person who knows that understanding is the most important step towards conquering fear.

Photo: Igor Revenko

What Maureen and I felt instinctively was that bears were not as dangerous and unpredictable as their reputation suggested. We felt that a great part of the problem has been that, ever since humans became organized enough to do such things, grizzlies have been managed, almost exclusively, in a way that assumes these characteristics are absolute. In a sense, bears and people have been deliberately trained to fear each other, in order to keep them a safe distance apart. This policy has been particularly troublesome for bears, because grizzlies and humans both need the same type of productive land—and the grizzly most often loses in competition for it.

We thought it would be helpful for bears if we did a study that would question the central assumptions about them. Whatever a grizzly is up to, its actions are considered threatening to humans who encounter them. But many years of watching them had suggested to us that they might really be peaceful animals, not vicious predators. That they occasionally strike out could in fact be a result of incessant human reactions to them based on fear. It is surely true

Sanctuary, and is one of the last great wildernesses in the world. We have never fully understood why we have been tolerated by our Russian hosts as long as we have in this strange and distant country, but the seventh year of our study has proven more enlightening than we had ever dared to hope.

We came to understand that the bears in our study area, whom we hoped would be innocent, in actuality had had encounters with poachers over the years, so they were very fearful of us at first. But they soon began to relax when they saw that we were not overly interfering with their lives. We never allowed ourselves to make mistakes, such as letting them into our food, because living well together required being hassle-free both ways.

In our second year in Russia, our project became meaningful in a whole new way: we were able to rescue three very small orphaned cubs from a zoo and bring them to our cabin, where we looked after them until they could be on their own. Since then we have remained a part of their lives. It was the first time such rehabilitation had been done successfully, that is, without the bears becoming dangerous to humans. Our work with the cubs has been—and still is—the most critical focus of our study, and has hastened the process of our understanding the subtleties of the true nature of grizzlies.

Typically, as our study progresses, we identify more questions needing answers. For instance, having to feed our cubs when they were young meant we were led into the thorny debate surrounding the issue. It is widely assumed that "a fed bear is a dead bear," meaning that every bear that tastes human food becomes obnoxious. But we discovered it is possible to feed bears without them becoming dangerous, if it is done in a systematic and careful way. More work must be done in this area, but often bears starve from natural food failures, and hundreds could be saved by knowing how to feed them in an appropriate manner.

With the success of the cub reintroduction project, we've also recognized the importance of ensuring that the South Kamchatka Sanctuary remains a safe habitat for bears. It's wonderful to experience the bears' openness to our presence, but unless we are able to change human attitudes, our work cannot be considered complete. Our presence in the sanctuary has discouraged much of the poaching that was happening prior to our arrival, but we worry that when we complete our project, our study

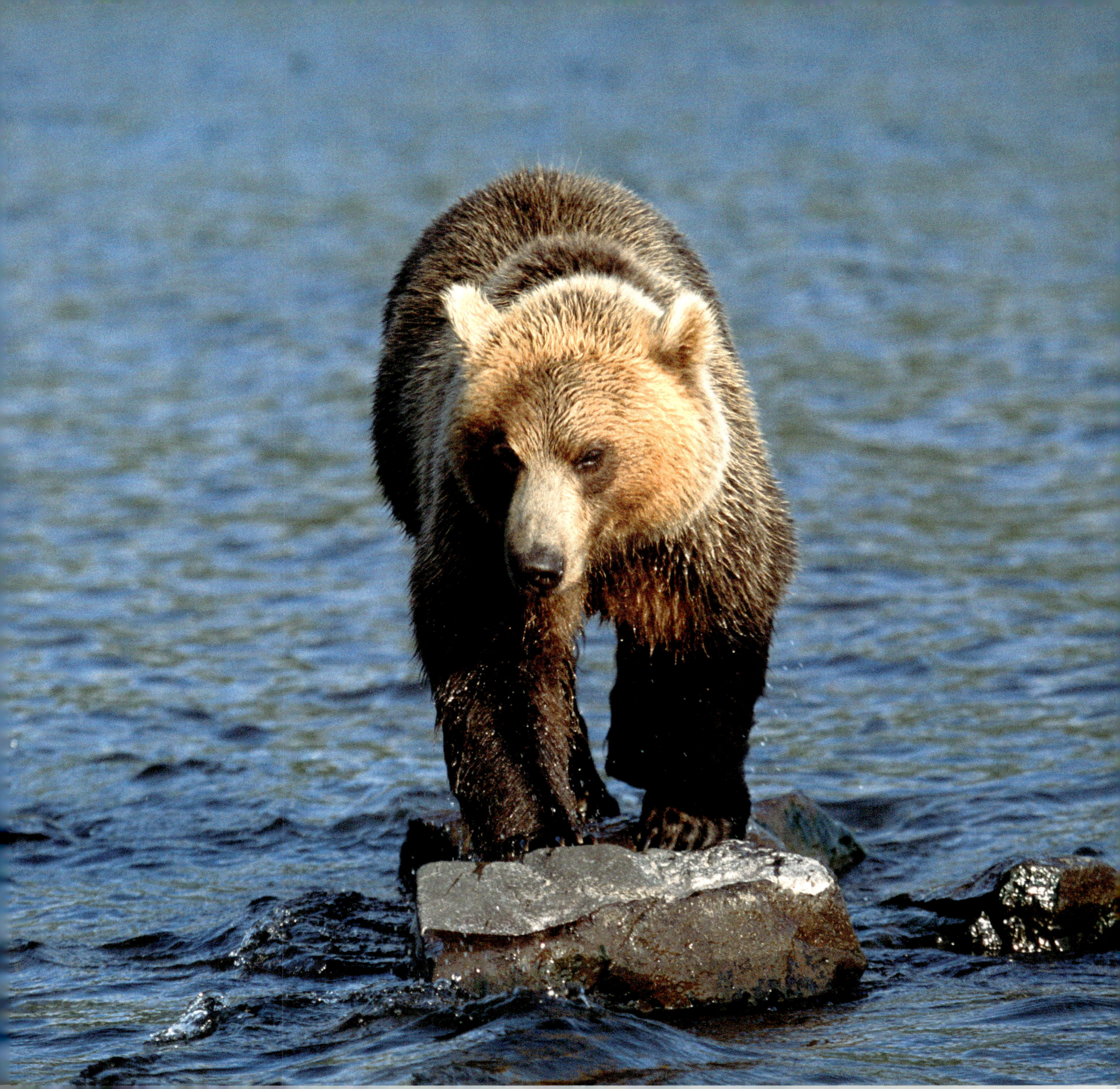

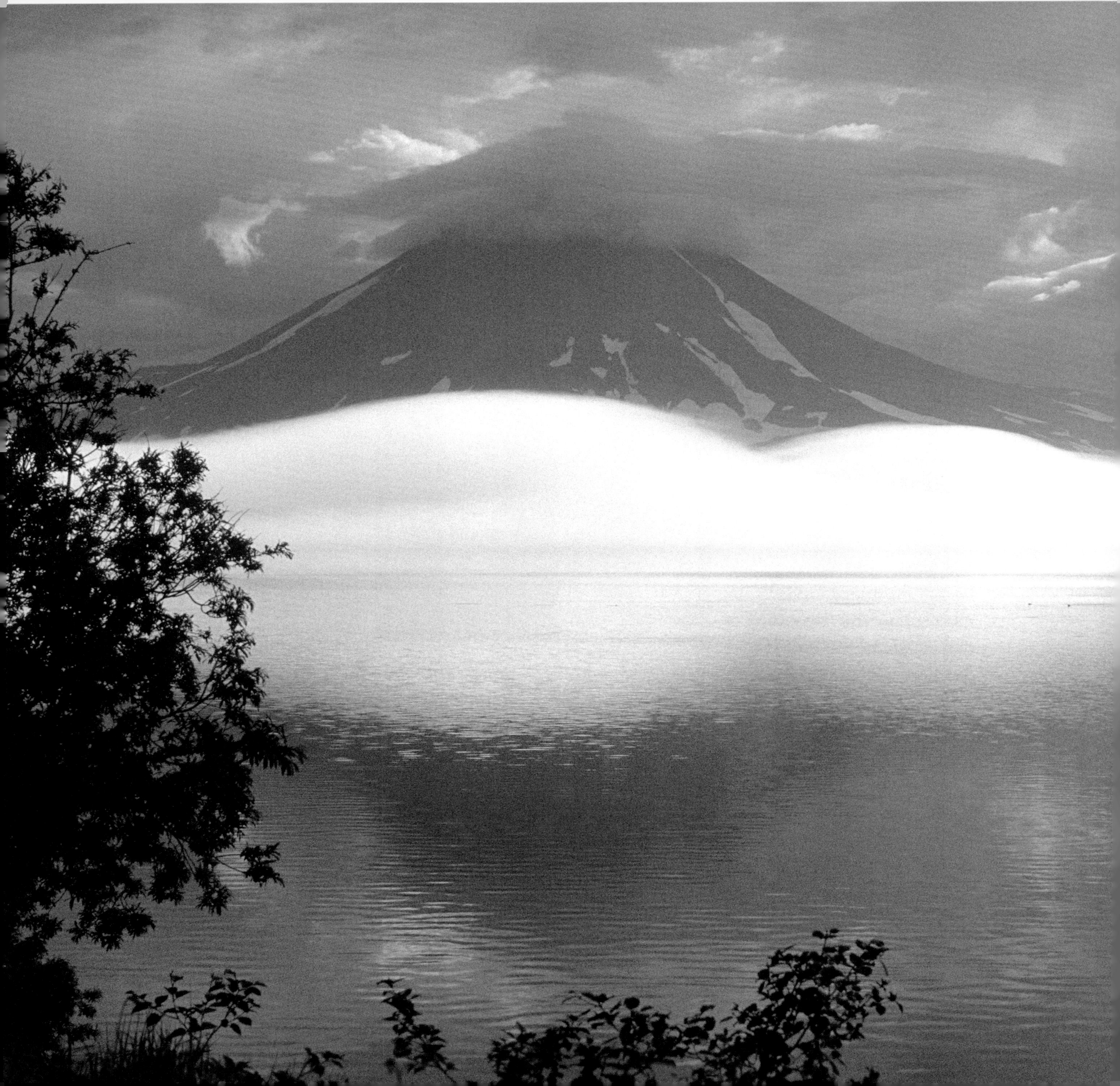

Discovering Kamchatka 1994-1996

We first travelled to the province of Kamchatka in the summer of 1994, with only a vague idea of what we would find there, and we were dazzled by what a precious jewel it was. The place was virtually unknown, even by Russians, and had been almost entirely protected by its remoteness. There are no roads or railways joining Petropavlovsk, Kamchatka's one city, with the rest of Russia.

The most startling of the region's features are its two hundred volcanoes, many of which are active. One of these, the Kluchevskoy Volcano, rises 15,600 feet above sea level, and is the highest active volcano in Eurasia. Lush greenness, highlighted with colourful washes of wildflowers, carpets the mountainsides. The clear rivers are so full of salmon it looks as if you could walk on top of them to get across. And everywhere you look are Asian brown bears, stuffing themselves on an incredible variety of foods, including salmon.

The only way to travel the whole of Kamchatka is by helicopter, which we did, from one end of the thousand-mile-long province to the other. Away from the city, we learned these were difficult, almost desperate times. The Soviet Union had only recently broken up and social conditions were changing quickly—and not always for the better. Most governmental jobs in Kamchatka, including those with the military, had vanished, and when the value of the ruble tumbled many citizens were left destitute. These people had to find new ways to live, and the Southeast Asia bear-gall trade was one of the very few sources of income available to them. A poacher we befriended calculated that from his fishing village alone, he and four others had killed a thousand bears in three years. The poacher even agreed with us: the bears could not possibly survive such pressure for long.

When we visited Kurilskoy Lake in the south, we discovered that the situation there was not as grim. The lake was located within the South Kamchatka Sanctuary, a somewhat protected zone dedicated to wildlife preservation

A summer evening at Kurilskoy Lake.

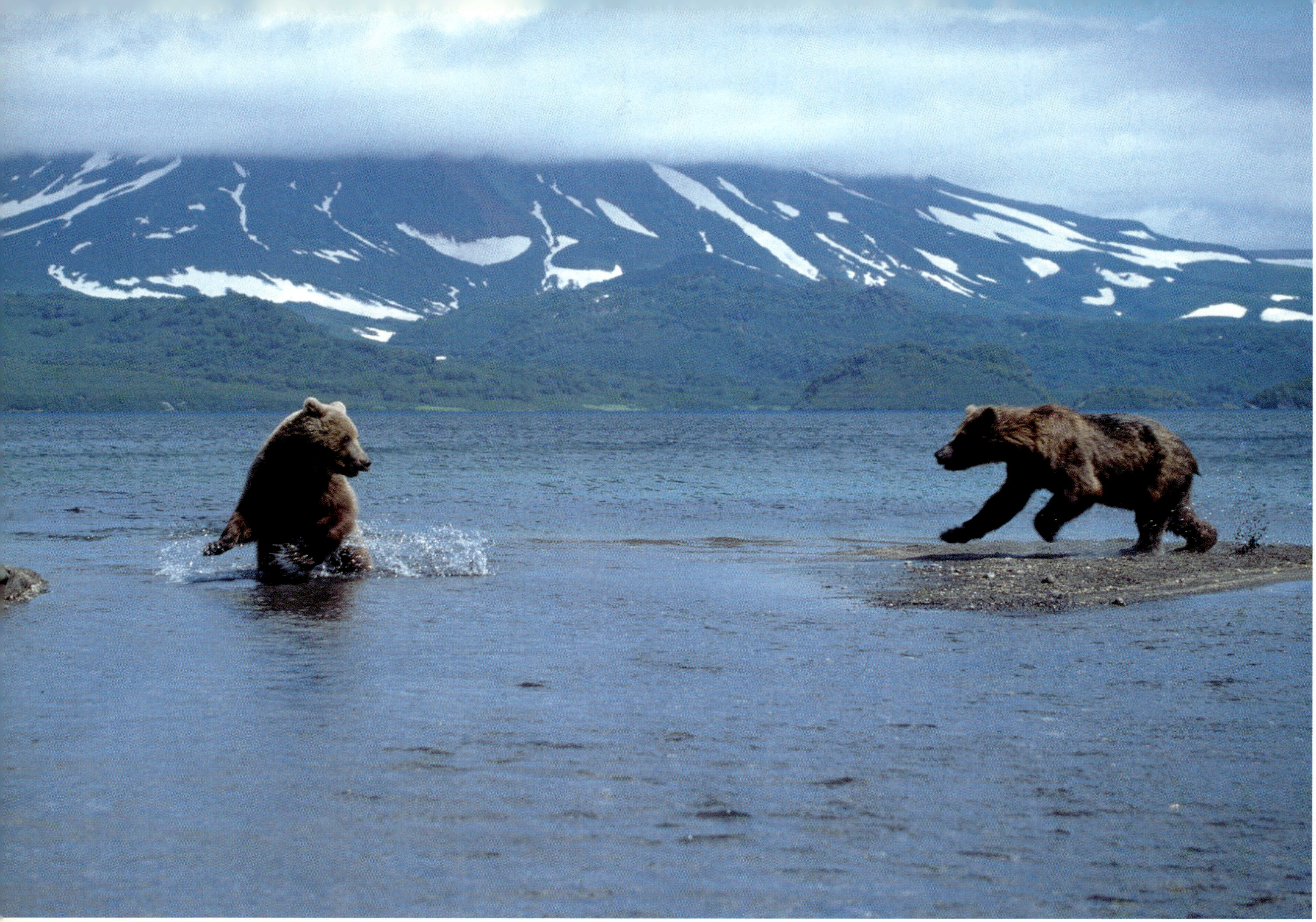

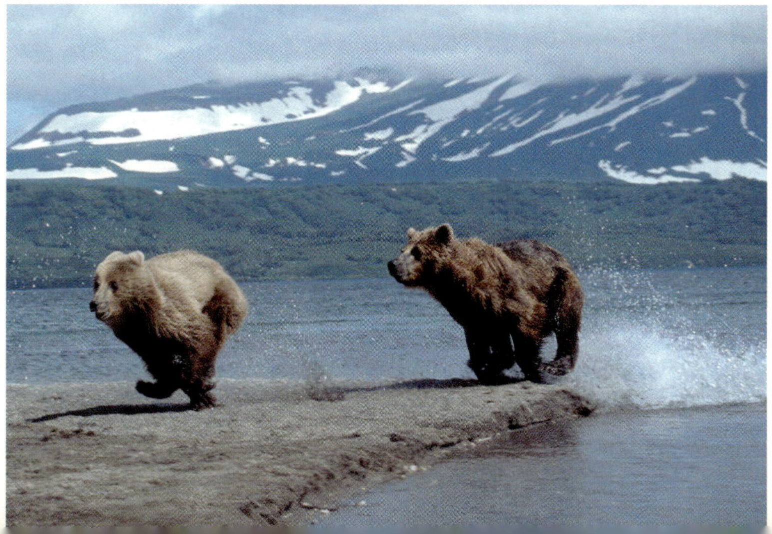

The shore of Kurilskoy Lake is a major thoroughfare for bears. By sitting quietly, one can observe a lot of bear behaviour in a very short time.

Here, a young bear gets too close to a cranky female at the mouth of one of the many salmon streams. Spurts of sand—appearing to be standing straight up—show the high speed at which the bears are moving.

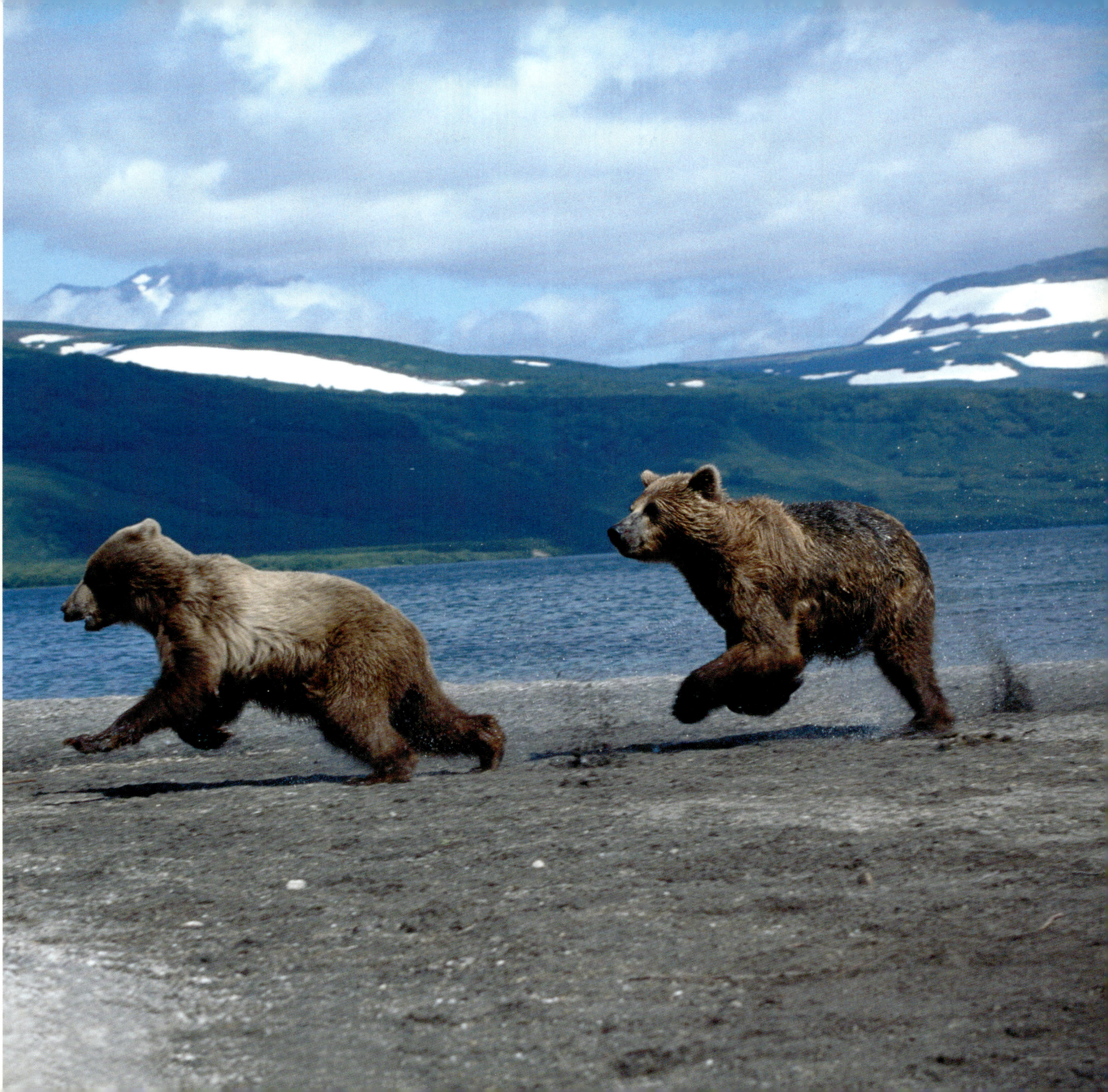

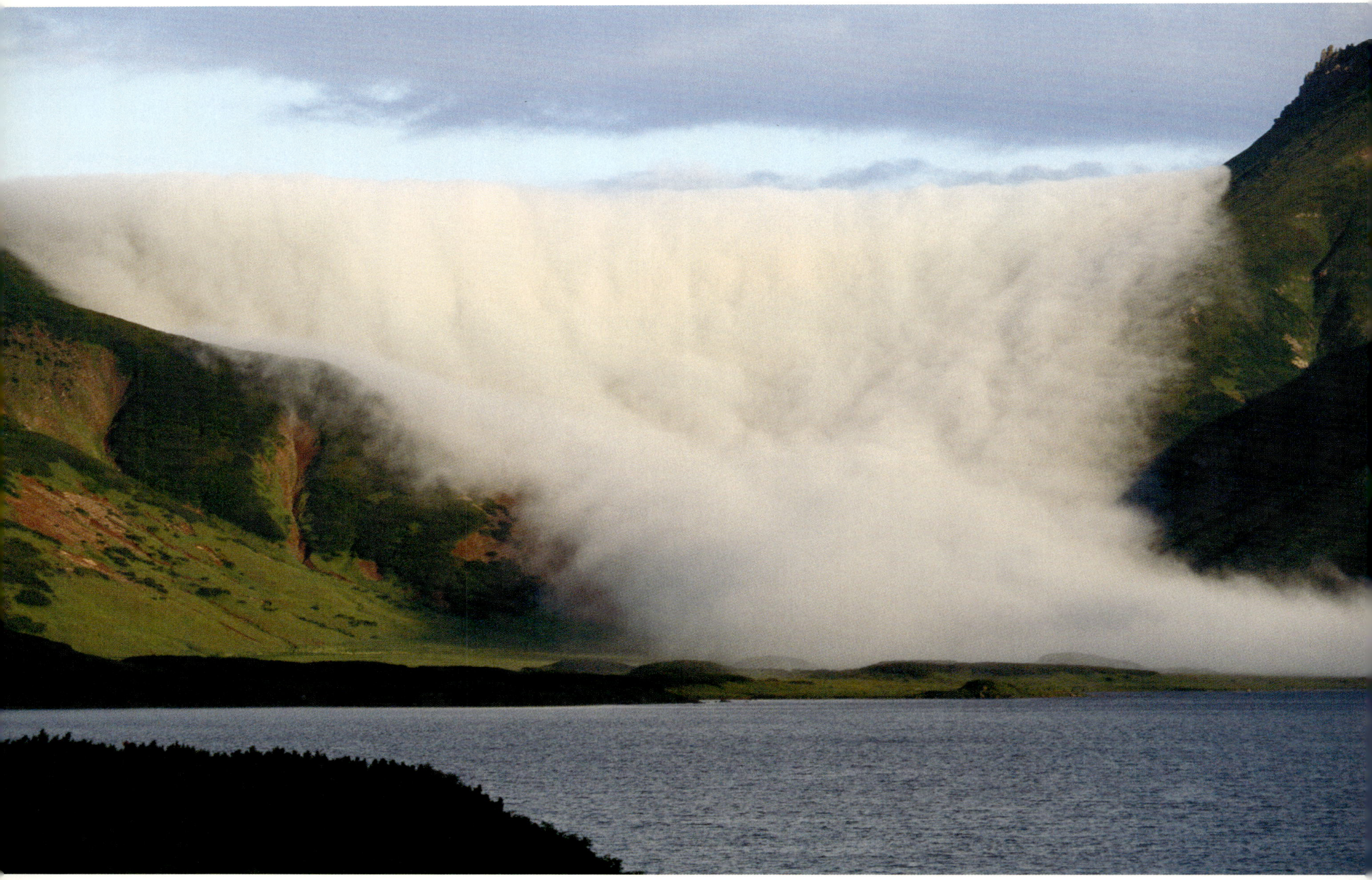

As seen from our porch, fog pours over the divide from the east, signalling a coming storm.

and scientific research. There were some signs of poaching, but the area appeared to be a bears' paradise in comparison to sites farther north. In one afternoon alone, we watched fifty bears fishing for salmon. In the evenings, after we too had stuffed ourselves with salmon, we huddled around the campfire talking to Igor Revenko, a biologist studying bears in the sanctuary. After carefully considering our proposed study and its stringent site requirements, Igor suggested Kambalnoye Lake, describing it as "the forgotten place." Only twenty-five miles to the south of Kurilskoy Lake, it sounded ideal for our project: remote, undisturbed, and populated by many, many bears.

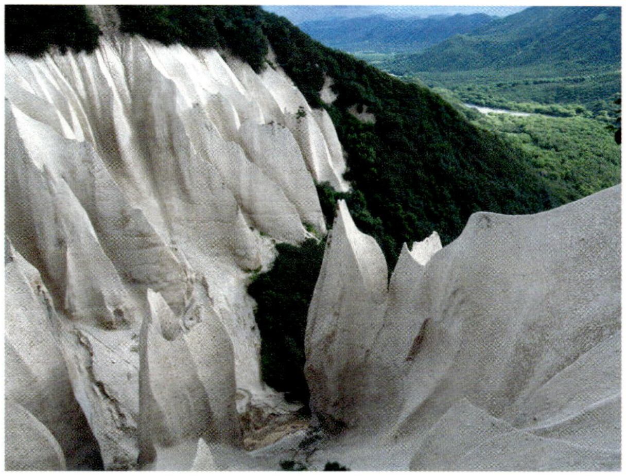

Due to bad weather, we could not visit Kambalnoye that summer, and it was not until 1996 that we finally were able to build a cabin there and begin to settle into the landscape. Amazingly, Russian officials allowed us to bring a Kolb aircraft and enjoy the extraordinary sights and freedoms flying afforded. Nothing happened for miles around our basin that we did not see happen. The views were breathtaking: Kambalnoye Volcano towered over us, and tundra plains stretched out beneath us all the way to the Sea of Okhotsk.

Igor had been right. There were bears everywhere: in the breakers of the two oceans to either side of us, high on the mountain slopes that surrounded us, and strung out along the river that spilled from Kambalnoye Lake. But we had a big problem. These bears were all very afraid of us, and we caused stampedes wherever we showed ourselves. This reaction was certainly not what we had hoped for, but we had already committed ourselves to seeing this project through, in Kamchatka. We had to start the process of forming some kind of rapport with the hundreds of bears, no matter how shakily our relationship with them had begun.

On the bright side, Igor Revenko gave us encouraging news. The price of gall in China

Volcanic pumice is easily carved by wind and water, and is as light as balsa wood. We've watched large pieces float down rivers to the sea.

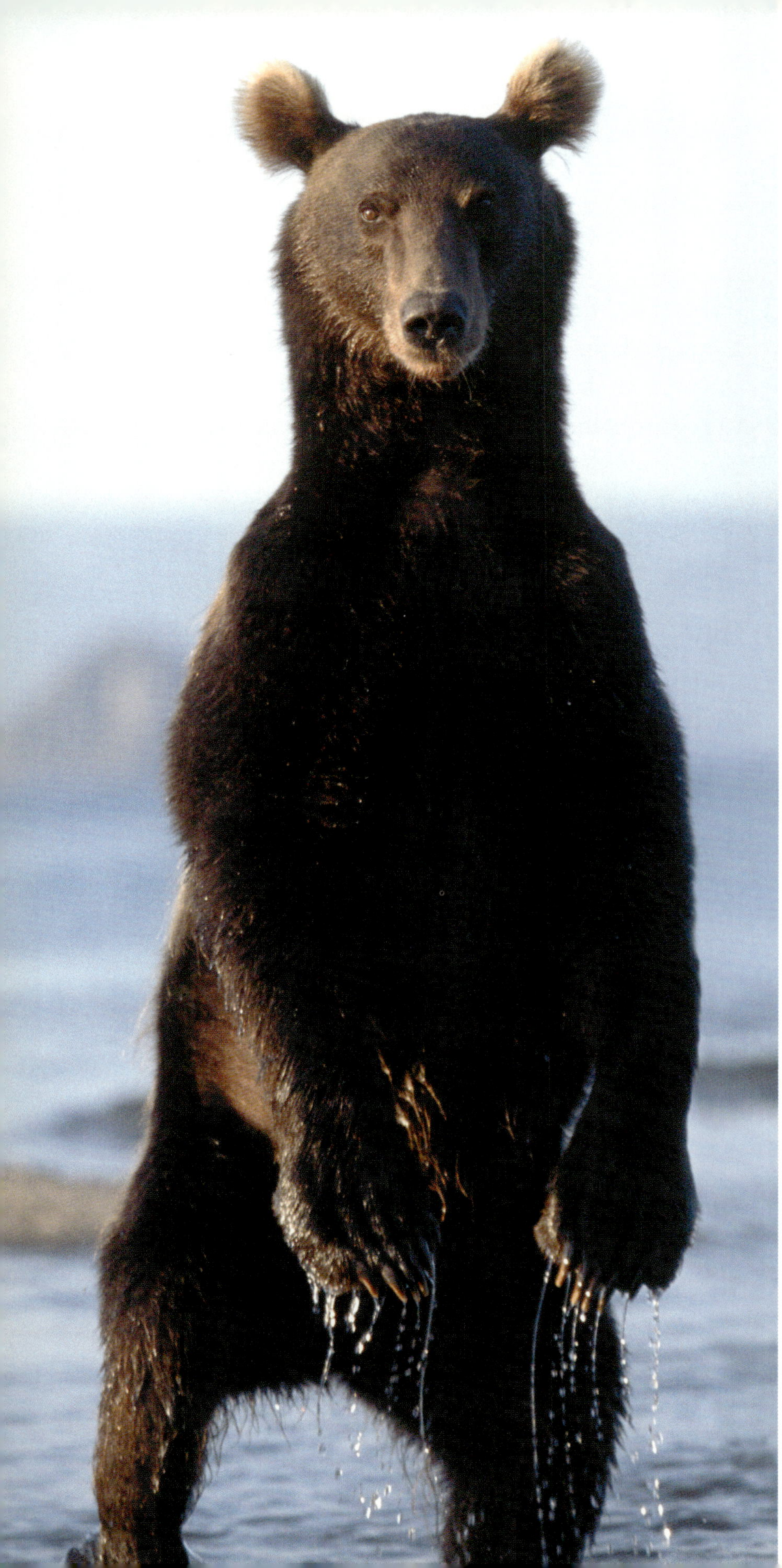

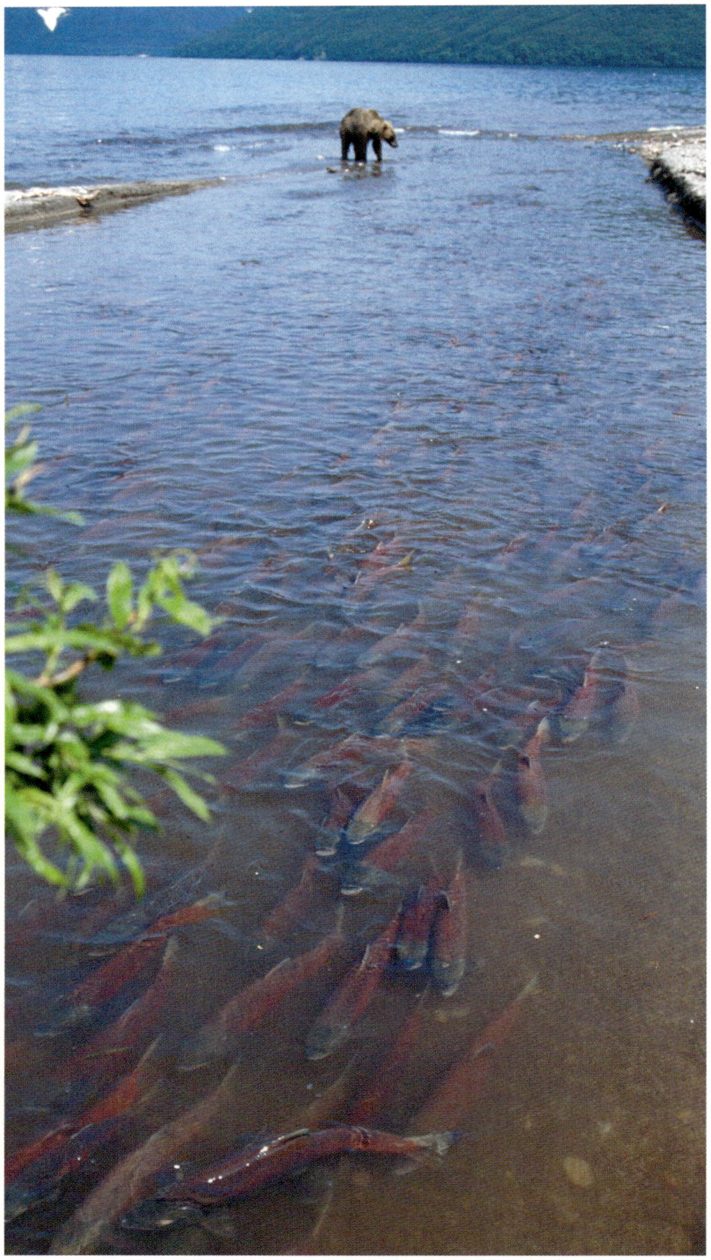

The sockeye at Kurilskoy Lake are so numerous that bears will just sit and watch them—until they finally become hungry enough to eat again.

Thinking that we may have caught a salmon right under his nose, a lanky male stands up for a better view. Only his ears have yet to shed their winter fur.

was dropping, and many poachers were turning to salmon fishing instead of killing bears. We hoped this change would be permanent.

Conventional thinking insists that bears that don't fear humans are inevitably dangerous, and to date most grizzlies that had decided to live near people had died for their transgressions. We had to show the world that this did not have to be the case, and in order to ensure a future for the grizzly, we had to do it soon. But in this respect, the first year of our study had been a failure. Much of what we wanted to understand depended on living among bears that were not afraid to explore a relationship with humans. With so many still afraid of us, it was clearly going to take a long time to earn the trust of a meaningful number of bears.

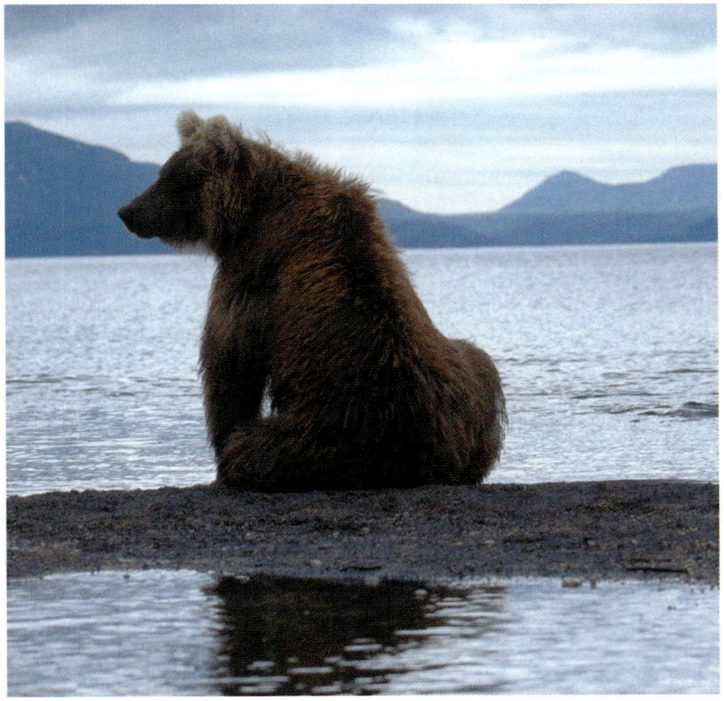

Heading home to Canada at the end of our first season, we knew that we had to find a new approach, so we stopped in Petropavlovsk to make a request of the Director of Preserves. Every year there were cubs orphaned by hunters and poachers, and the zoo was where they ended up, entertaining people until they outgrew their cages and were killed. We asked that the following spring we be allowed to take any available cubs to our cabin, to be reintroduced into the wild. To our surprise, the director was open to the idea, so we spent the winter planning how to spend our second season as new parents. The prospect of raising cubs was exciting; if it happened, our learning about bears would accelerate tenfold, and if we were successful, it would be the first time grizzlies would make the transition from a zoo environment to being truly wild.

A mature female rests at the shore but remains alert to her surroundings. We named her Sitting Bear because that was how she spent much of her time, enjoying the view across the lake.

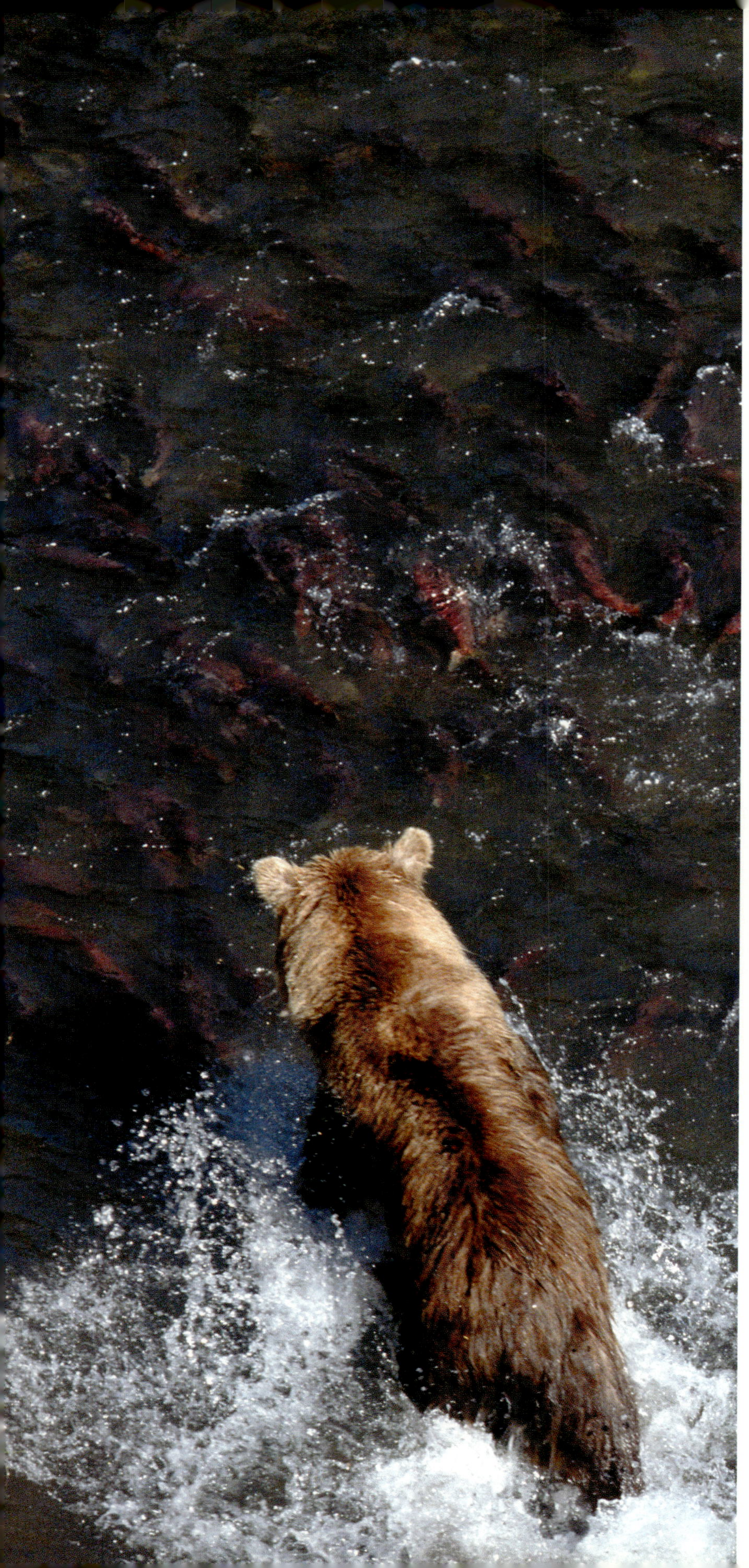

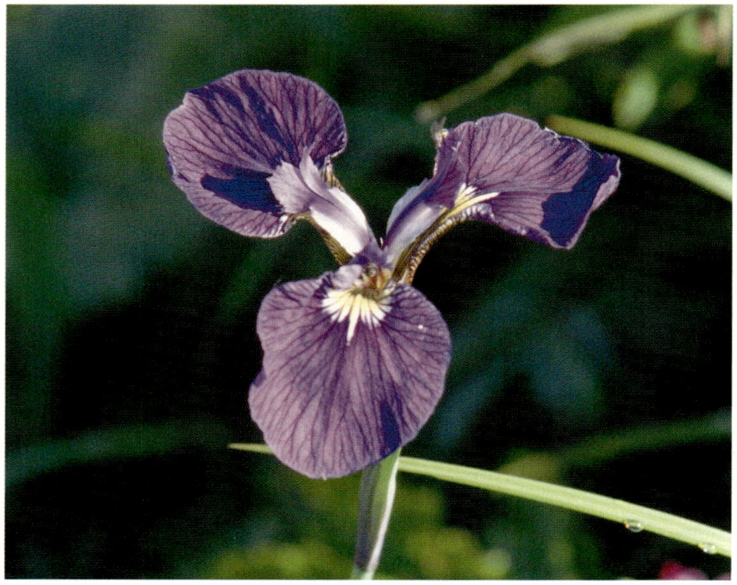

Irises will bloom from the middle of July and into October in areas where snow lingers.

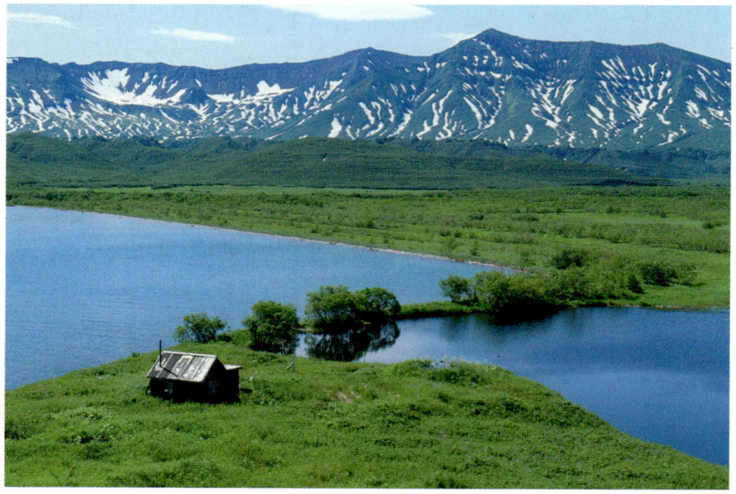

Igor Revenko's cabin on the shore of Kurilskoy Lake. Kambalnoye Lake is twenty-five miles over the ridges to the south.

Kamchatka's severe winters with deep snow and cold winds are redeemed by the bounty of the summers. Bears' ability to sleep for six months makes it easy for them to thrive in the region.

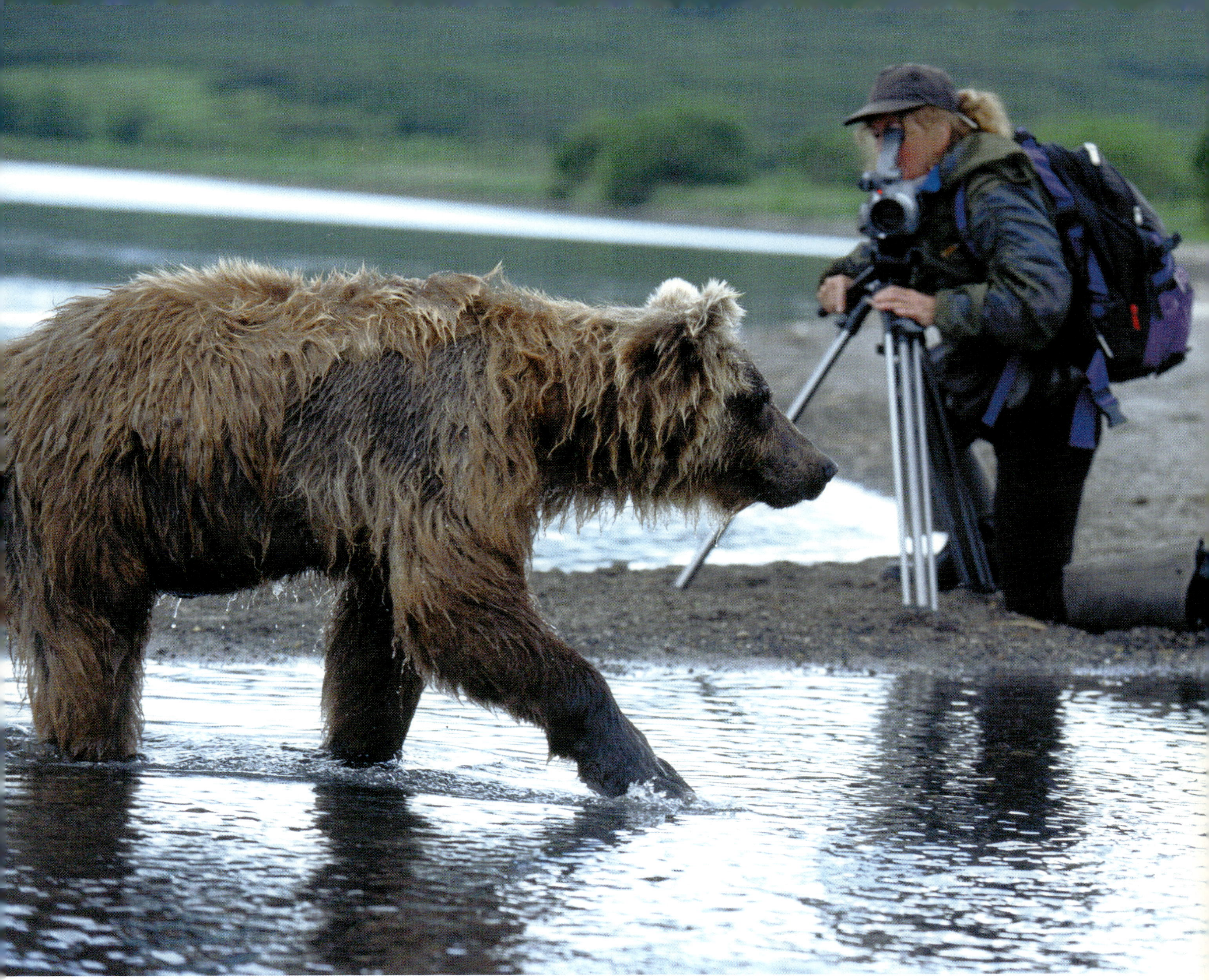

When Maureen was working on a documentary about grizzlies in the Rocky Mountains of Alberta, she would go weeks without seeing a brown bear. In Kamchatka she could photograph fifty in a day.

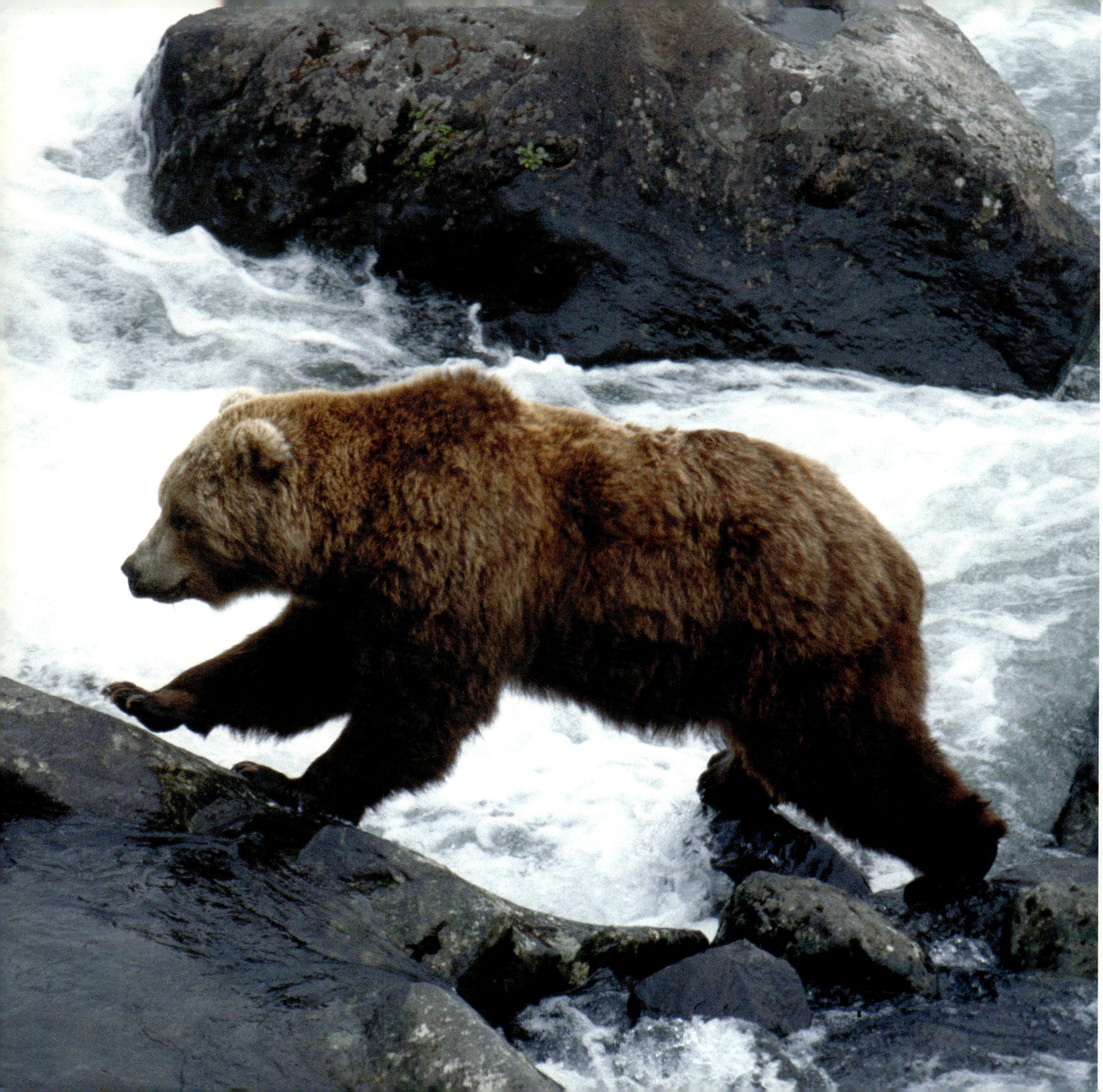

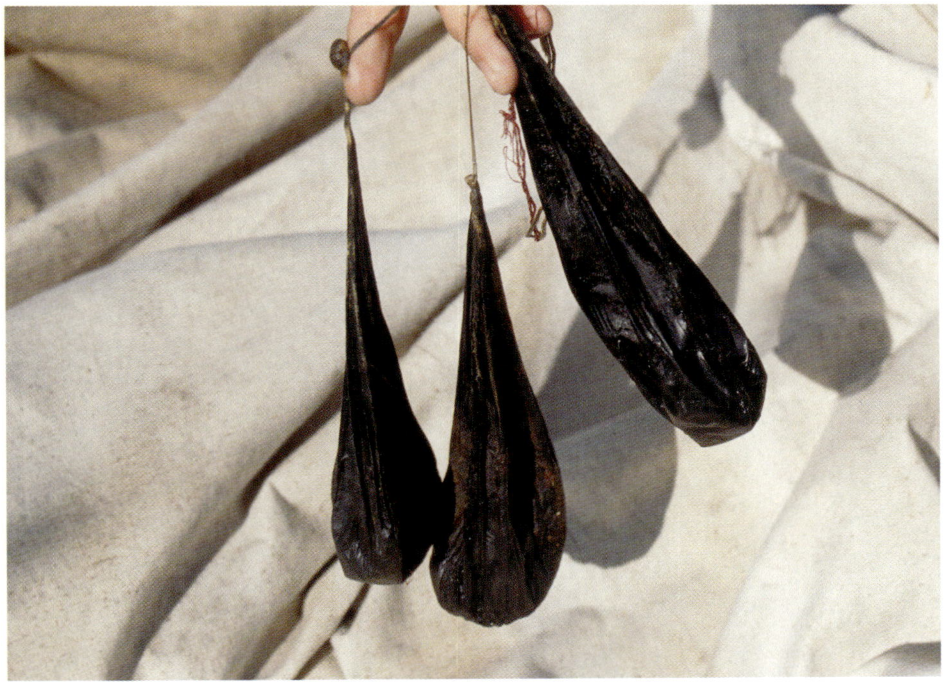

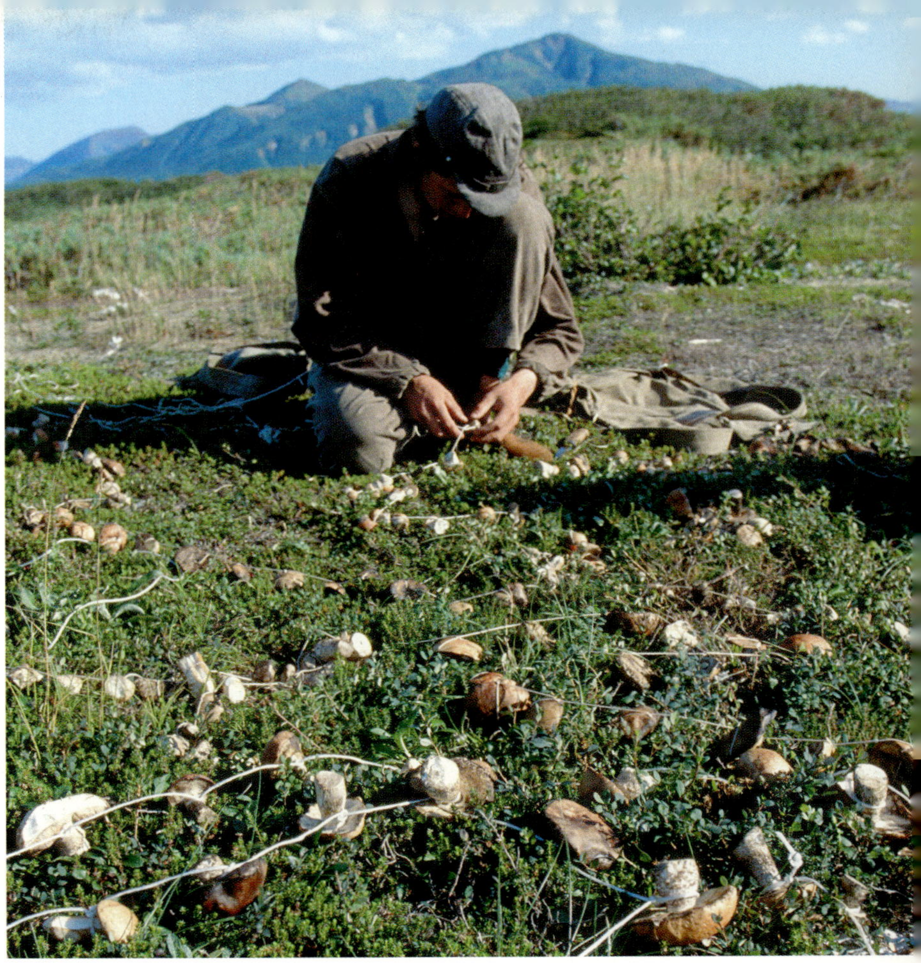

A young Itelmen gathers mushrooms for drying. The Itelman were indigenous to the area around Kurilskoy Lake. Eventually they were forced to pay a tax of sable skins to Russian conquerors, so they moved north to forested areas.

It was not a perfect world for the bears of South Kamchatka Sanctuary. Poachers took advantage of world markets to supplement their meagre incomes by killing bears for their gallbladders, which are sold into Southeast Asia as a traditional stomach medicine.

An Itelmen hunter's bag, displaying eagle feathers and a wolf skull.

The big males spend most of their time at the river. A bear will even sleep all night on a favourite perch, so as not to have to reclaim it the next day.

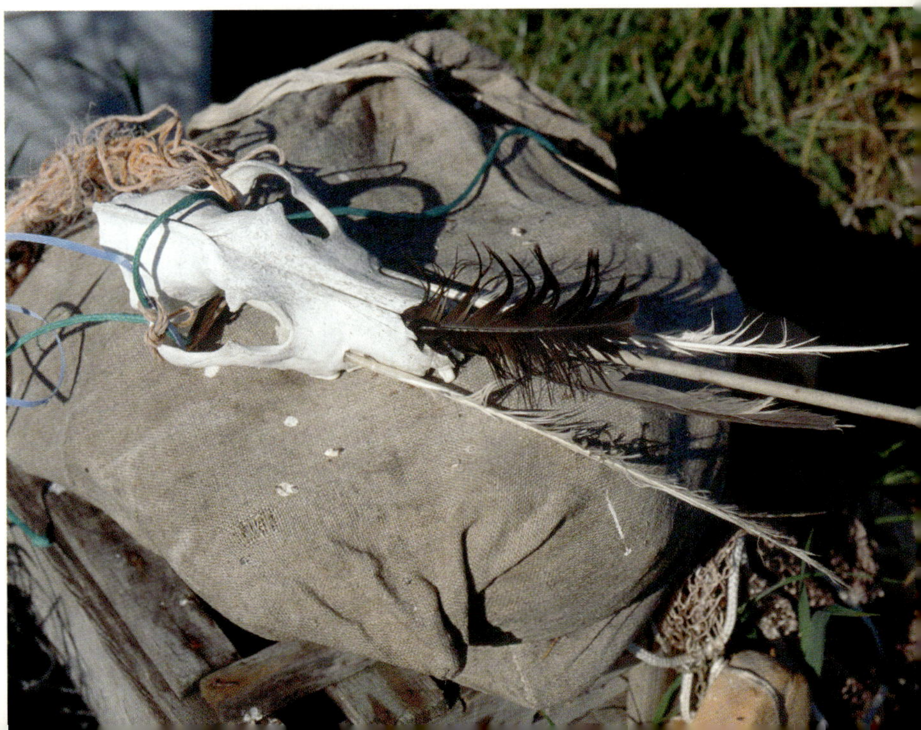

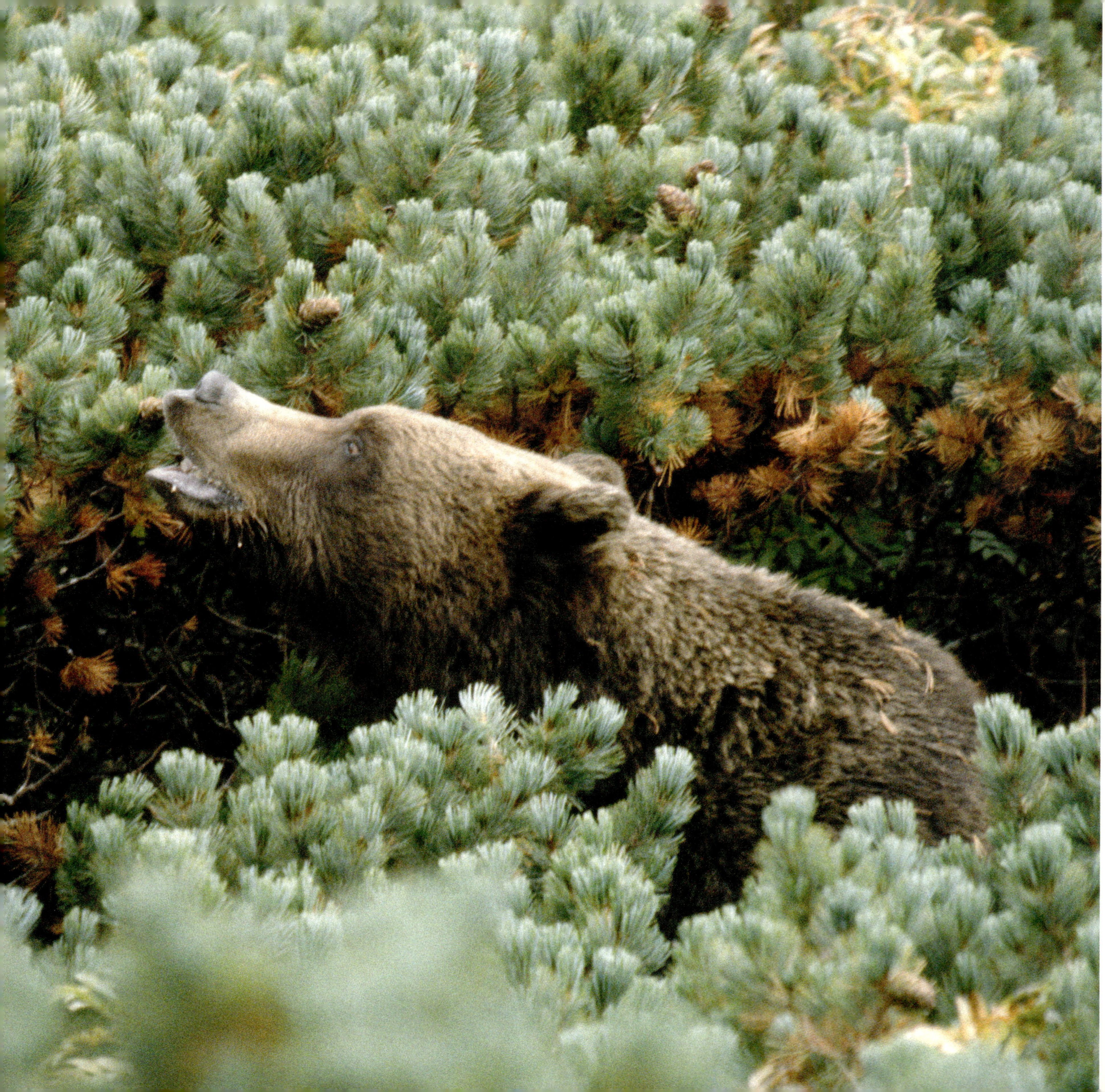

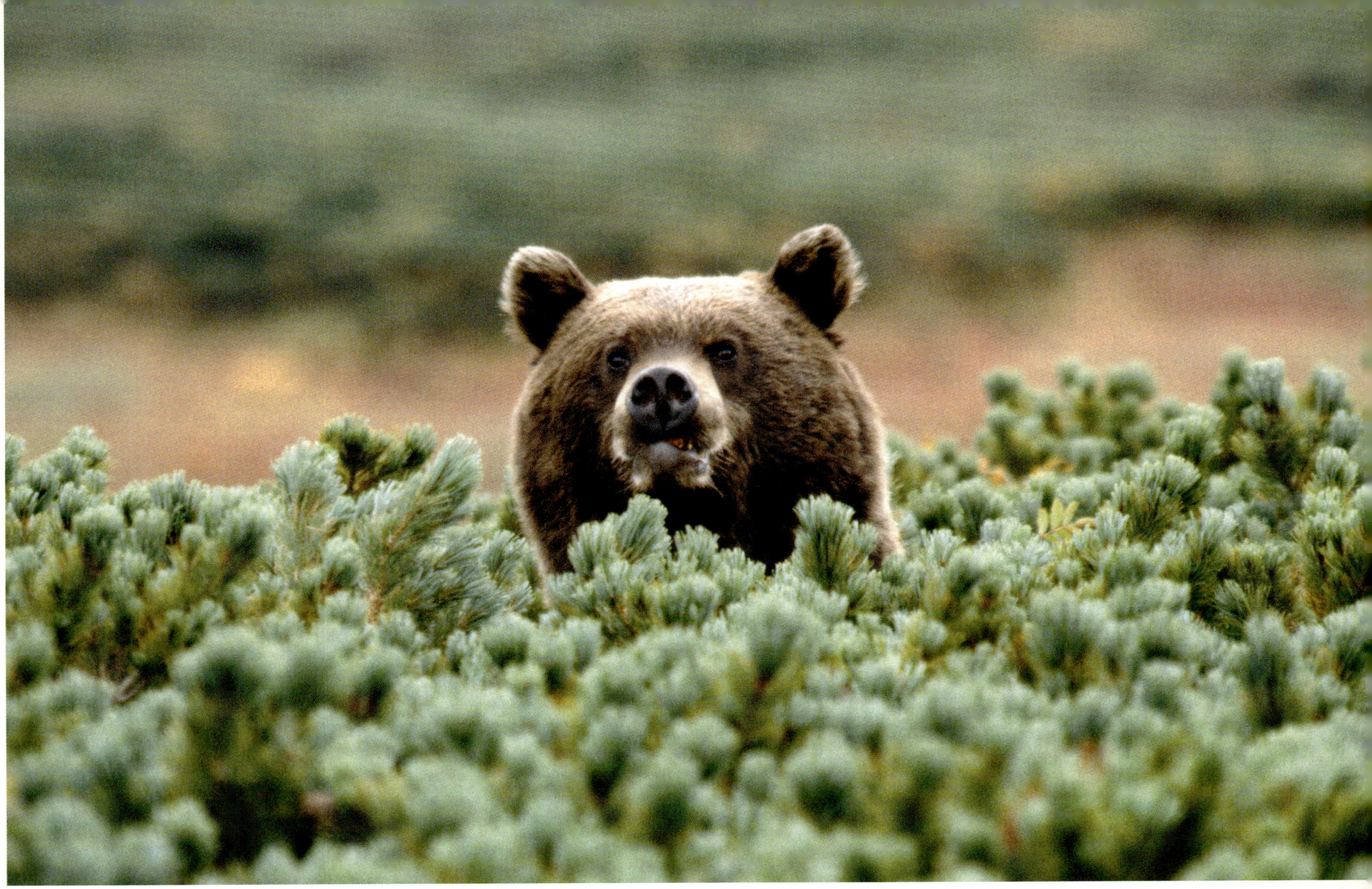

In September, brown bears will cease fishing for a week or more to disappear into the pines to eat nuts. Some Kamchatkan bears never eat salmon; all of them eat pine nuts.

Bears have several ways of removing nuts from cones. This female is using her tongue to roll the cone around in her mouth until the nuts fall out. She then spits out the husk like a wad of chewing tobacco, and breaks the nuts with her teeth so they can be digested more quickly.

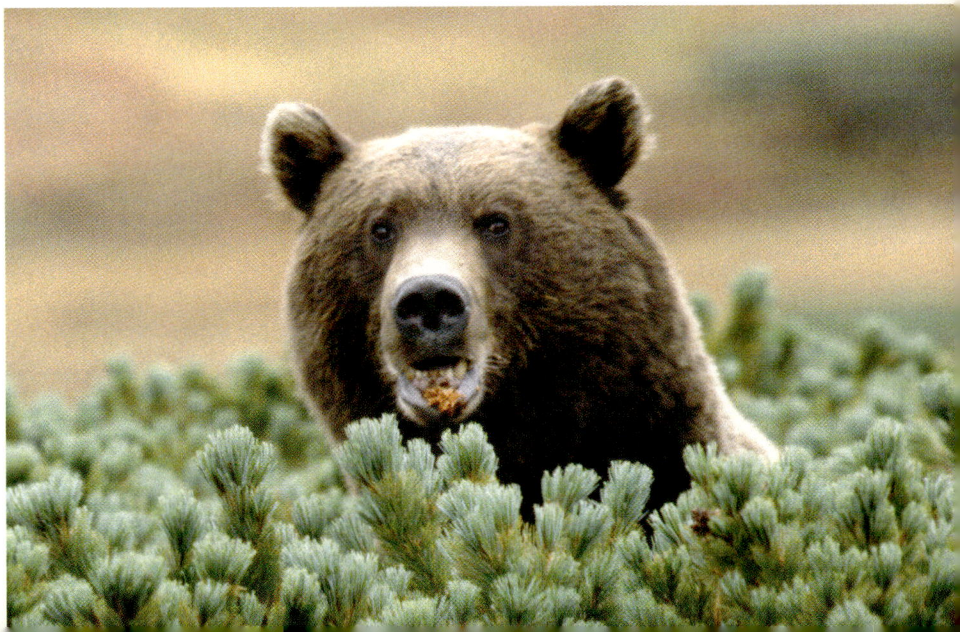

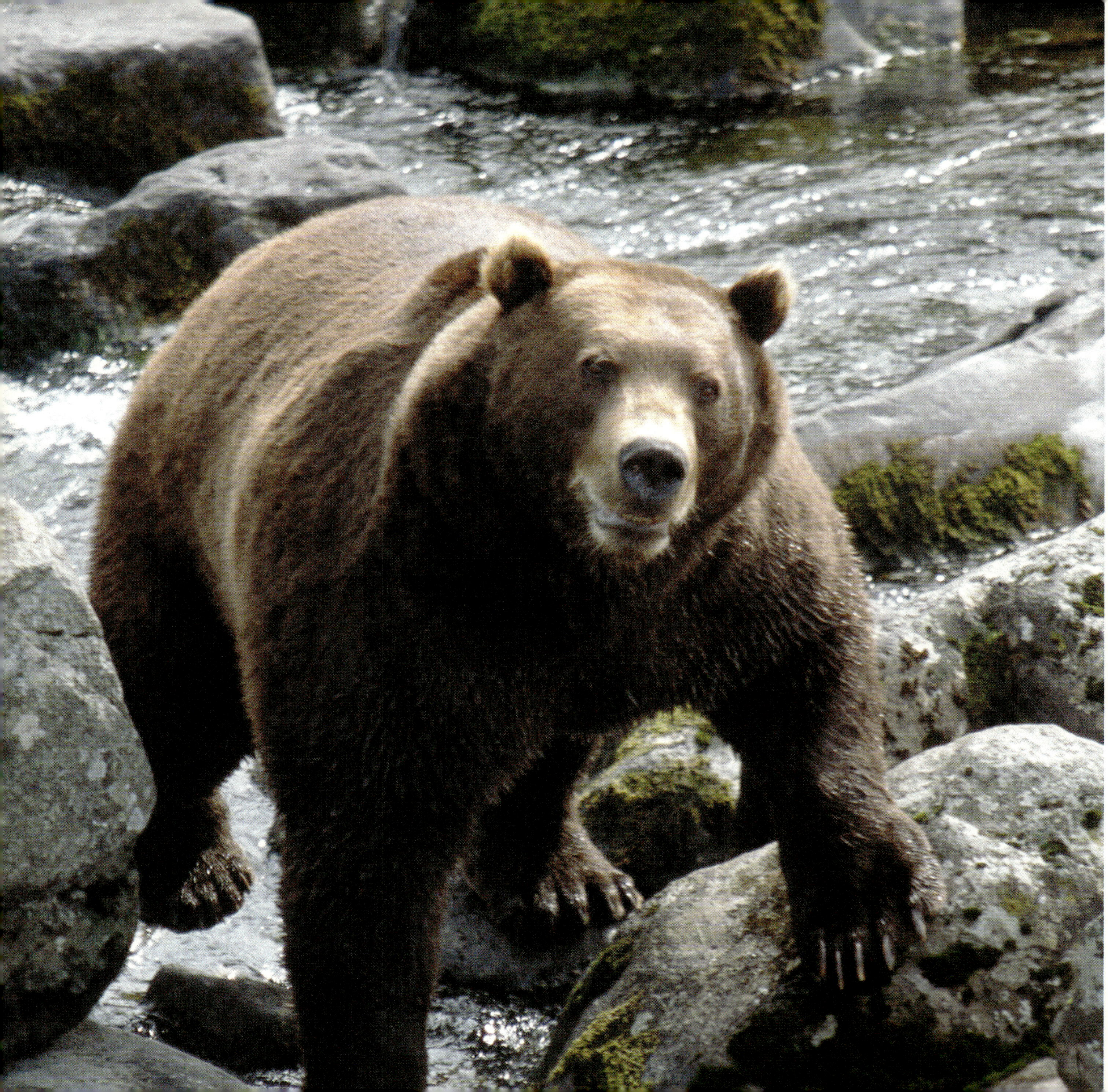

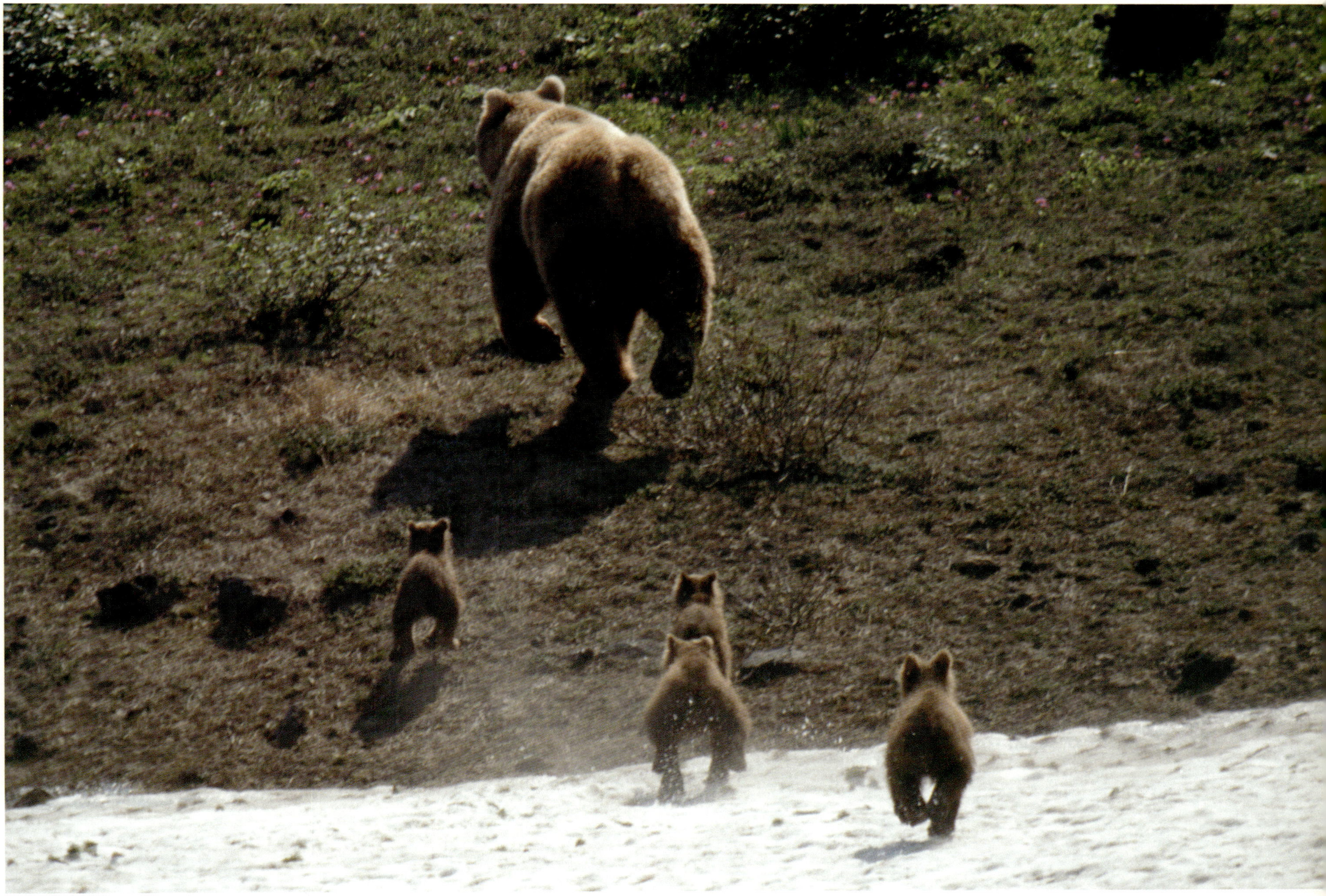

During the first year of our study, it was very discouraging to have bears constantly flee our presence.
This female has four cubs, which is quite common, although three is the norm.

Mature males weigh between one thousand and fifteen hundred pounds, and can look very menacing.
Although some of the males make a practice of killing and eating cubs, those predator bears have never threatened us.

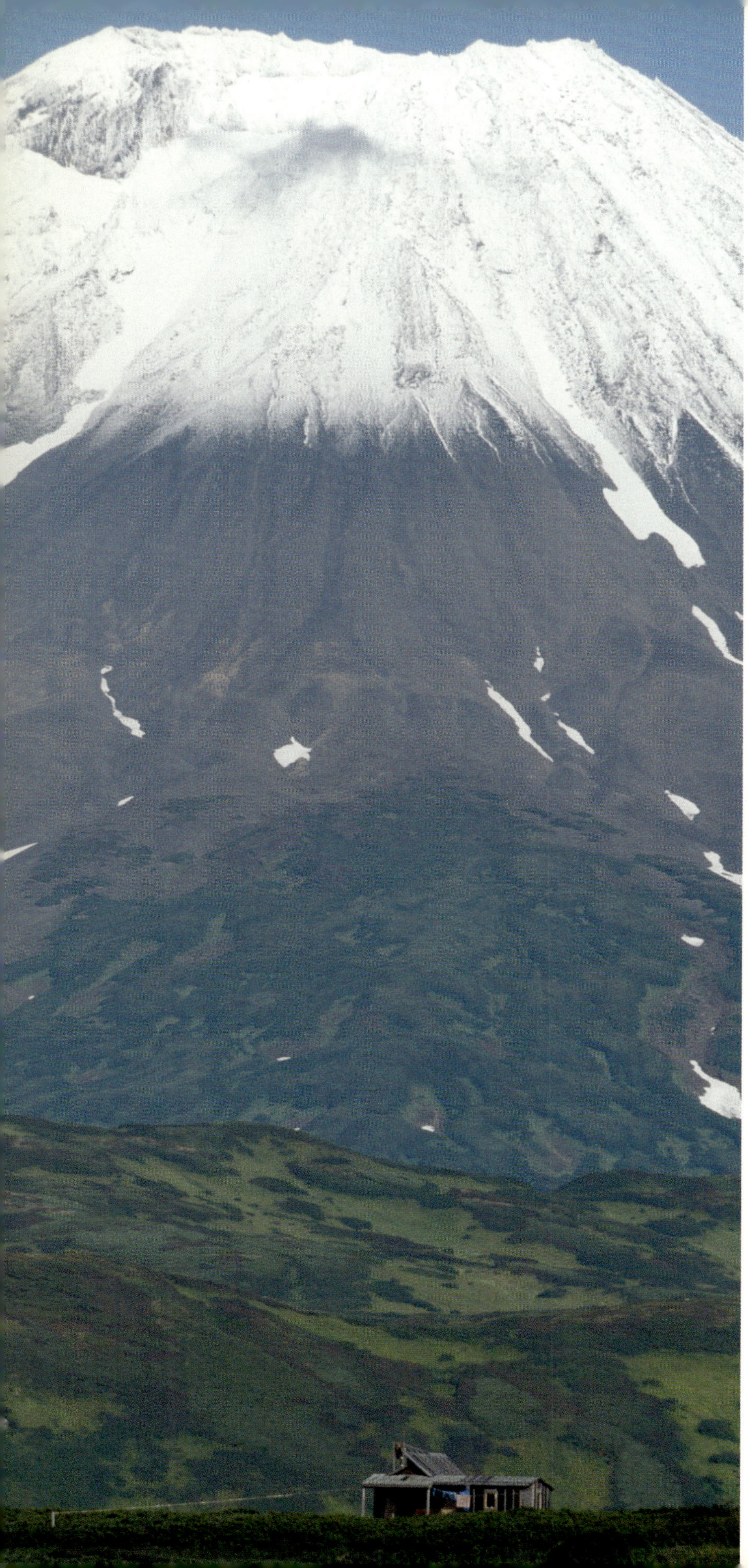

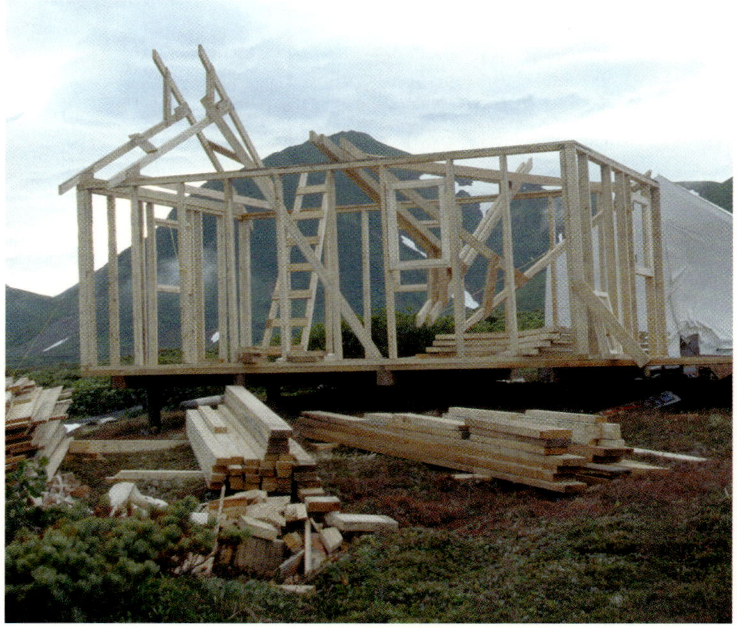

We built our cabin in just three weeks;
violent storms had made it impossible to stay in a tent.

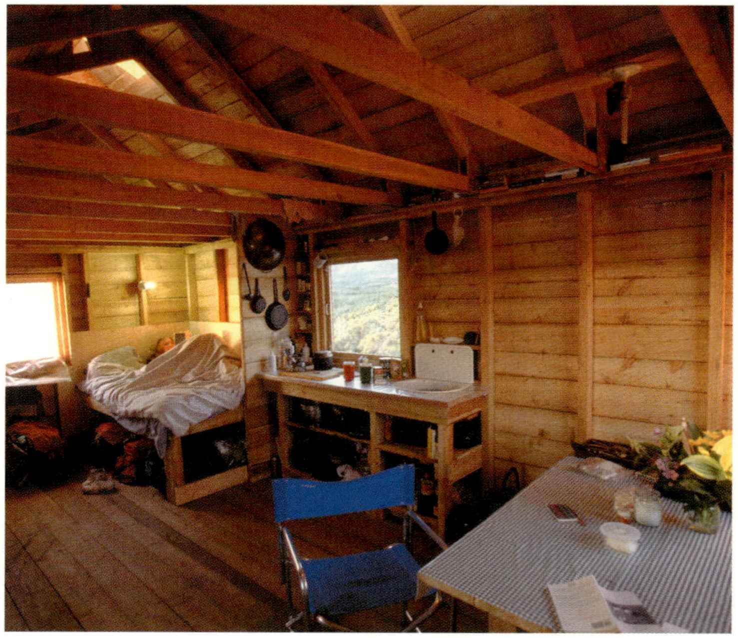

The cabin, as seen from Kambalnoye Lake.

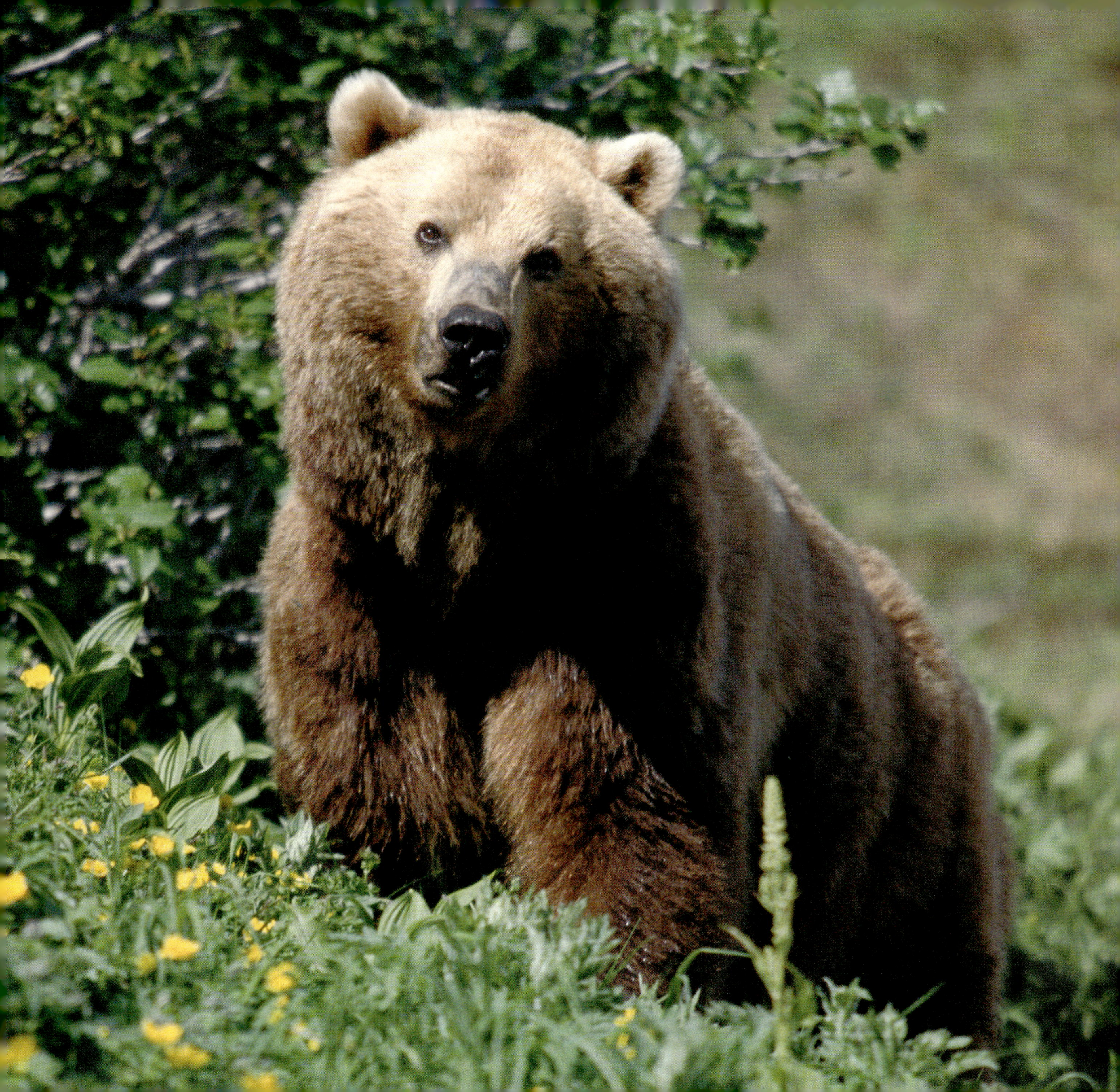

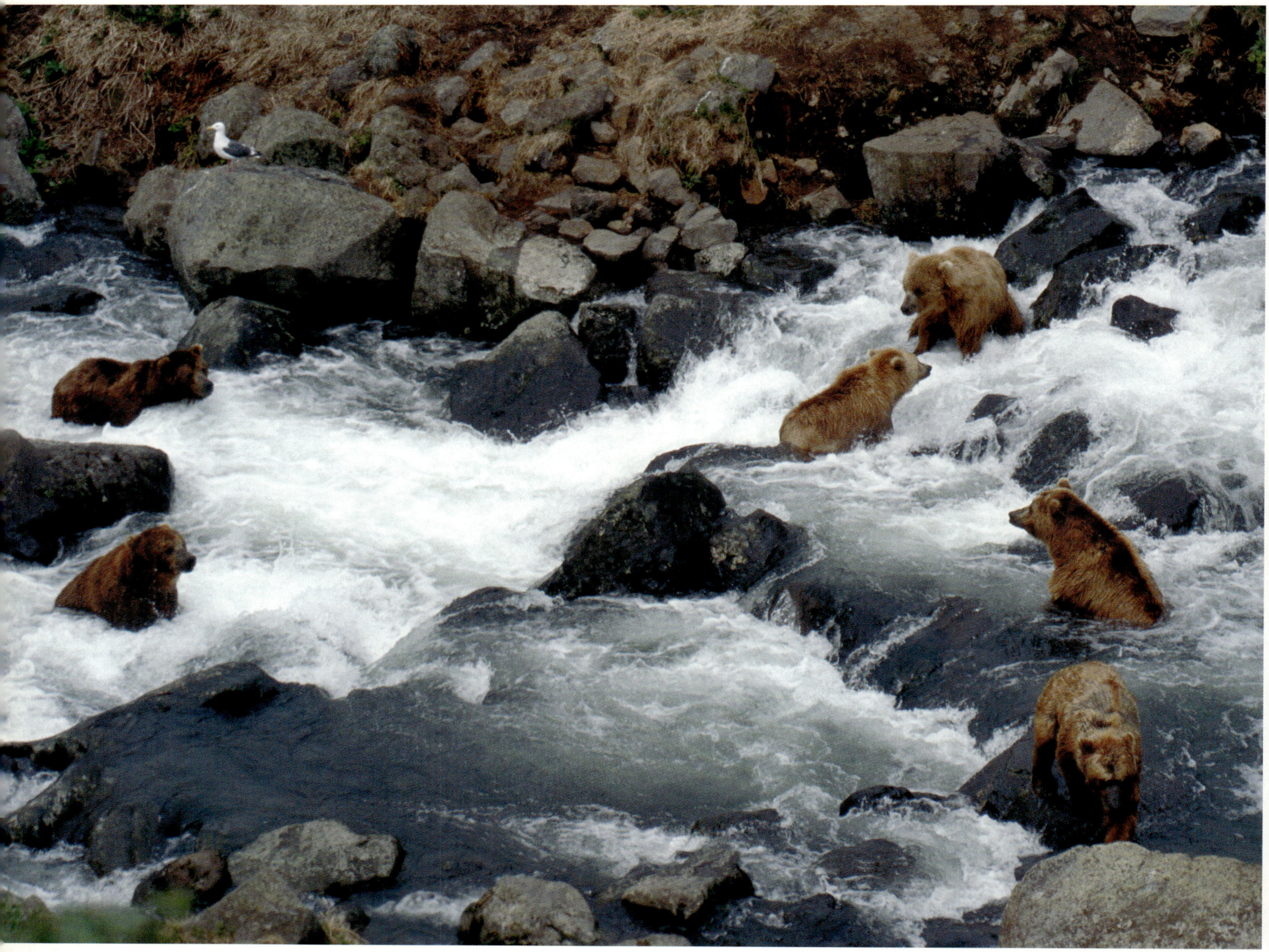

Kambalnoye River is a conduit for the sockeye salmon that spawn in the lake.
To complete their journey they have to survive a gauntlet of as many as 125 bears.

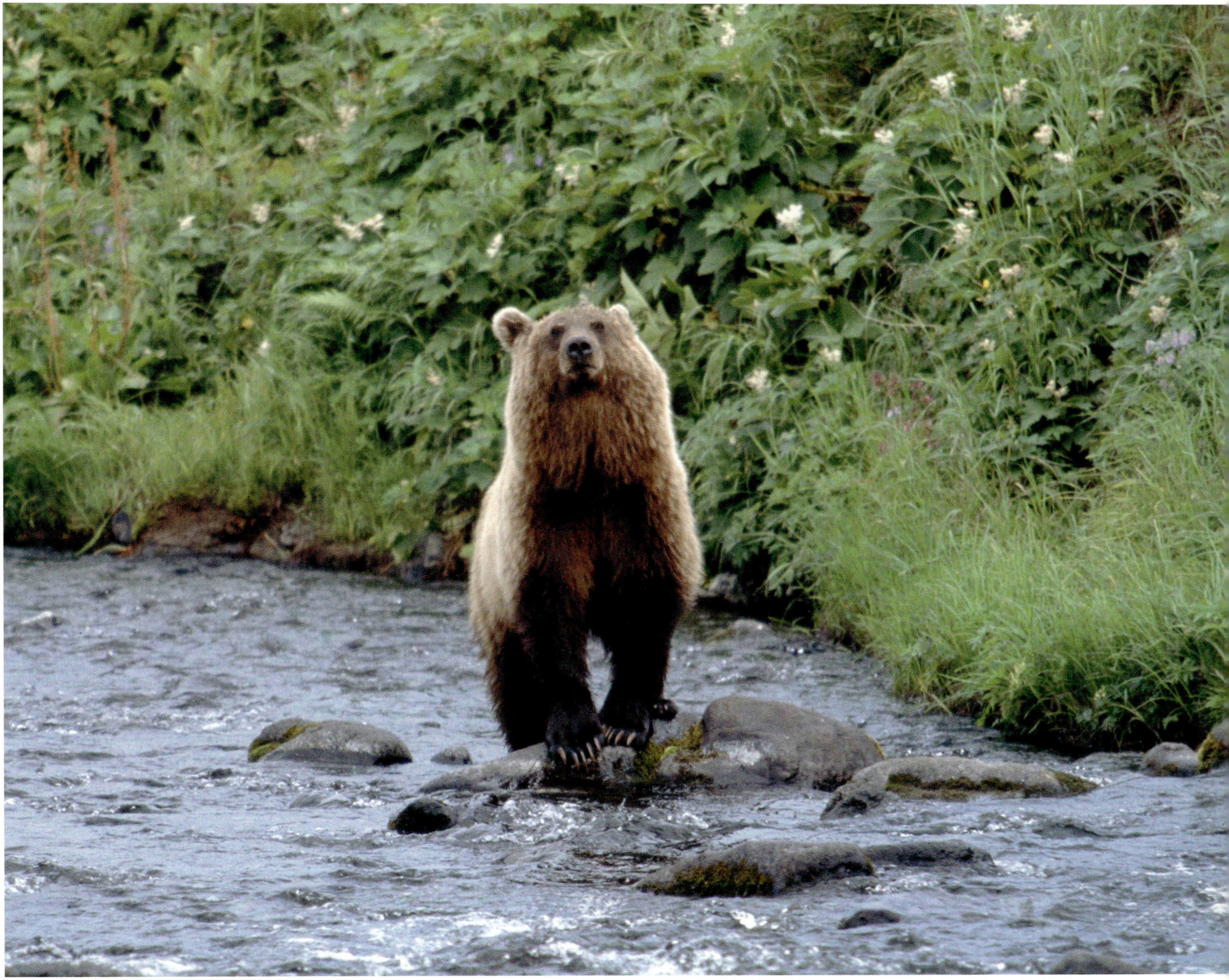

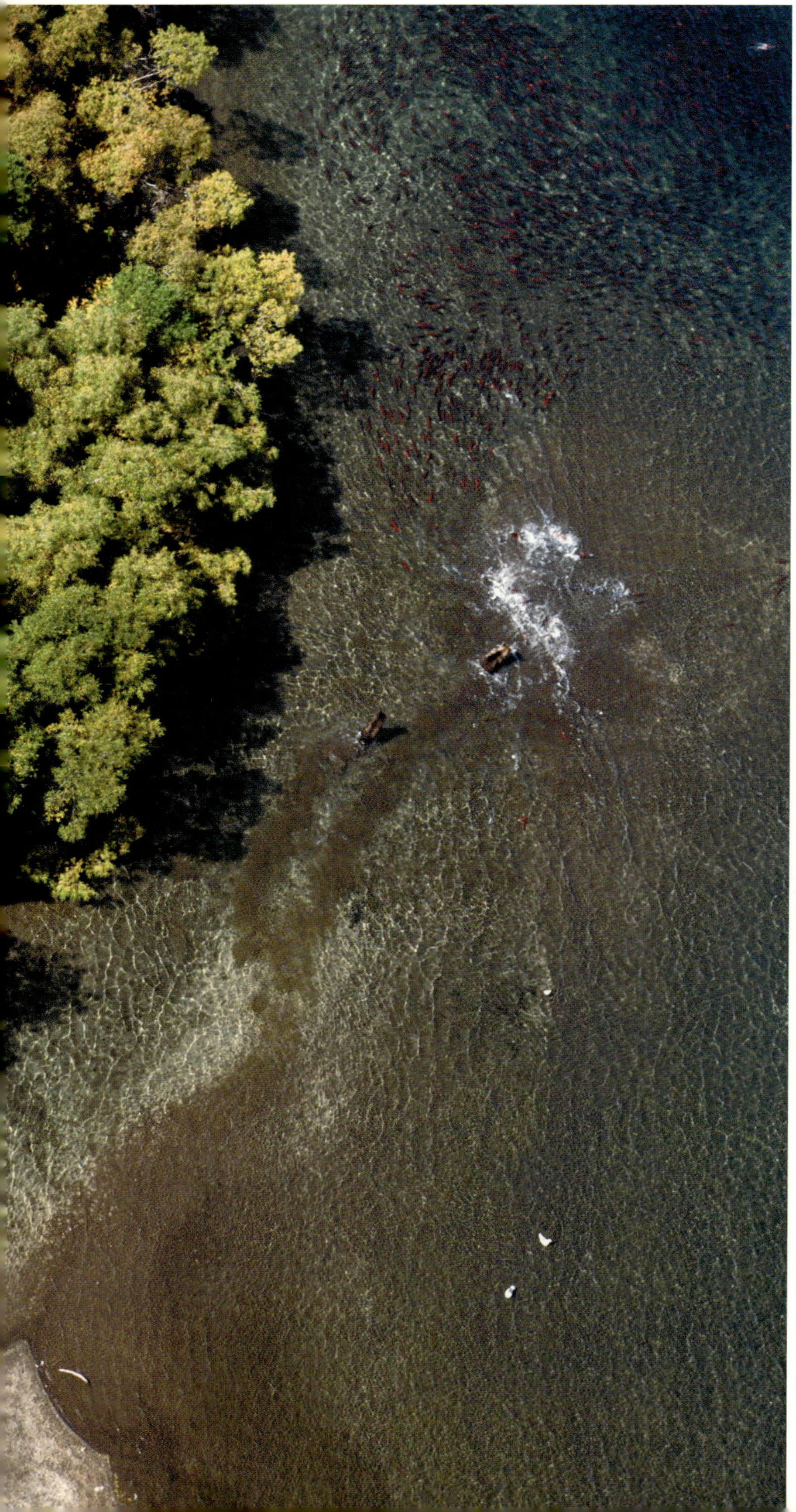

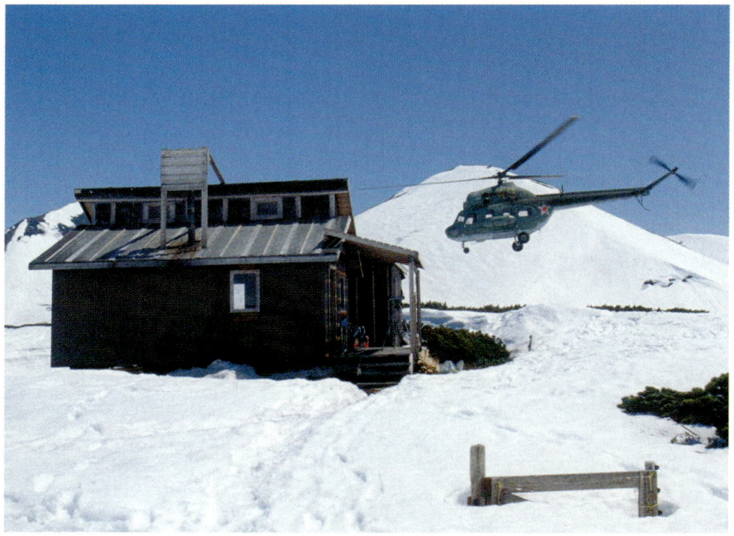

We rarely have visitors, but when
we do, they always come by helicopter.

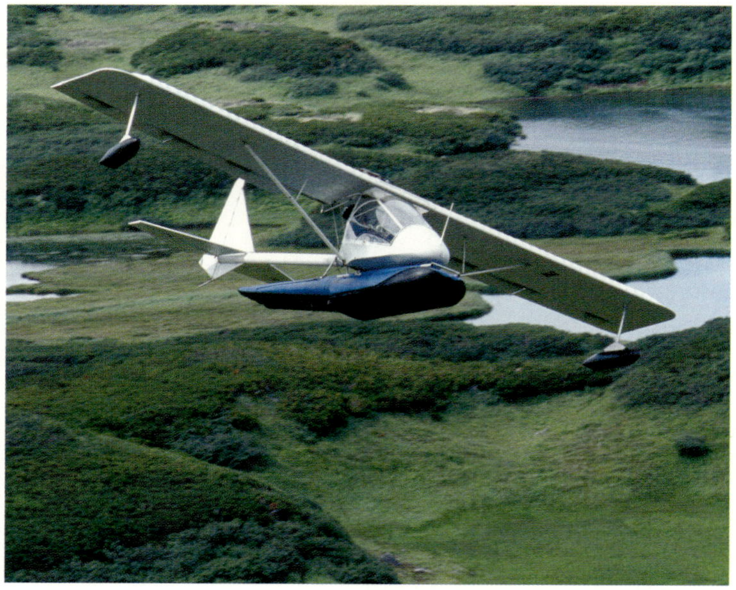

Built by Charlie in 1992, the Kolb has worked in
the wilderness without technical support for ten years.

From the Kolb, we could photograph bears (and salmon!)
from directly overhead. Usually the bears paid no attention.

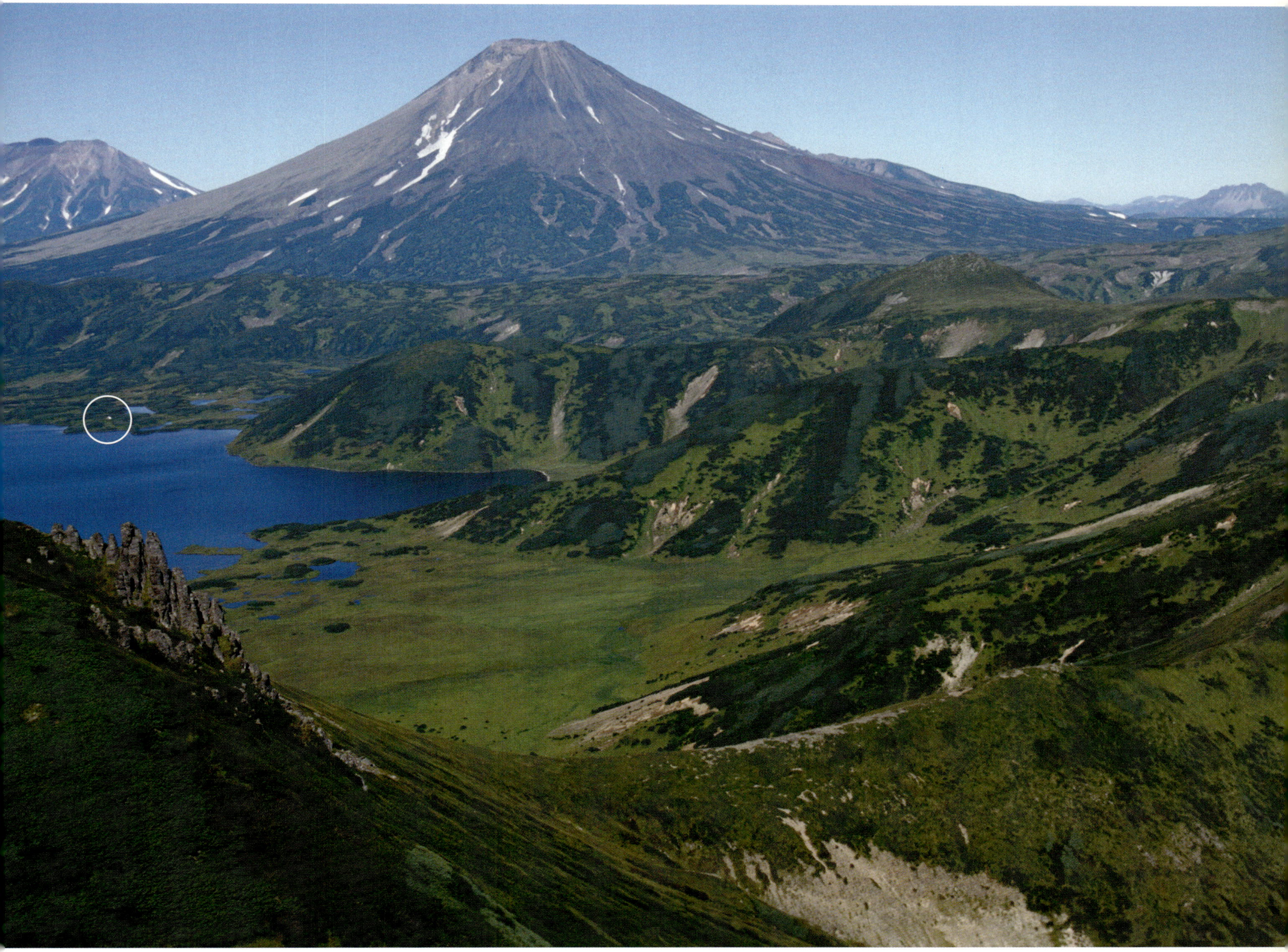

The valley surrounding Kambalnoye Lake has been home ground for seven years. Our cabin is a white dot on the left (circled).

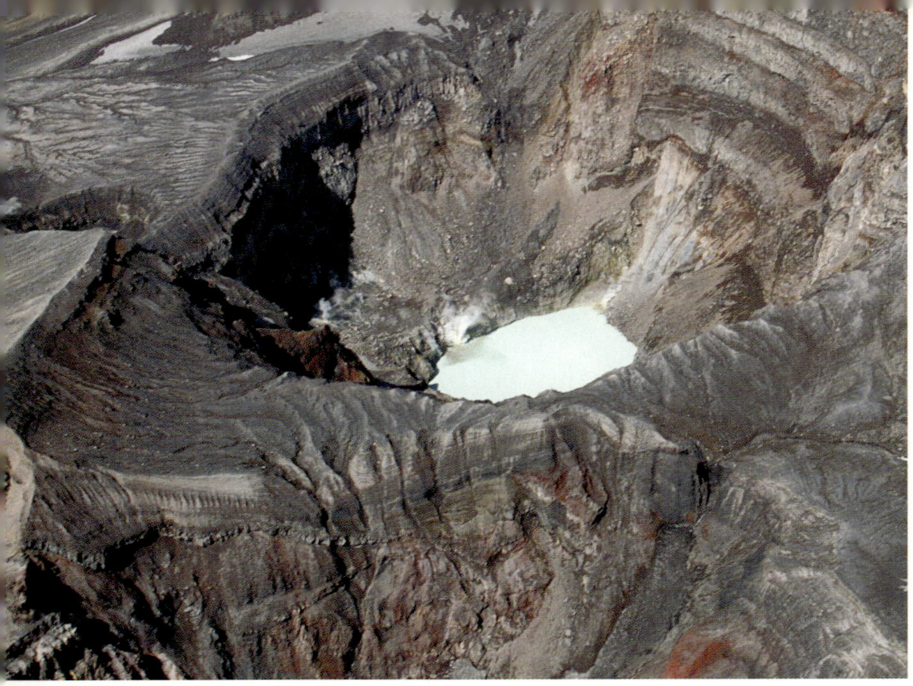

Gorelaya Volcano. As seen from the air, its lake appears turquoise, due to its chlorine and sulfur content.

A bear fishes in the Sea of Okhotsk, at the mouth of a spawning stream. The 7000-foot volcano in the background makes up one island in the long string of Kuril Islands.

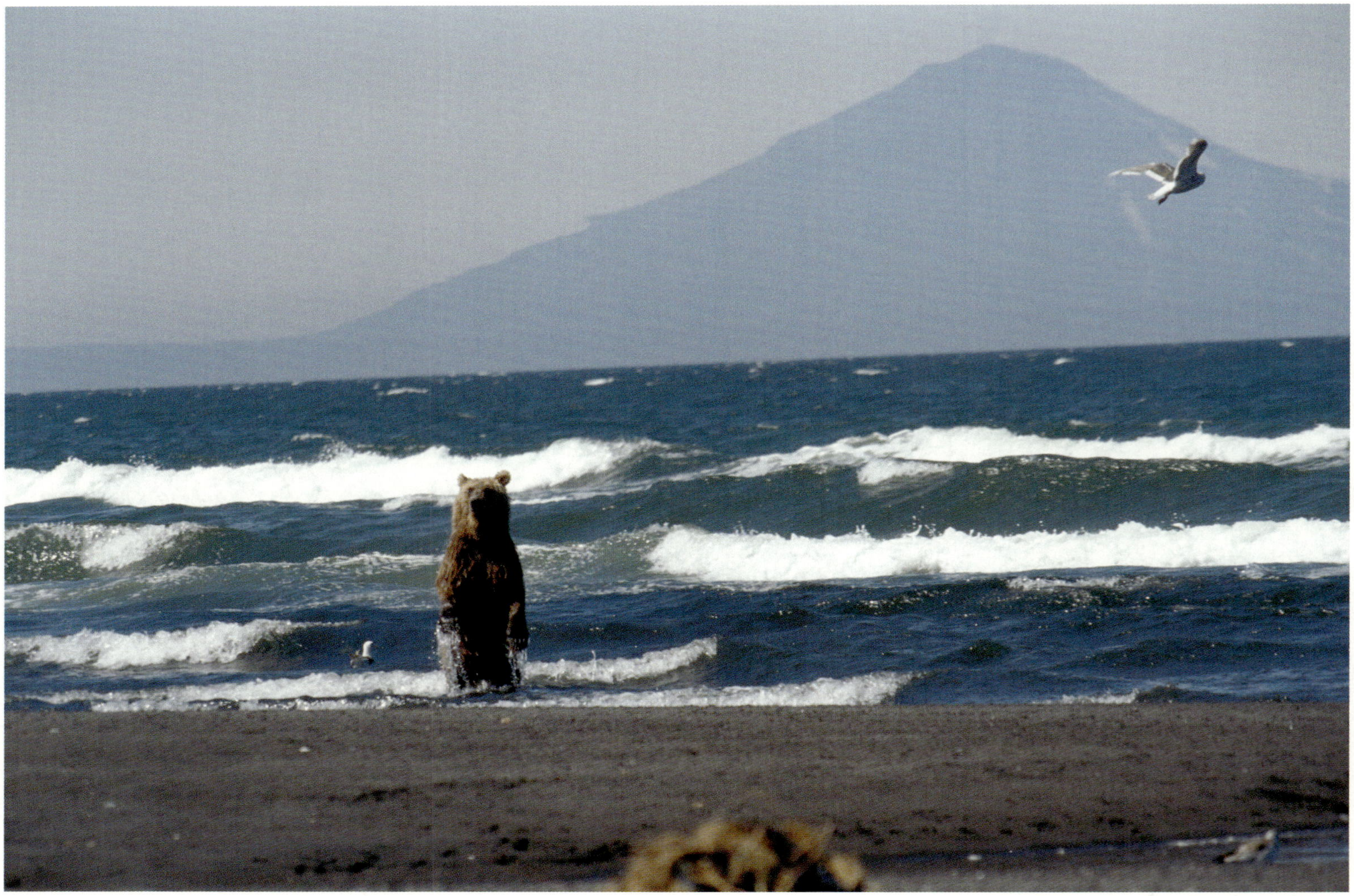

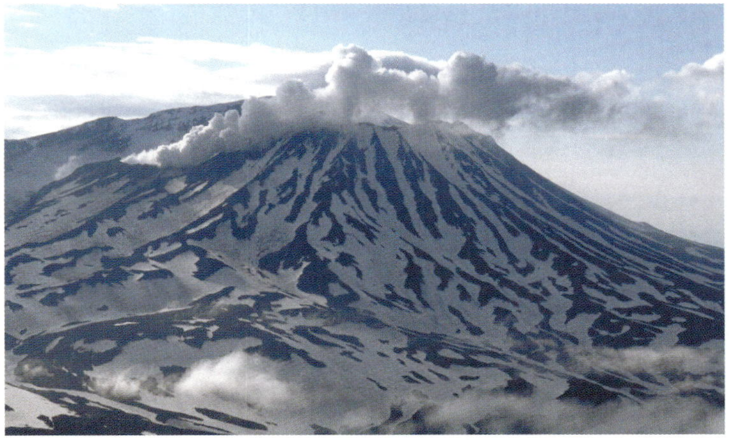

A smouldering Mutnovskiy Volcano, located along the flight path between Petropavlovsk and Kambalnoye Lake.

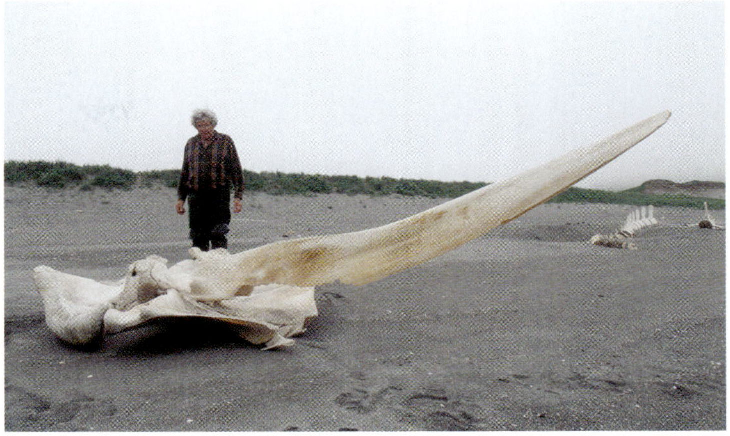

The skeleton of a blue whale, recently picked clean by bears. Within one year, storms would clear away everything except a couple of vertebrae. The whale skull was seventeen feet long.

One of the two lakes in the Ksudach Volcano crater.

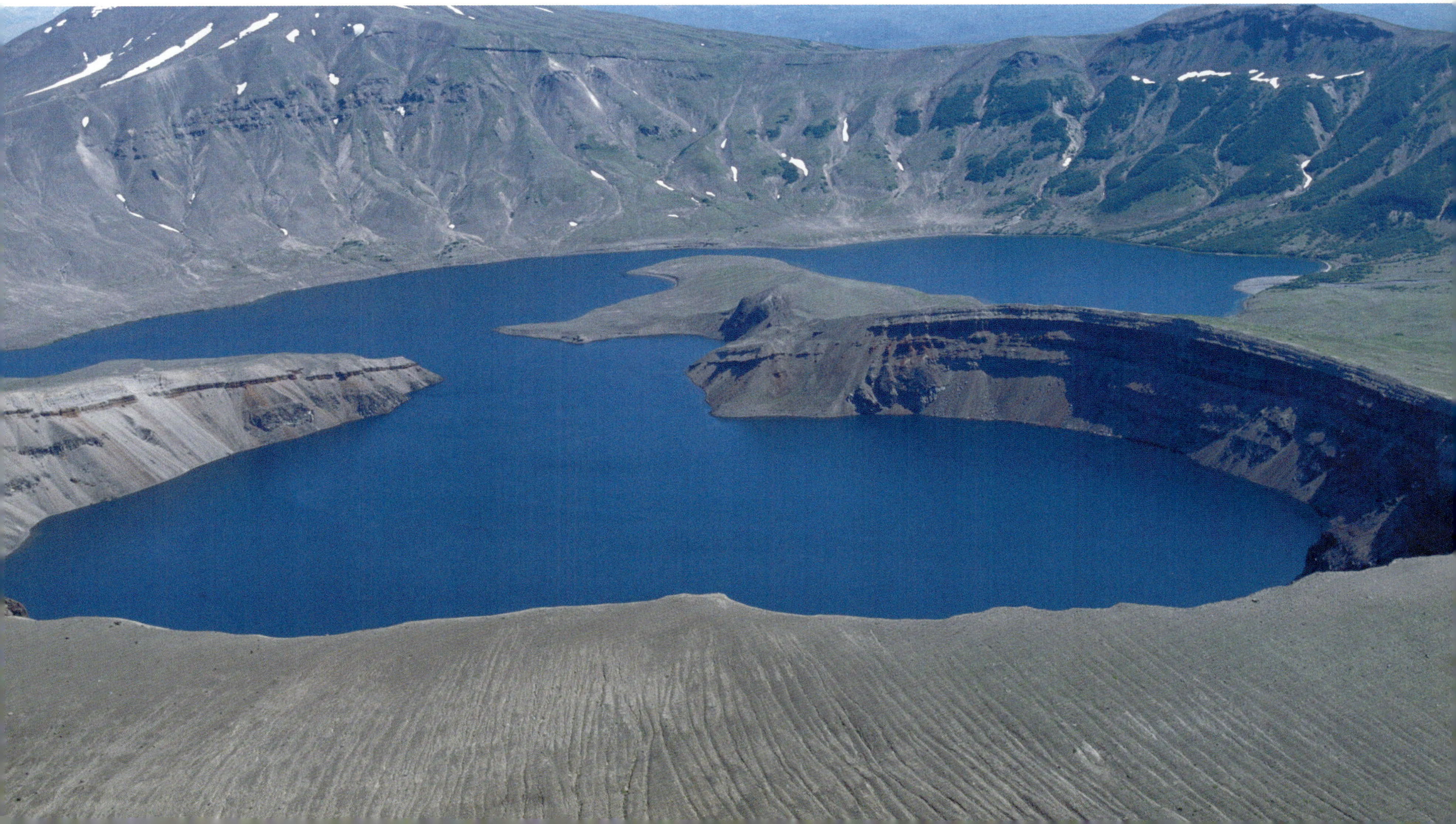

A trail made only by bears.

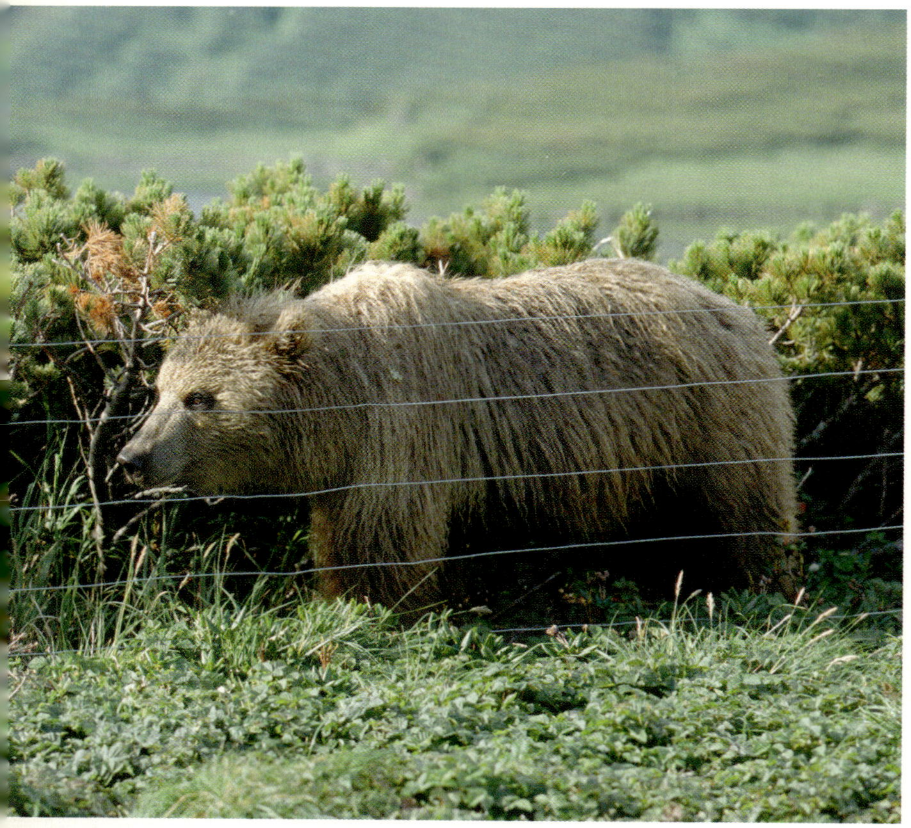

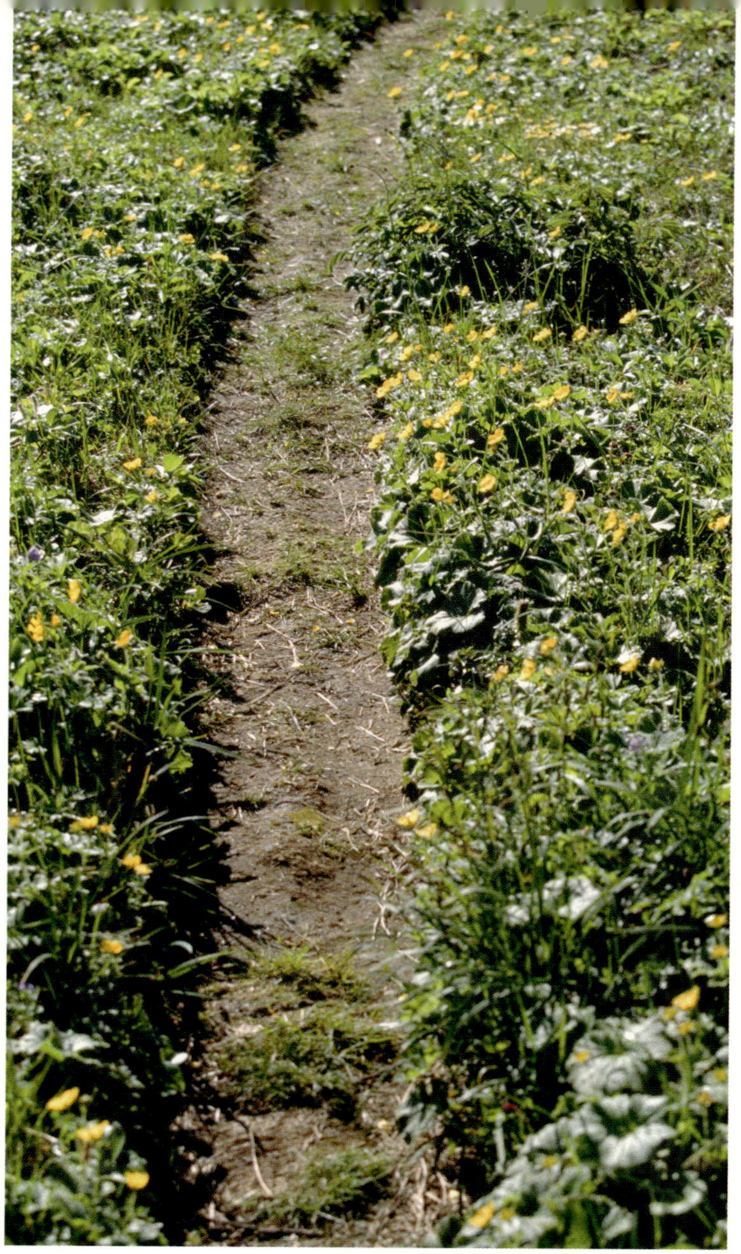

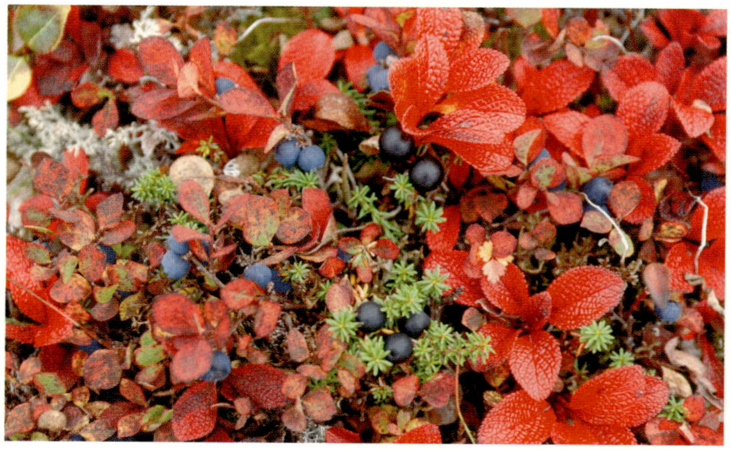

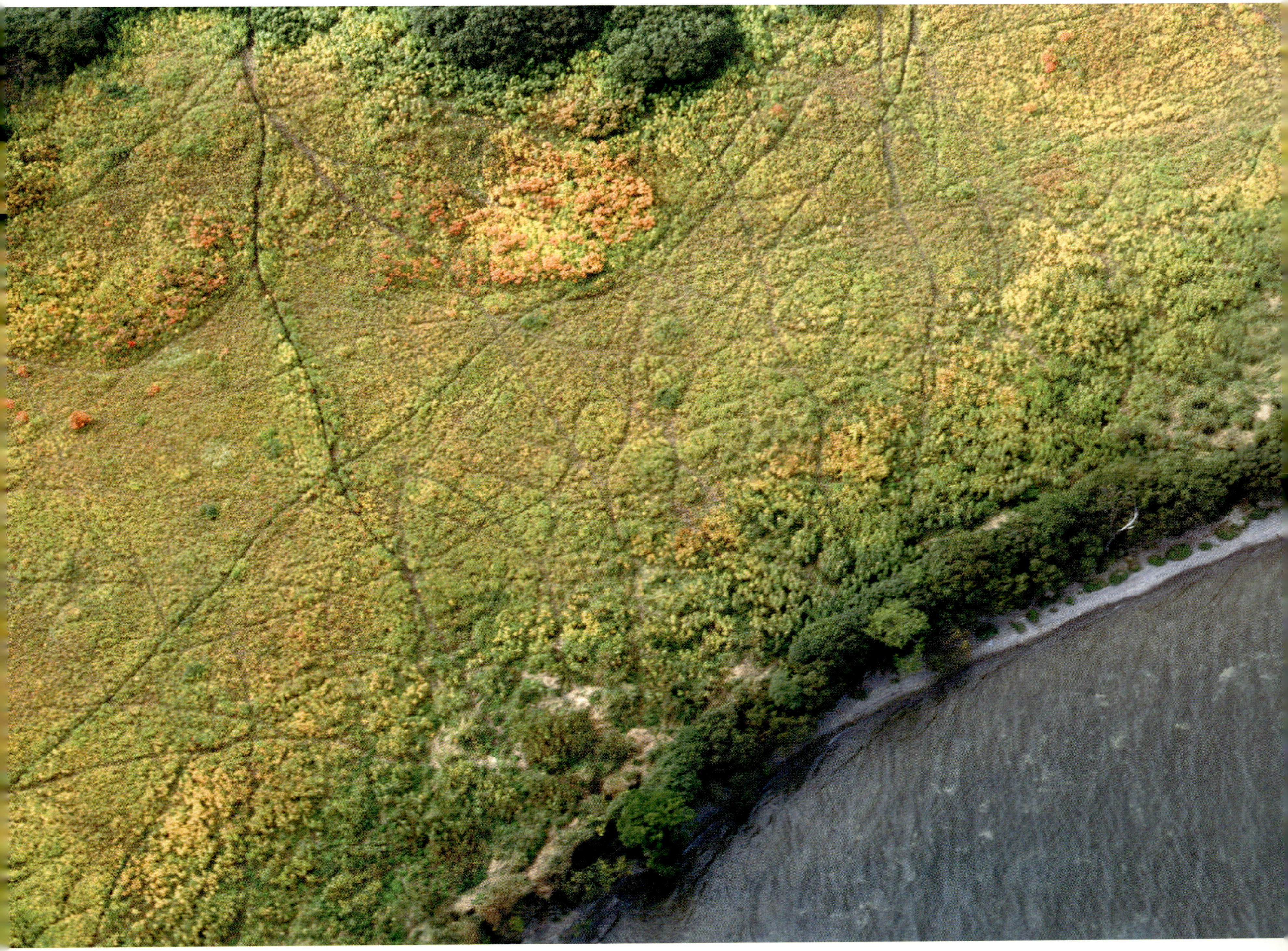

Bear trails through the brush. Some have been worn into the hard ground a foot deep from centuries of use.

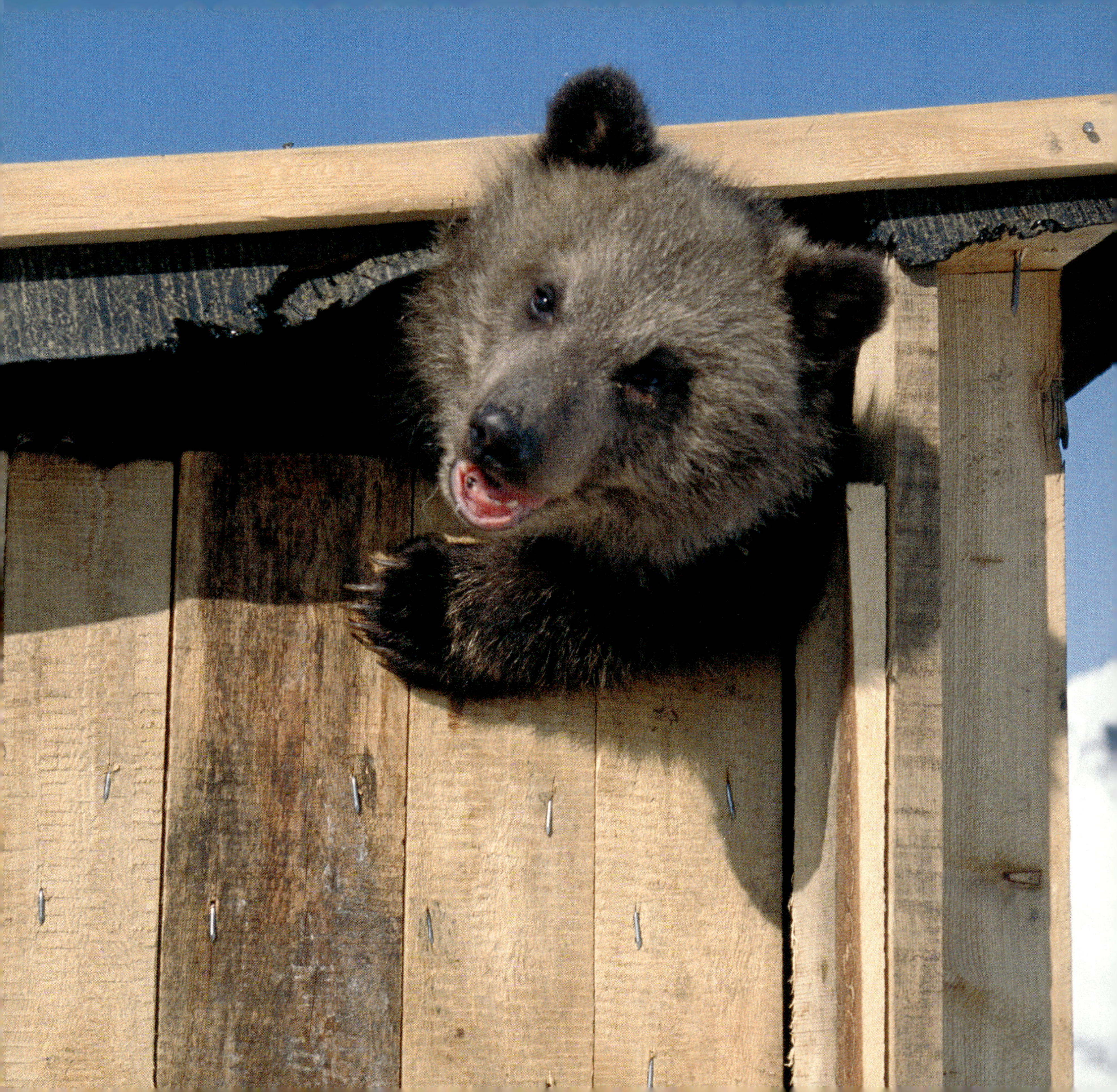

Our First Year with the Cubs—1997

Returning to Kamchatka in early May of 1997, we learned that there were three young female cubs who had recently been placed in a zoo after their mother was killed by a hunter. We were ecstatic at the chance to be their guardians; however, our request for orphaned cubs seemed to have been long forgotten. But one look at the cubs and the deplorable condition of the zoo was all it took to fix our resolve. After a great deal of negotiating—and a little bending of the rules—the cubs were lifted free of their cage to come with us to Kambalnoye Lake.

What followed was the launch of our cub reintroduction project, and a summer that we will always remember as the happiest time of our lives. Instead of us being parents to these three young bears, it was more as if they taught us how to be children again. Their joy for life was contagious, and through their eyes and their experiences we were finally able to enter into the world of bears—a world in which human presence was not only tolerated but accepted as a natural part of daily life.

Naming the cubs Chico, Biscuit and Rosie, we set about creating a home for them at Kambalnoye. We built them a small cabin for shelter, within a large pen surrounded by electric fencing, making sure they had alders to climb and soft earth in which to dig. The precaution of the pen was necessary, because small cubs roaming on their own would be vulnerable to any predator bears in the area. At first we were afraid to let the cubs out at all, as if even the vastness of the land could swallow them up, but our fears soon proved unfounded. Though delighted with their new freedoms, the cubs stuck close to us, often running in big circles while keeping us at the centre.

When the cubs had adjusted to their new home and learned to come when we called or whistled, we began to introduce them to the rest of the basin. Each day, we took Chico, Biscuit and Rosie on long walks into the rich wilderness that surrounded the cabin, trying to

It didn't take Chico long to climb the door of her new cabin and find the narrow gap we'd dismissed as too small for a cub to fit through.

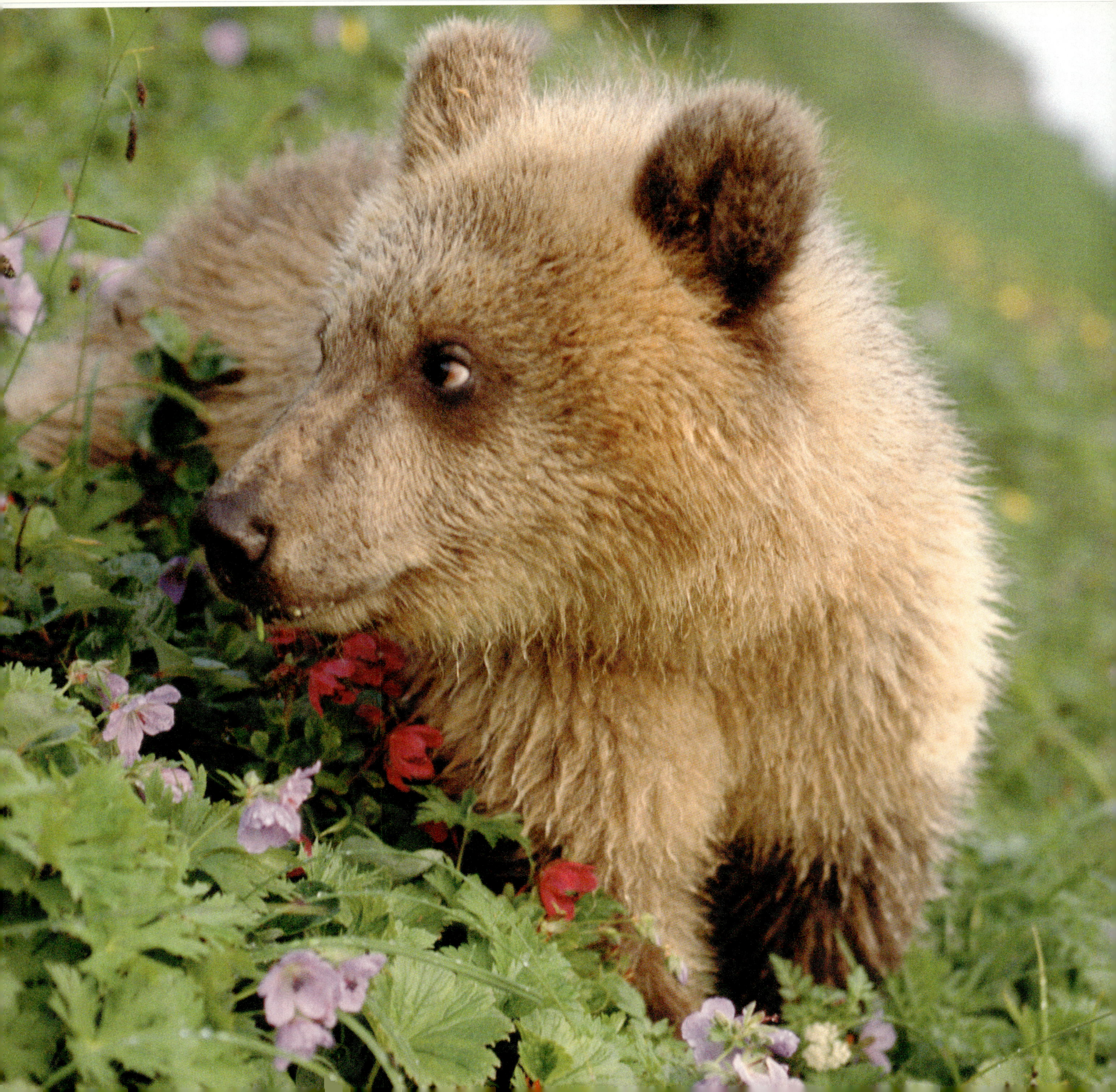

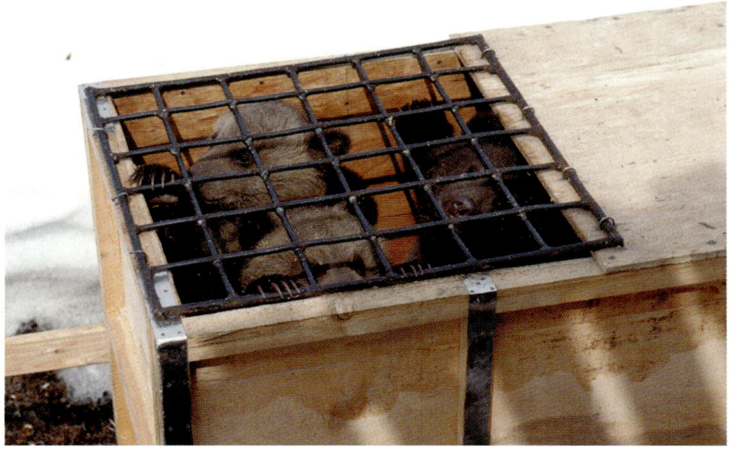

The cubs' travel box (their halfway house between the zoo and freedom) was cramped, but their quiet, watchful patience seemed to indicate they knew there were exciting adventures ahead.

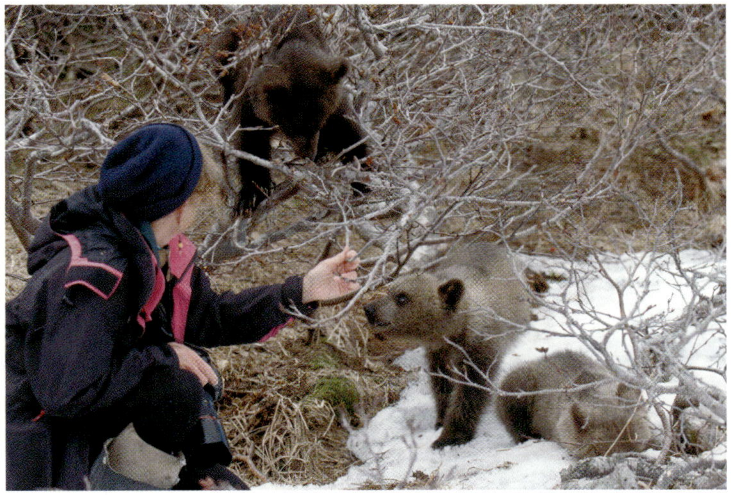

The cubs were always entertaining, and their joy infected us as well.

Rosie.

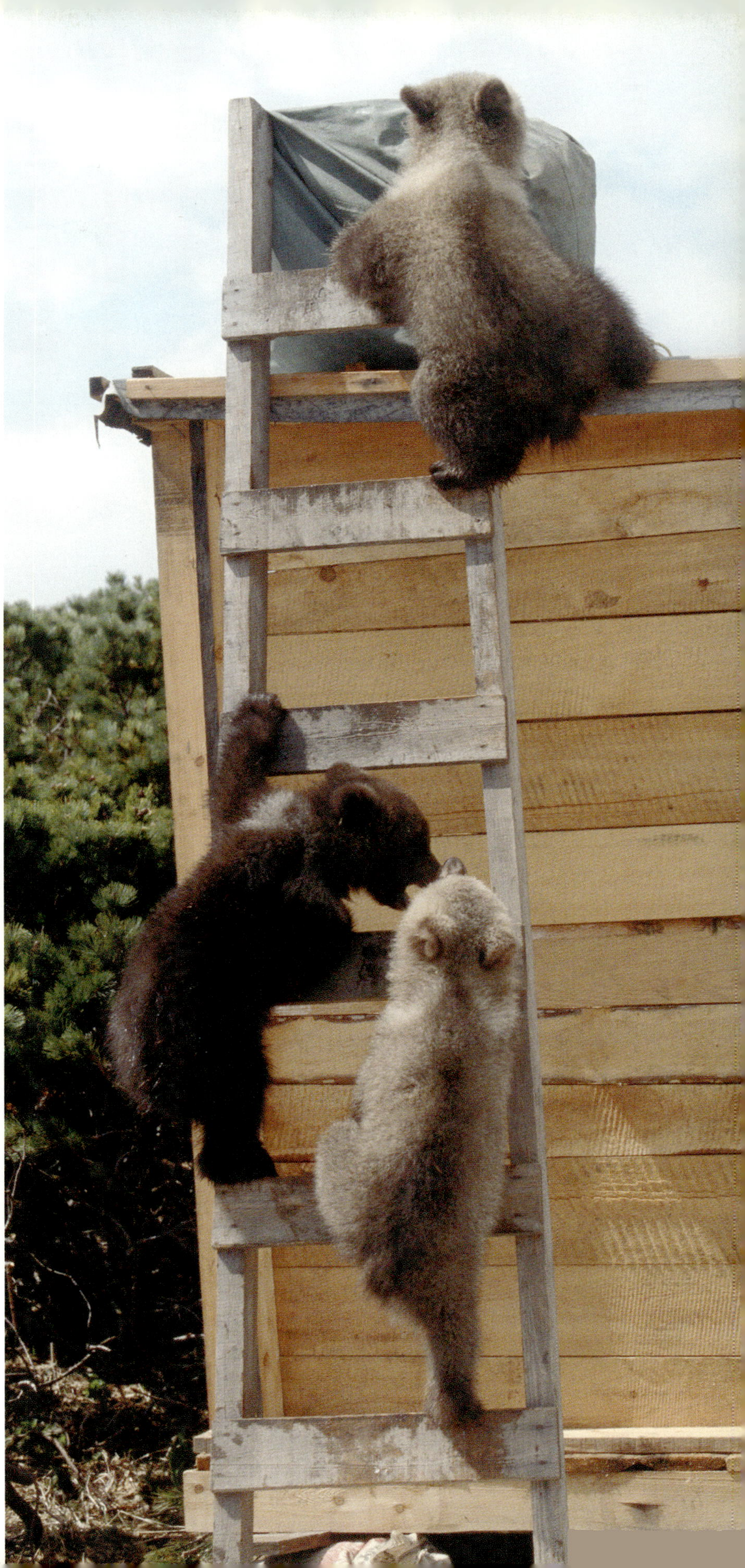

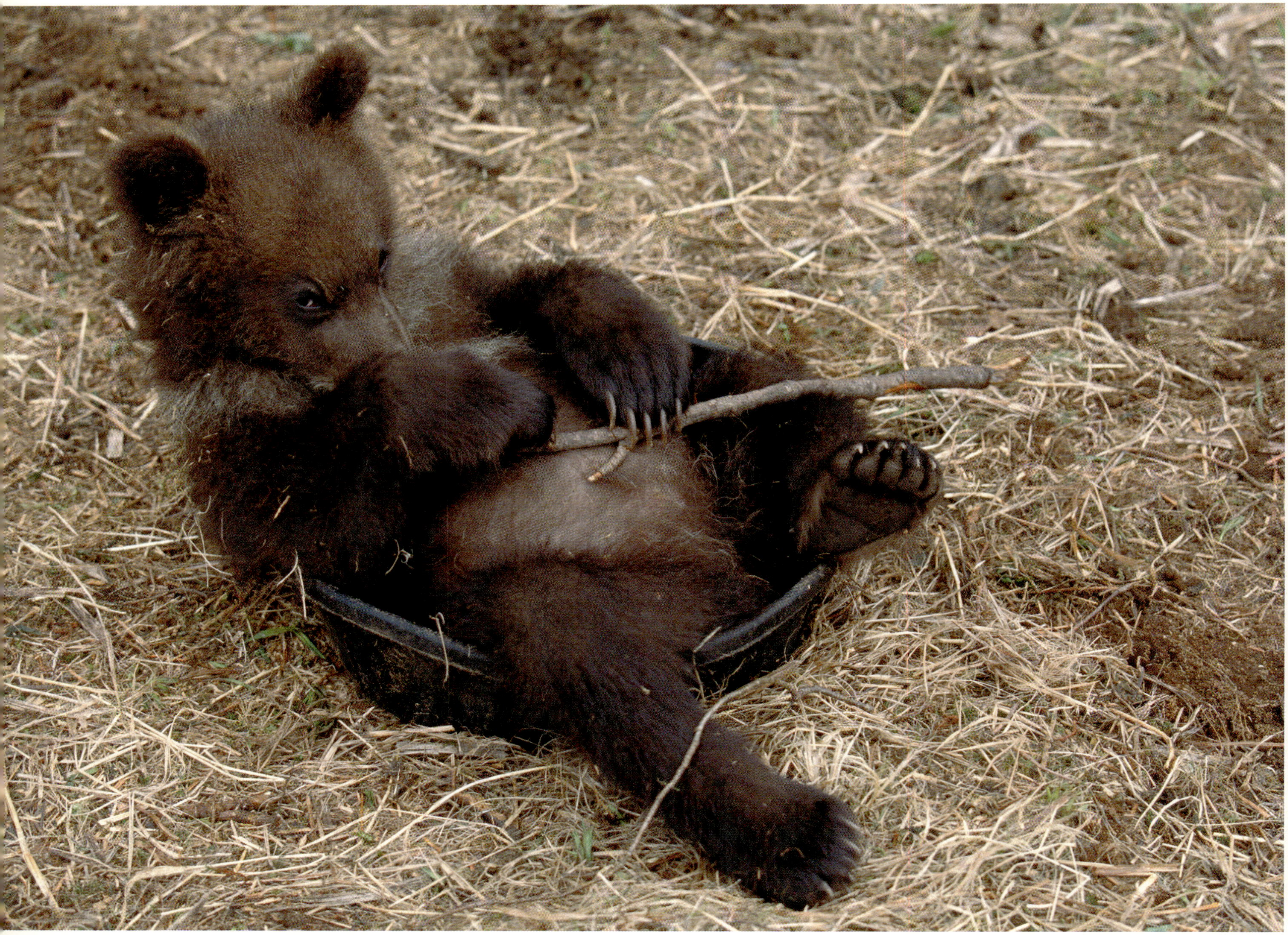

Chico, trying to be patient, waits in her bowl to be fed.

Each day, the cubs repeated their cycle of hard play and sleep. At this age bears have two speeds: full throttle ahead and complete stop.

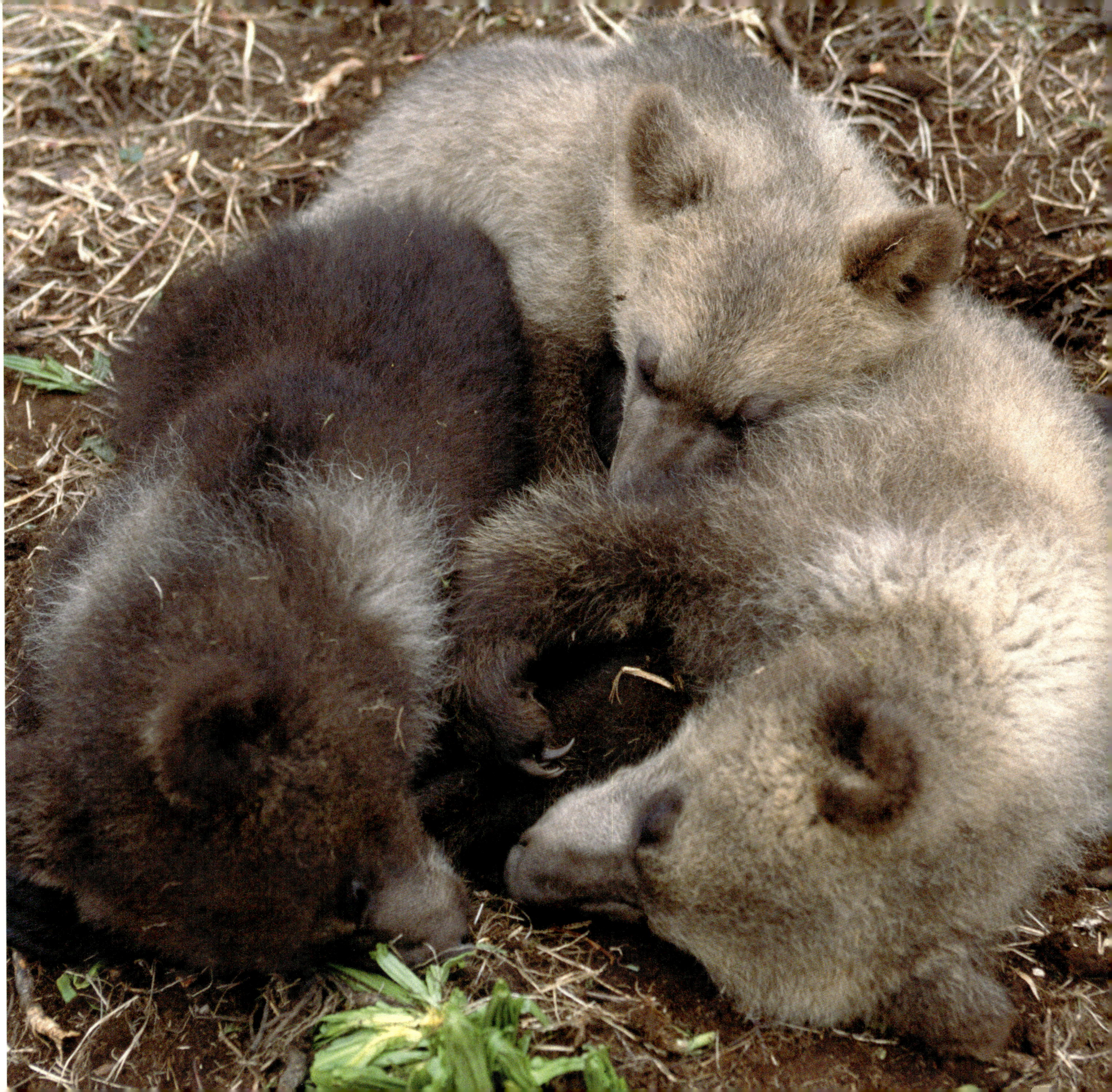

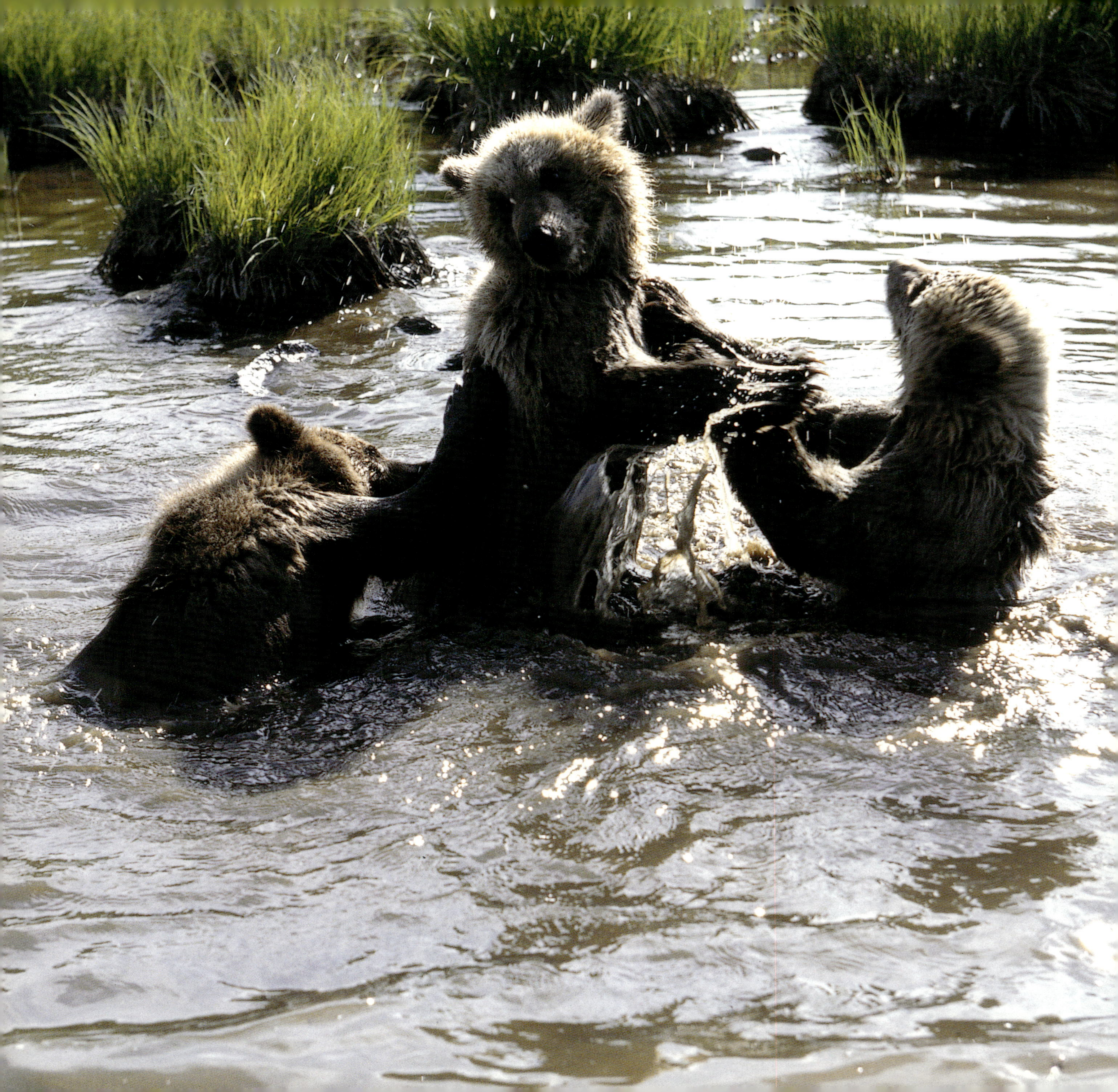

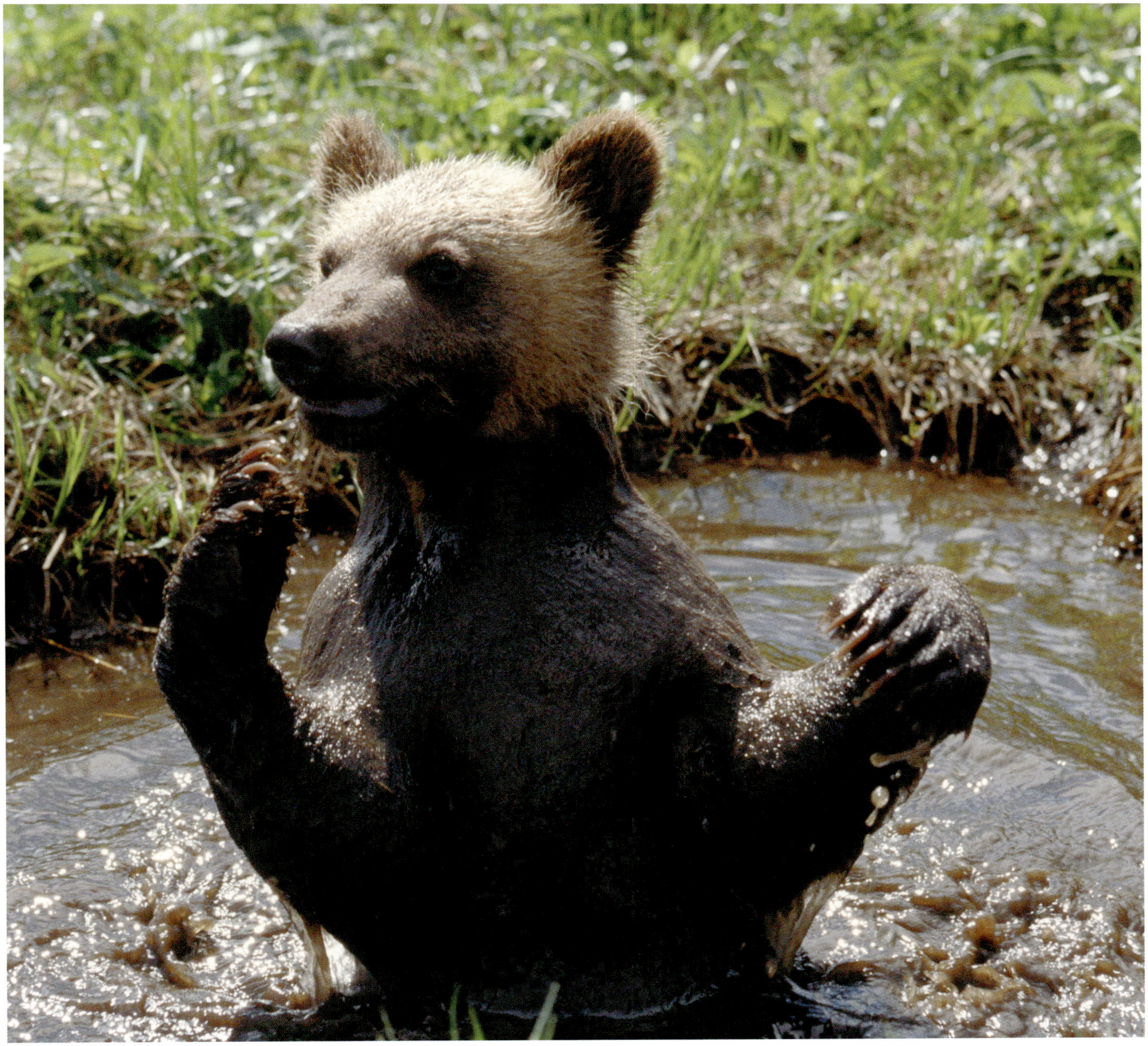

Chico, Biscuit and Rosie all loved the water, and the excitement it added to their games. Our daily walks often took the form of pool-hopping.

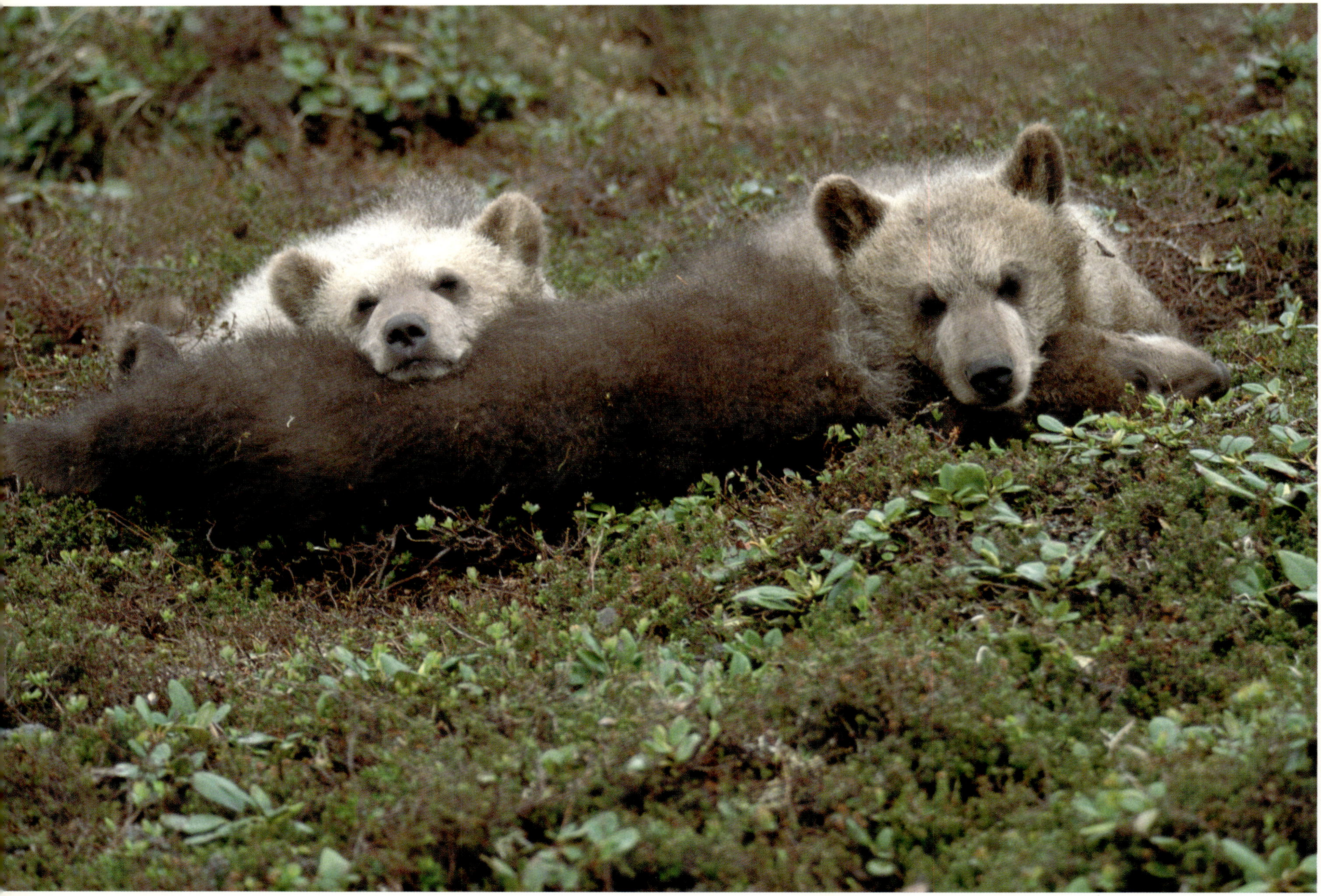

Rarely were the cubs out of sight of each other for more than a few seconds, and they usually slept in a pile. For one nap, Chico was a convenient pillow.

As they discovered edible and nutritious plants in the area, the cubs began to push for more independence. They'd always come when we whistled for them, but often seemed to wonder what all the fuss was about.

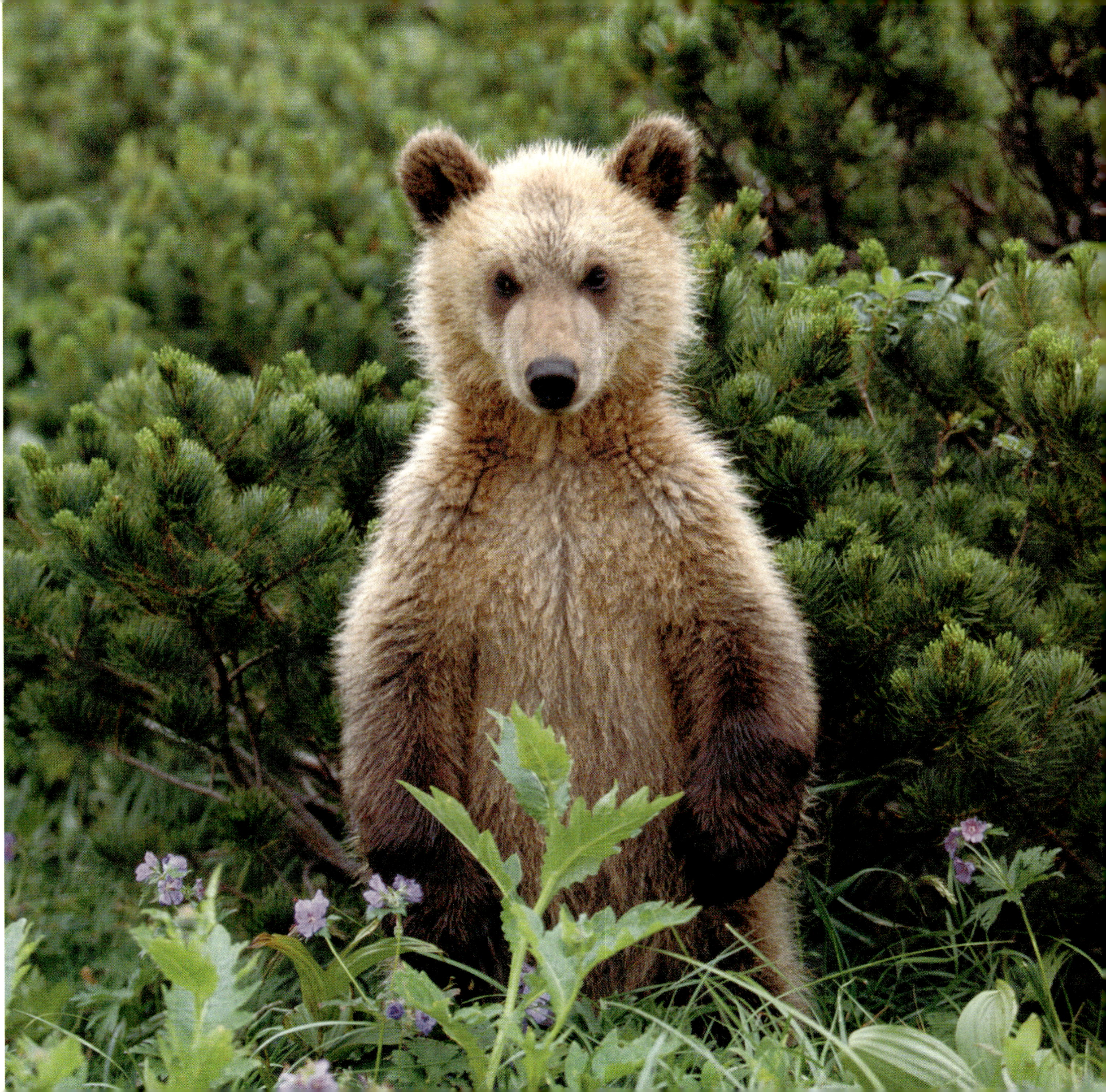

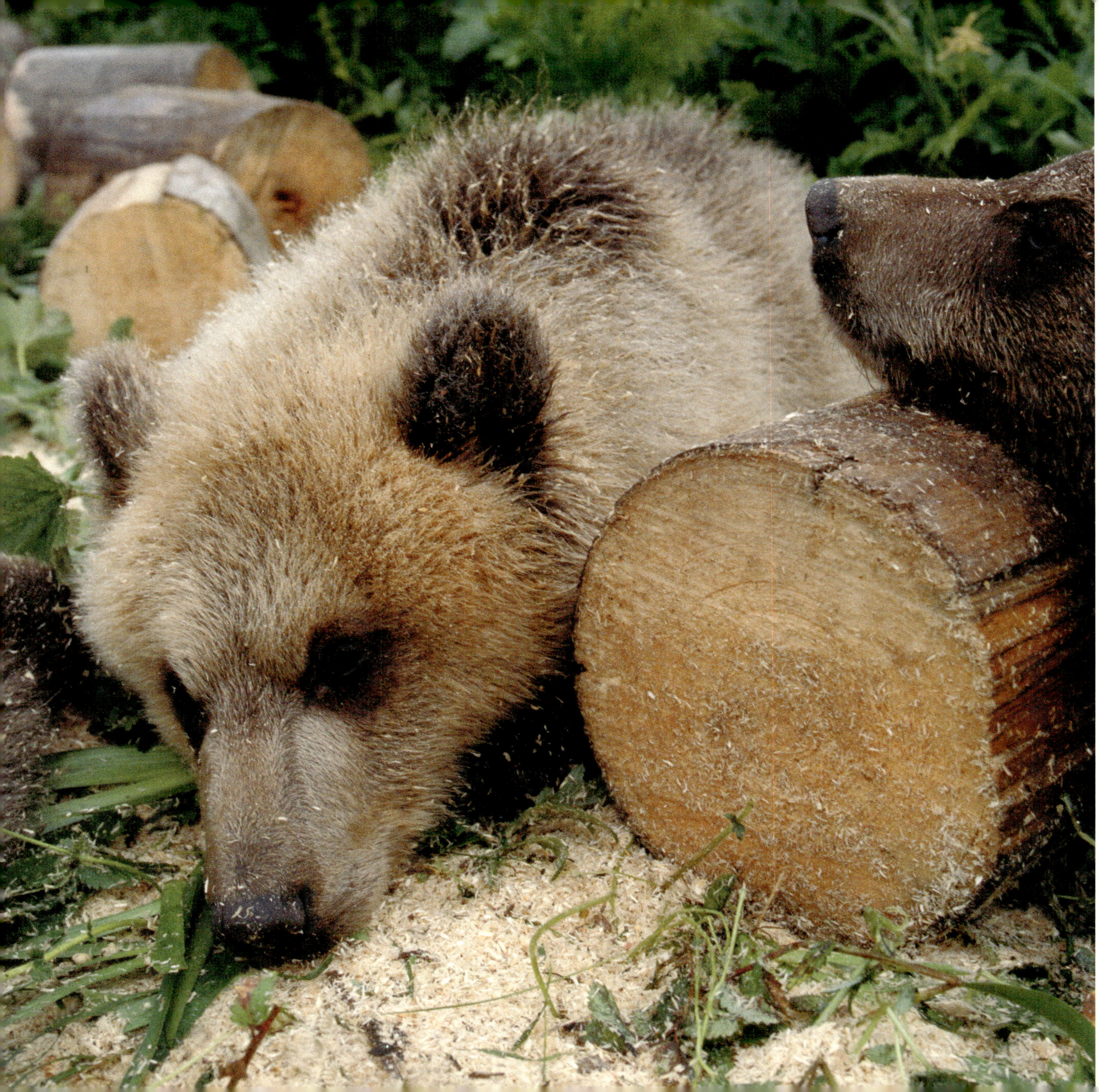

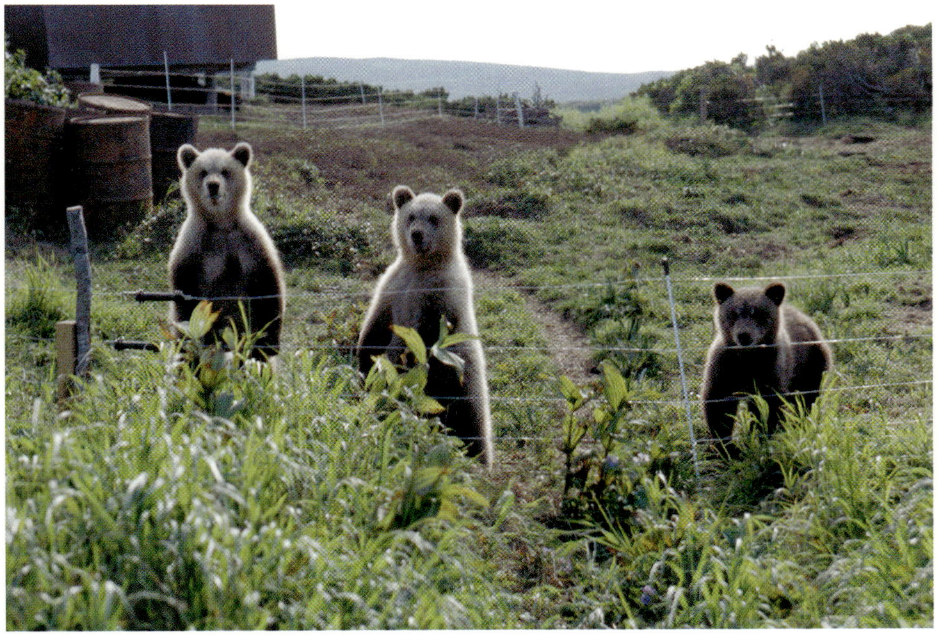

An electric fence kept the cubs safe from predator males.

As Chico, Biscuit and Rosie got bigger, they only sought the shelter of the cabin during extreme storms, but they did sometimes use it for play. Here they seem to be waiting for Goldilocks to drop by.

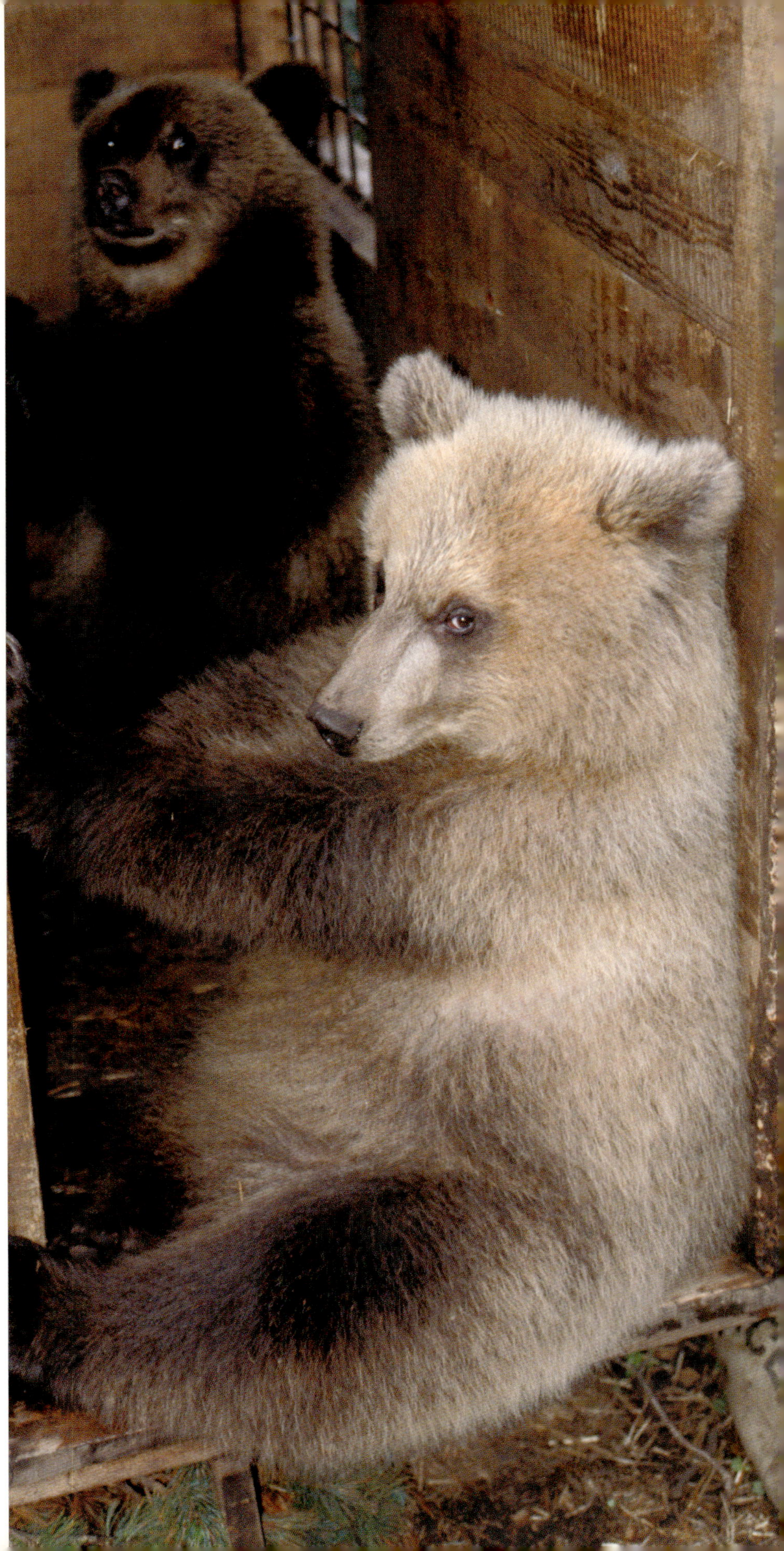

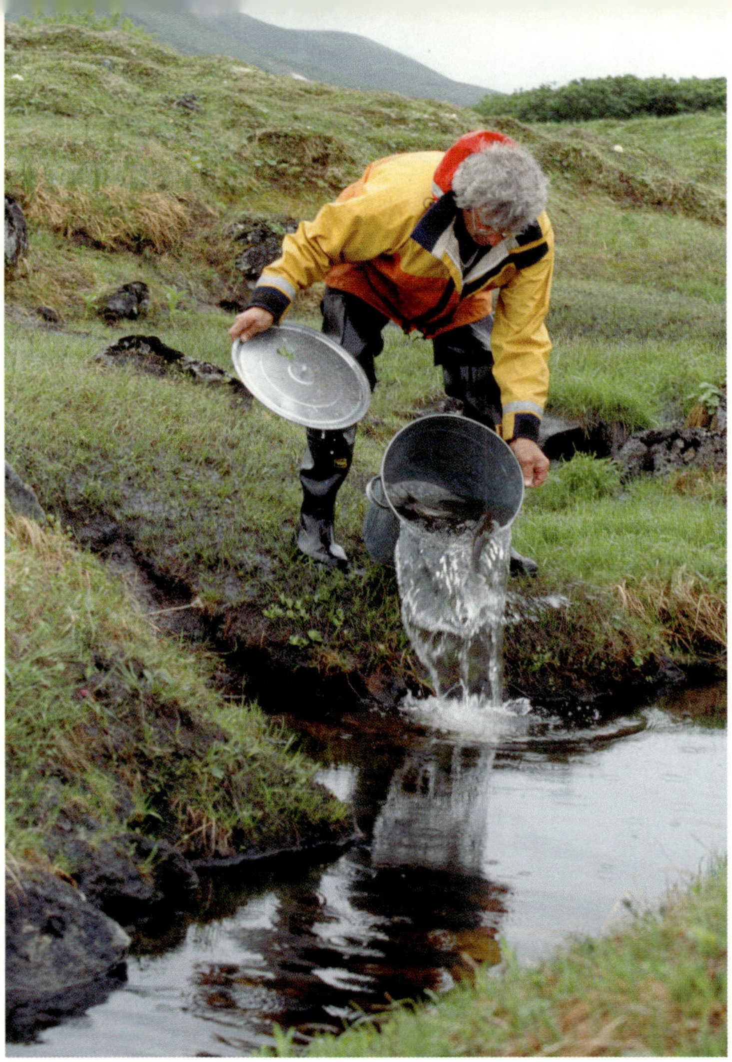

In order to teach the cubs how to fish, Charlie would catch a tub full of trout and put them in a shallow, contained pool, where they could be caught more easily. Below, Charlie and biologist Igor Revenko urge Chico on.

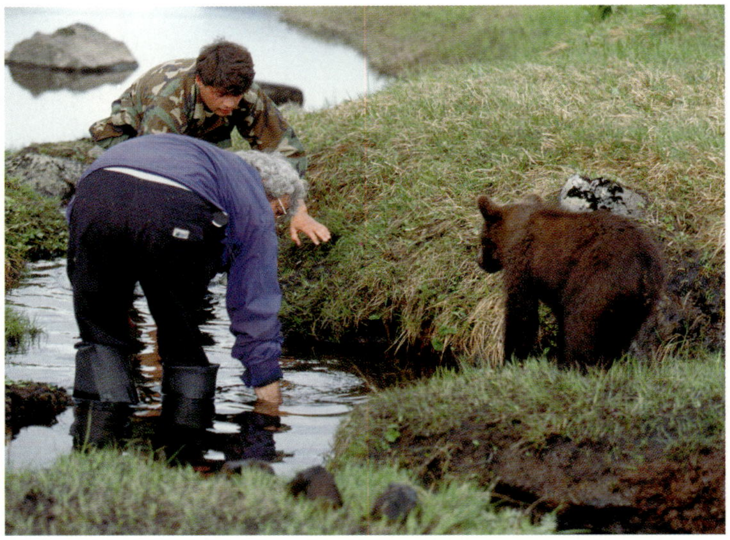

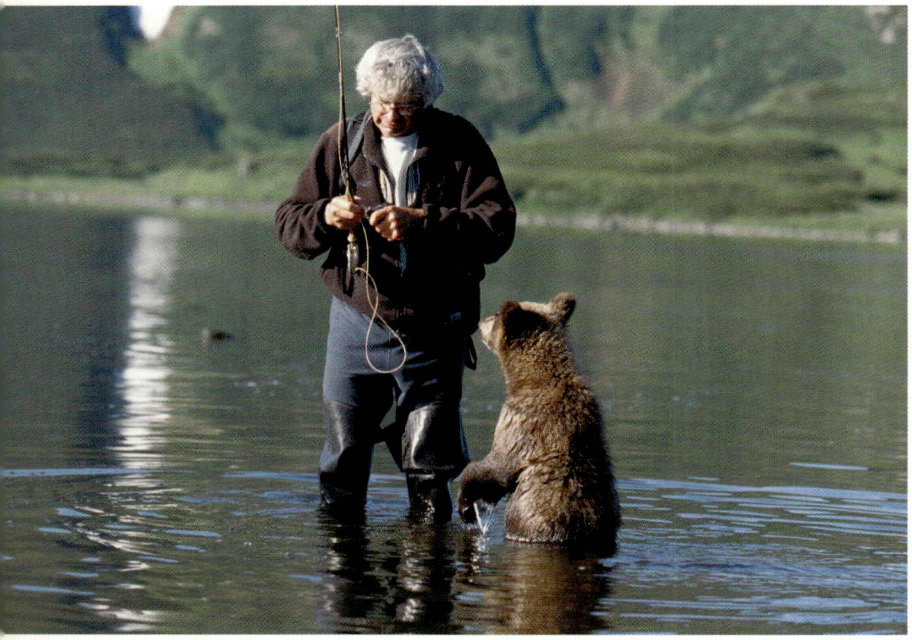

Chico displays remarkable patience waiting for her fish, which I tossed to shore for her to eat. The very tricky responsibility of feeding the cubs without them becoming aggressive later was possible only because we never fed them anything by hand.

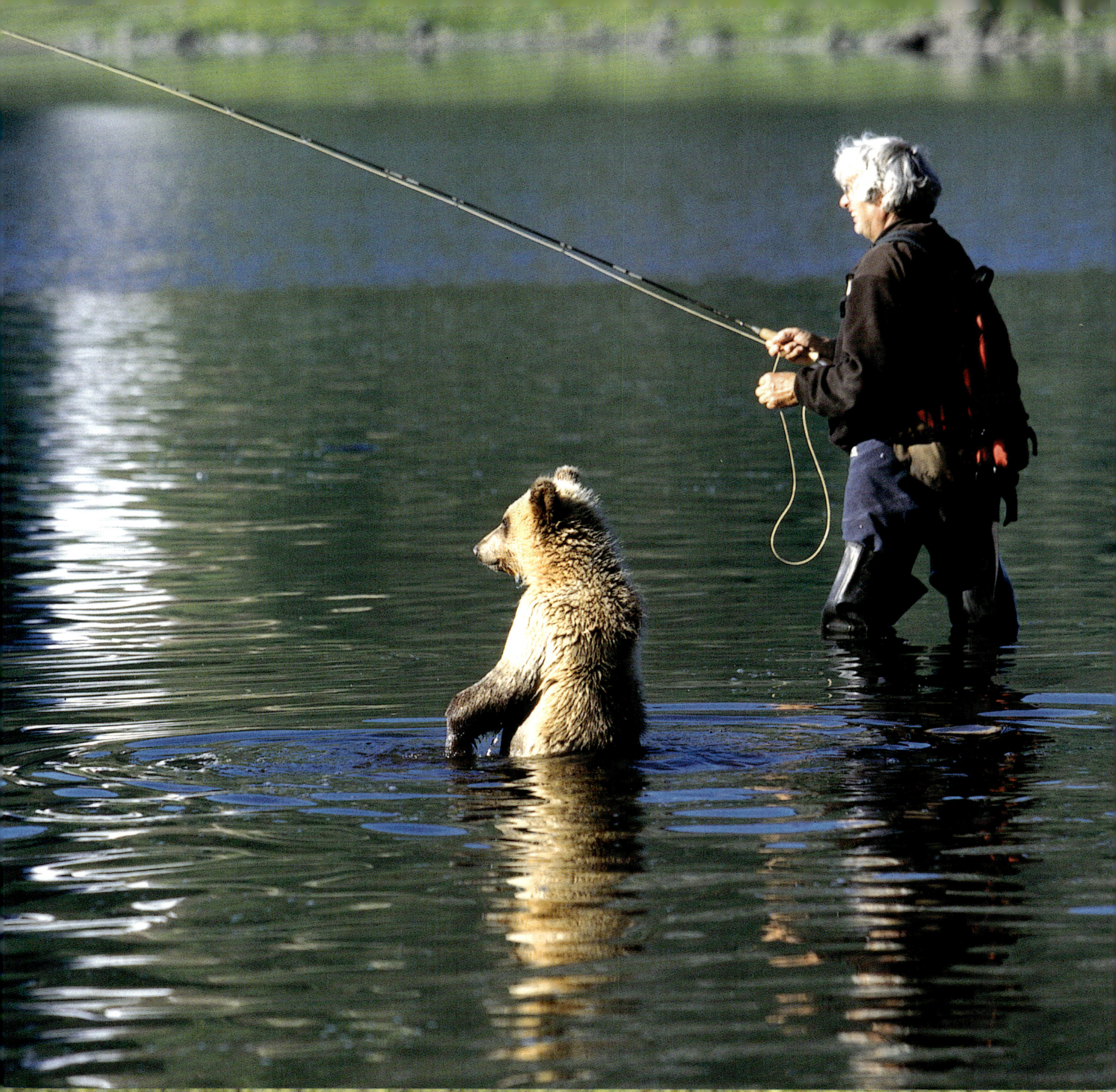

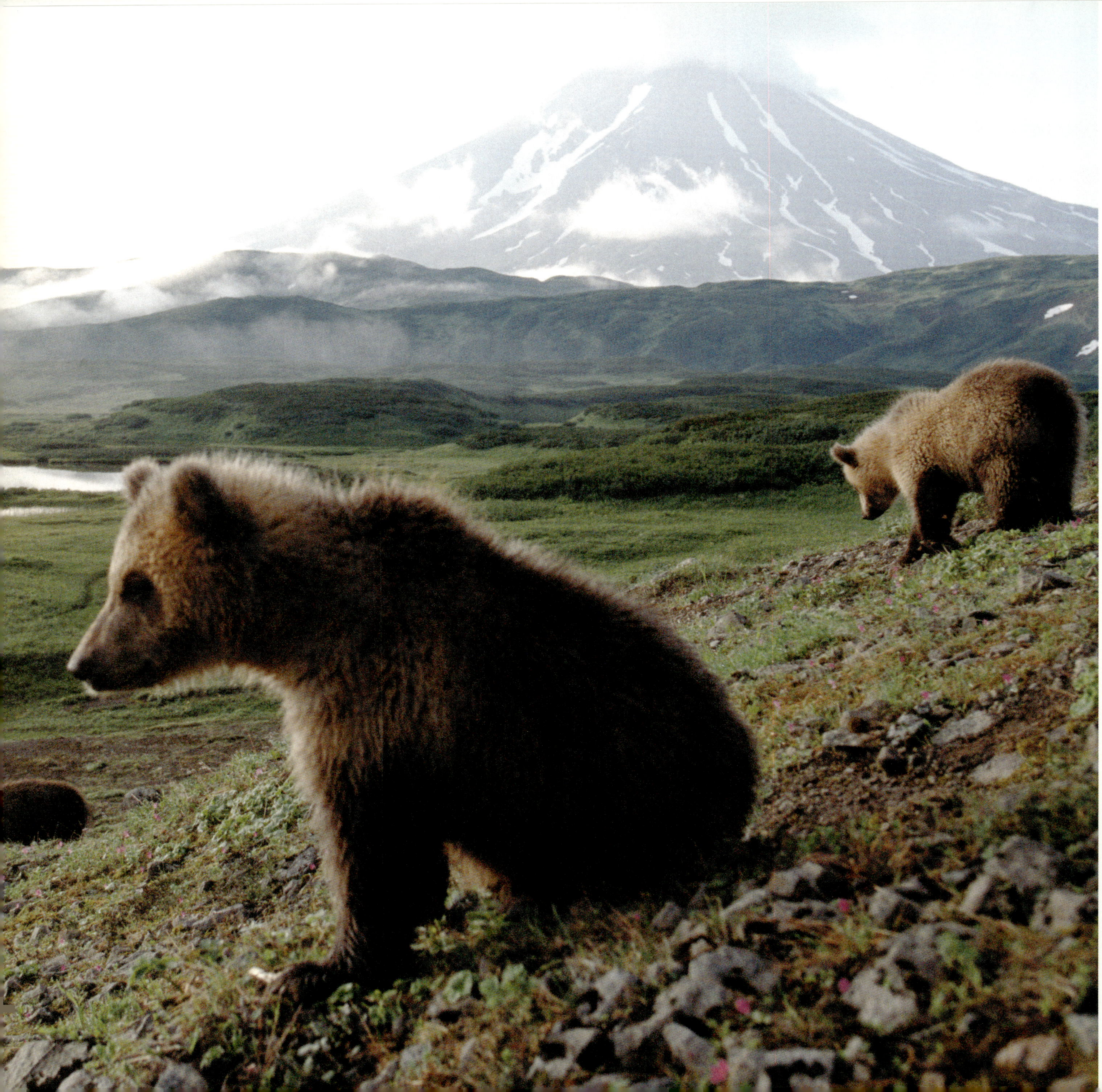

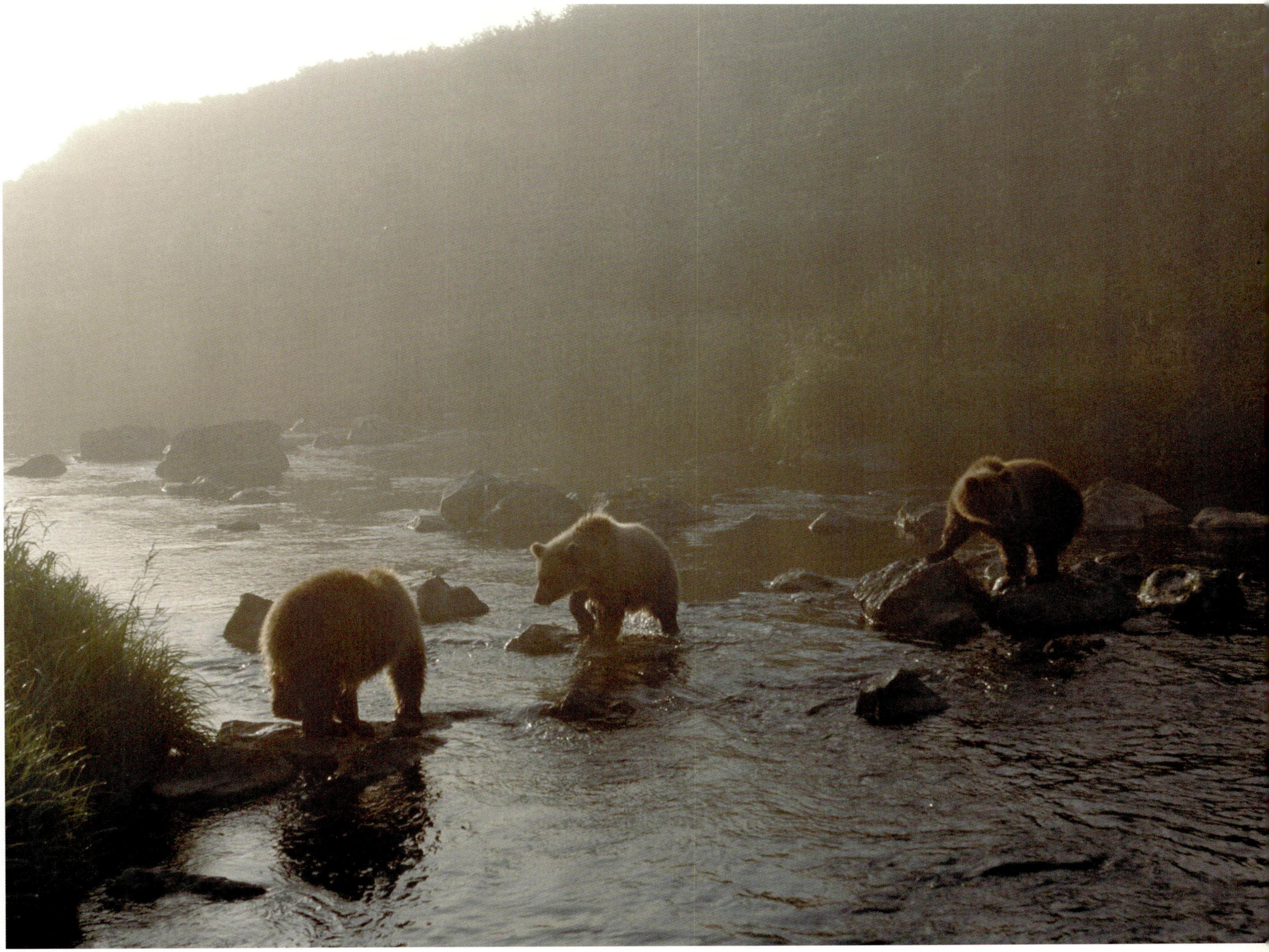

It's a humbling experience to recognize the intelligence bears display in their awareness of their natural surroundings.

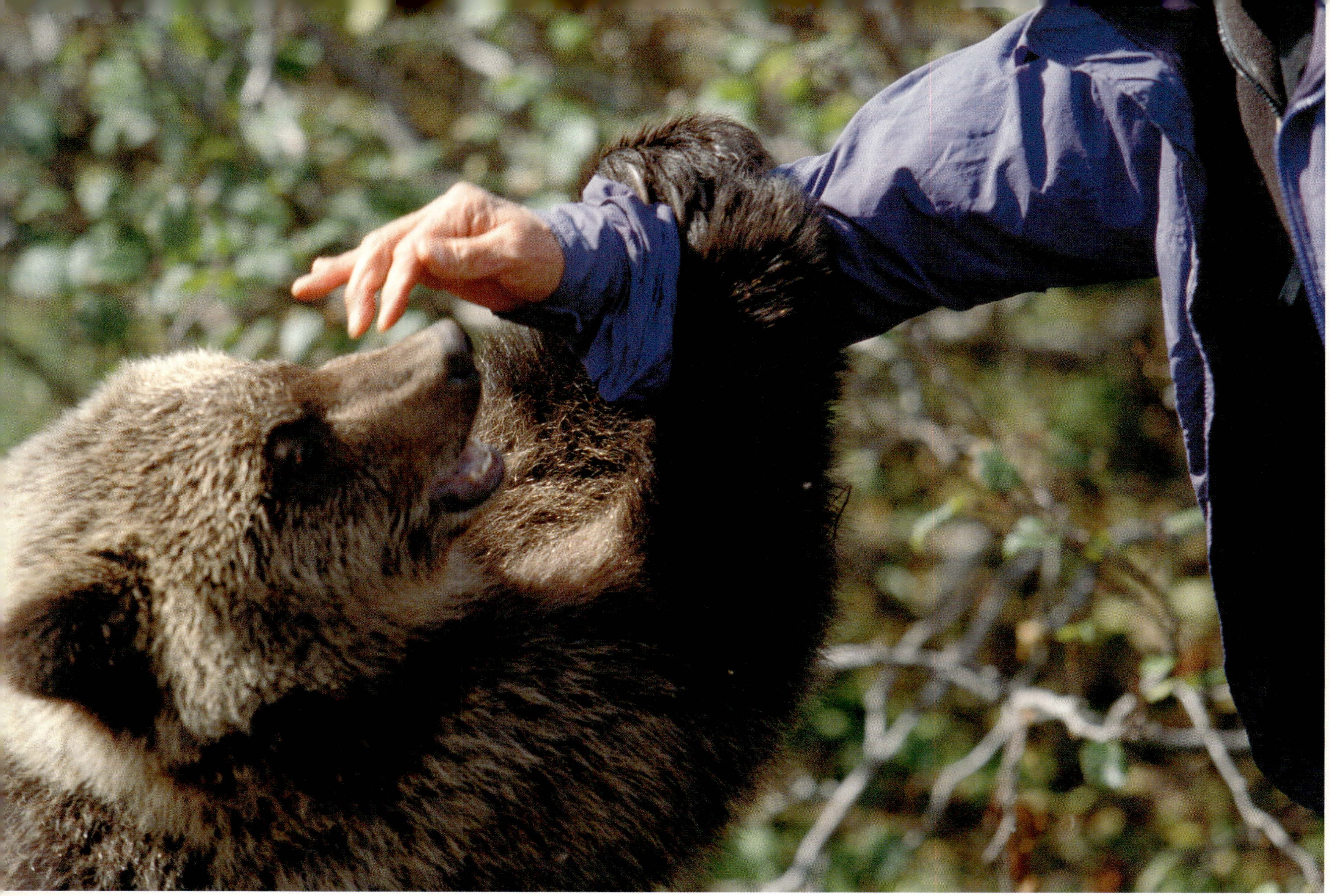

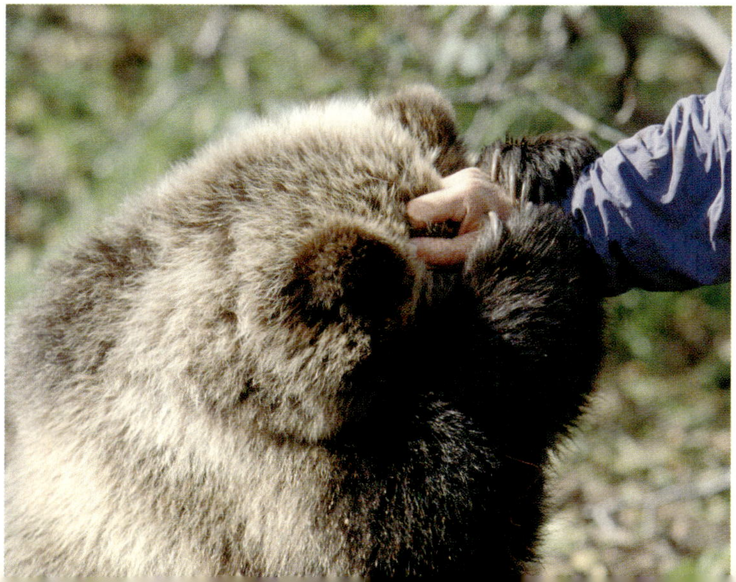

The main focus of our work with the cubs and with all of the bears in the area was trust. We worked with Chico in particular to explore the limits of human-bear interaction—limits that were to be tested with her only. In one game, Charlie would grab a handful of fur between Chico's ears and she would place her claws on his hand and slowly begin to apply pressure, until he had to let go.

Having learned that she was allowed to touch us, Chico enjoyed what to her must have seemed a special advantage.

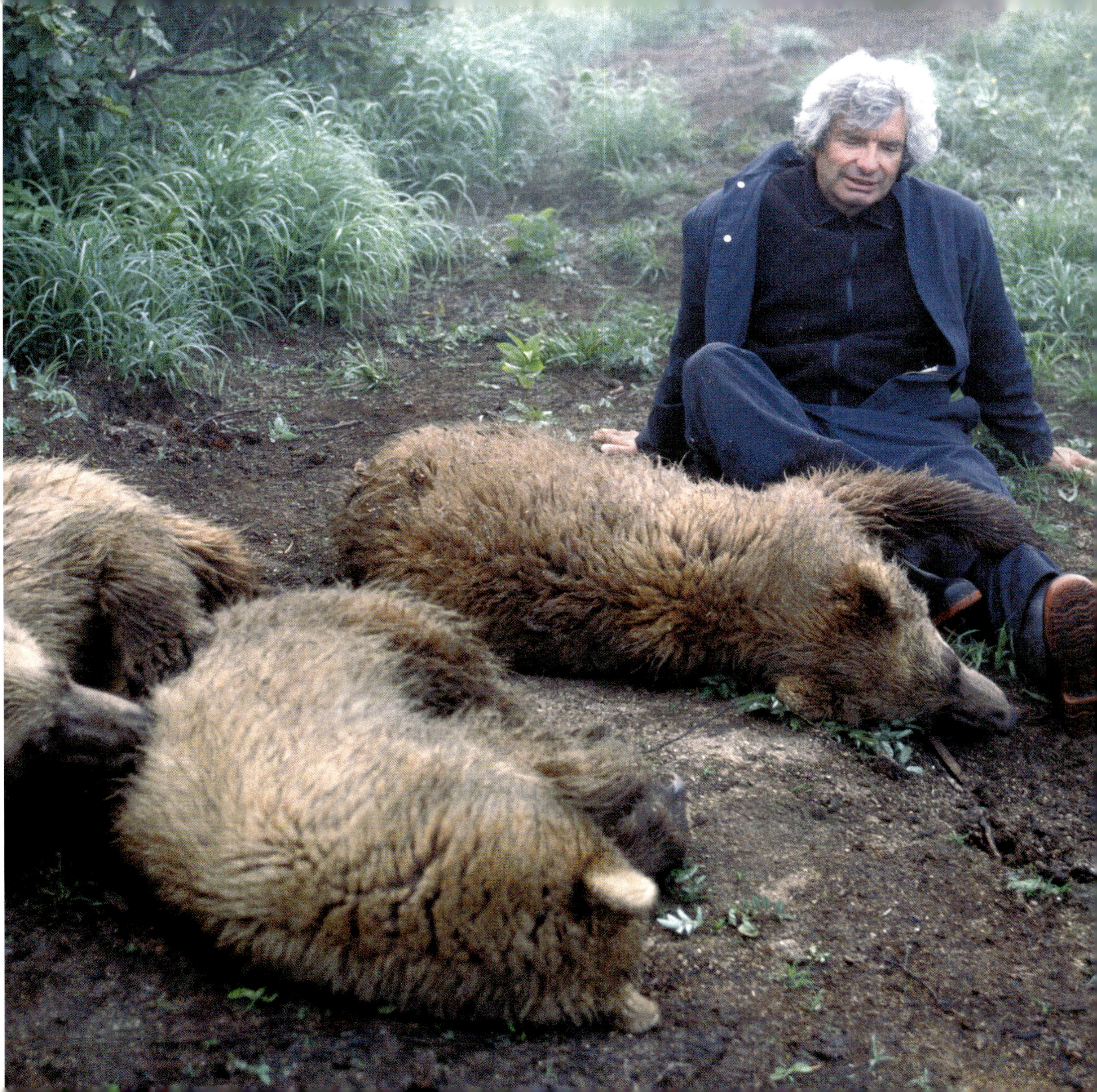

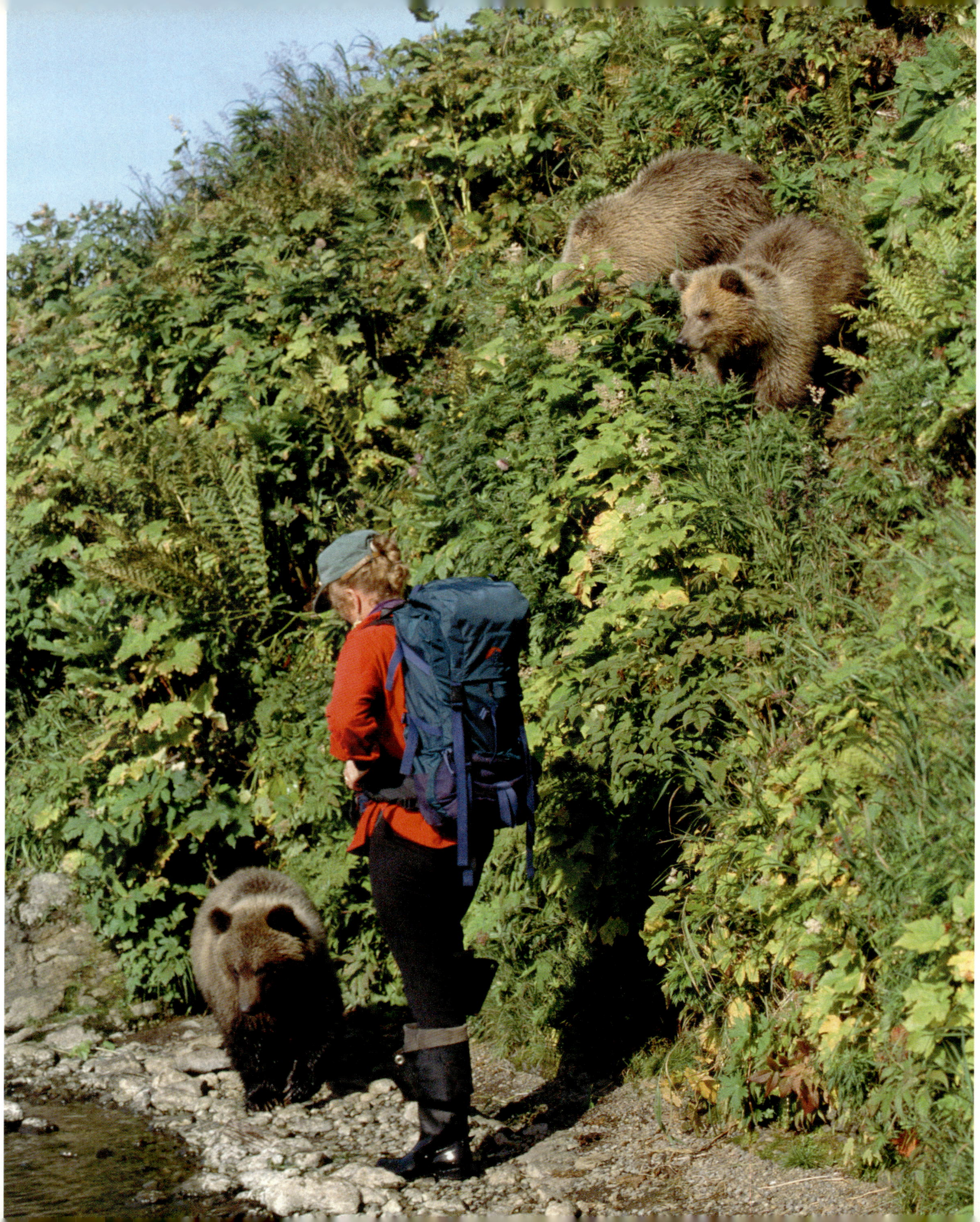

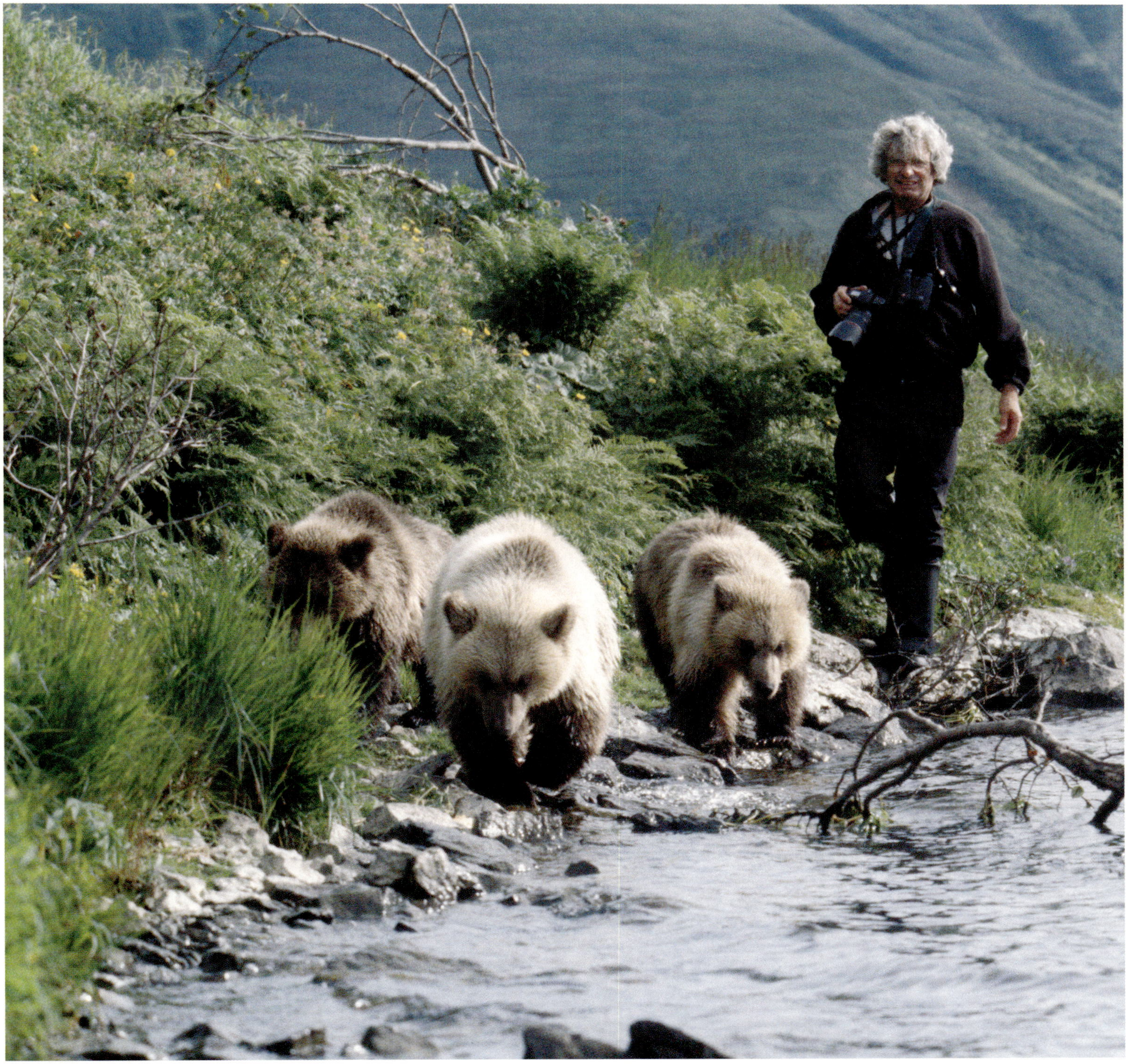

Our daily walks with the cubs took on the feeling of supreme privilege for us, and were not the mundane chore the word rehabilitation might imply. It was never clear: were we the givers or the receivers?

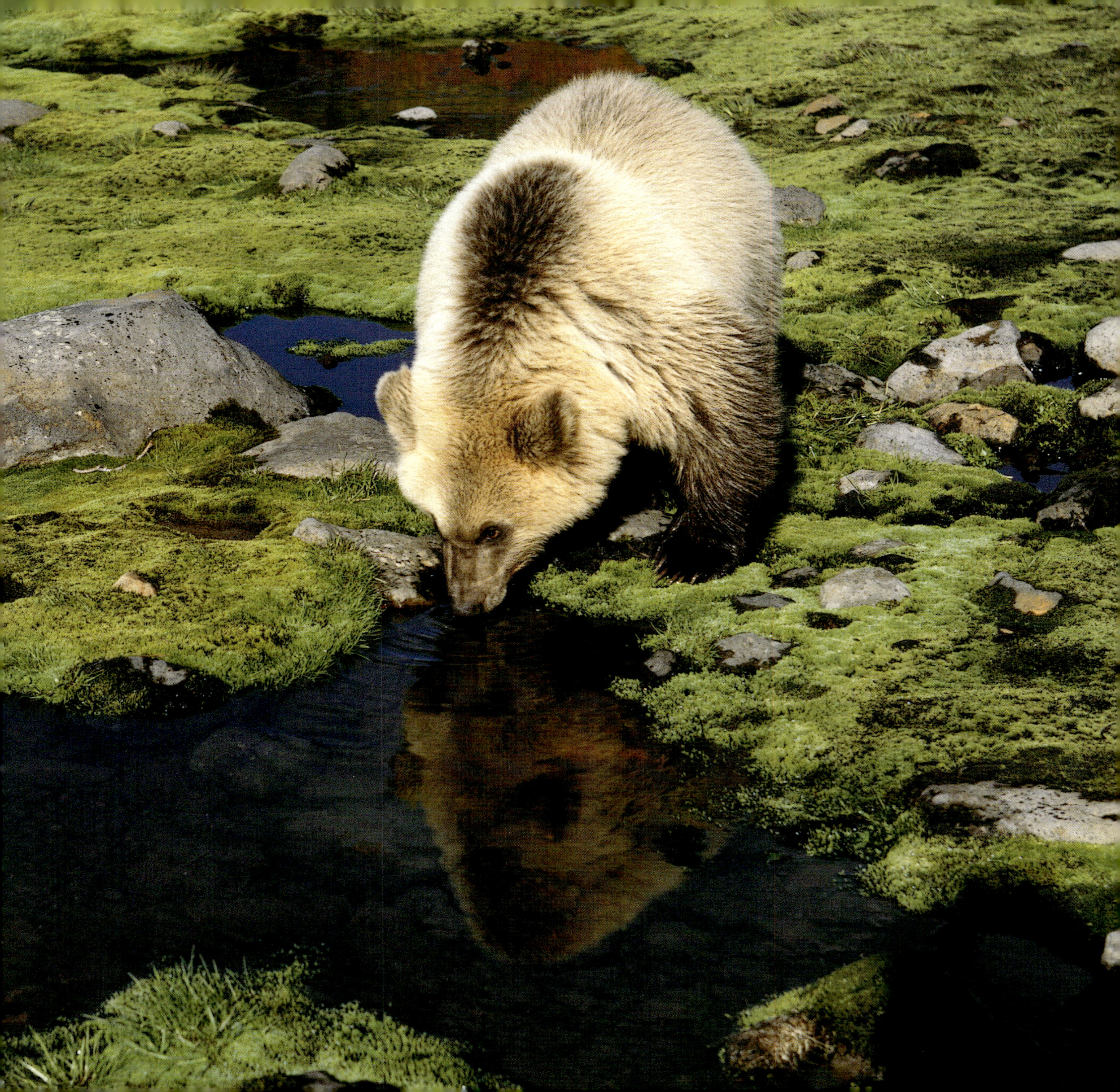

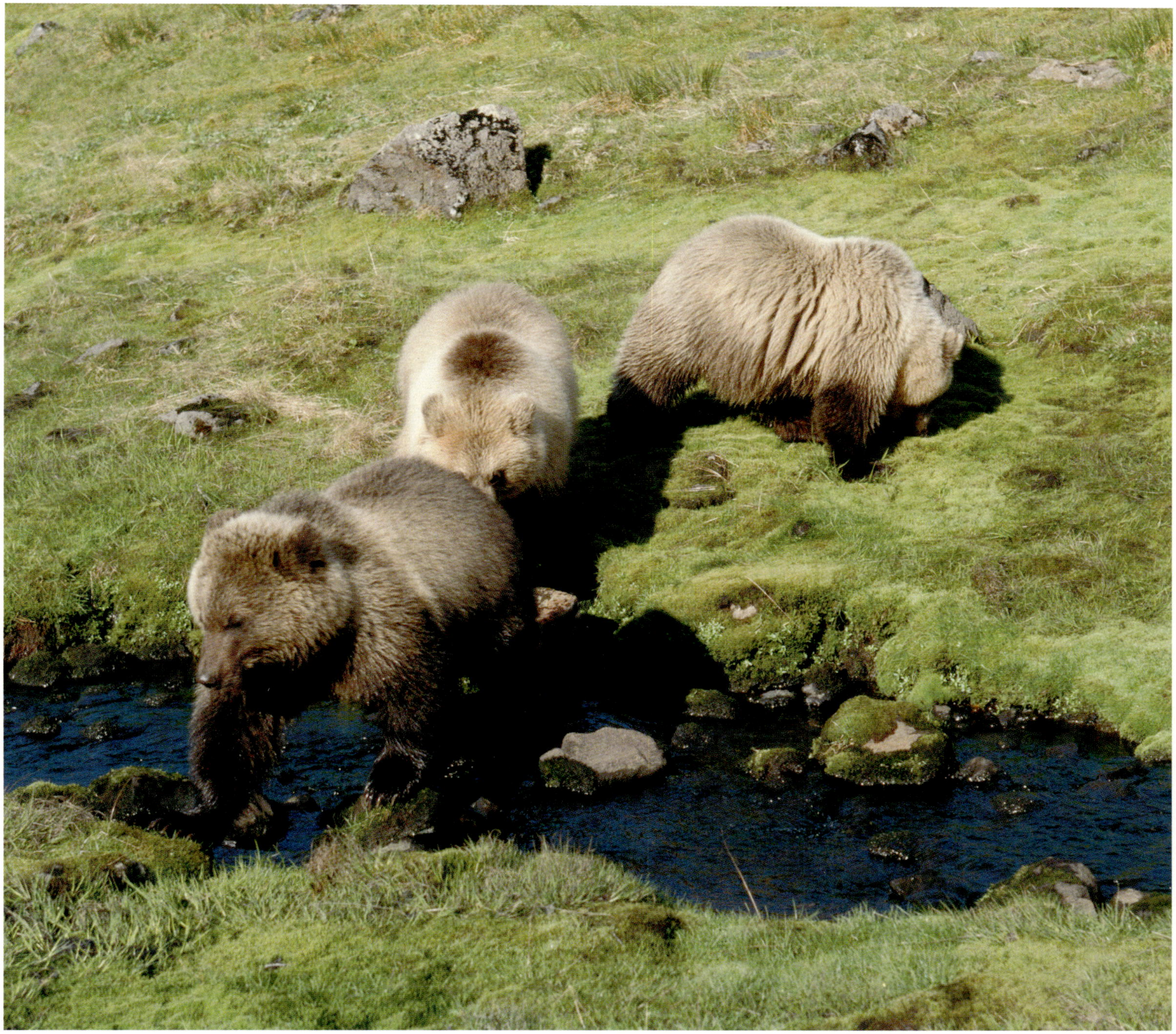

By September, the cubs were in beautiful condition.
They would soon be fat enough to den successfully—providing they could figure out how.

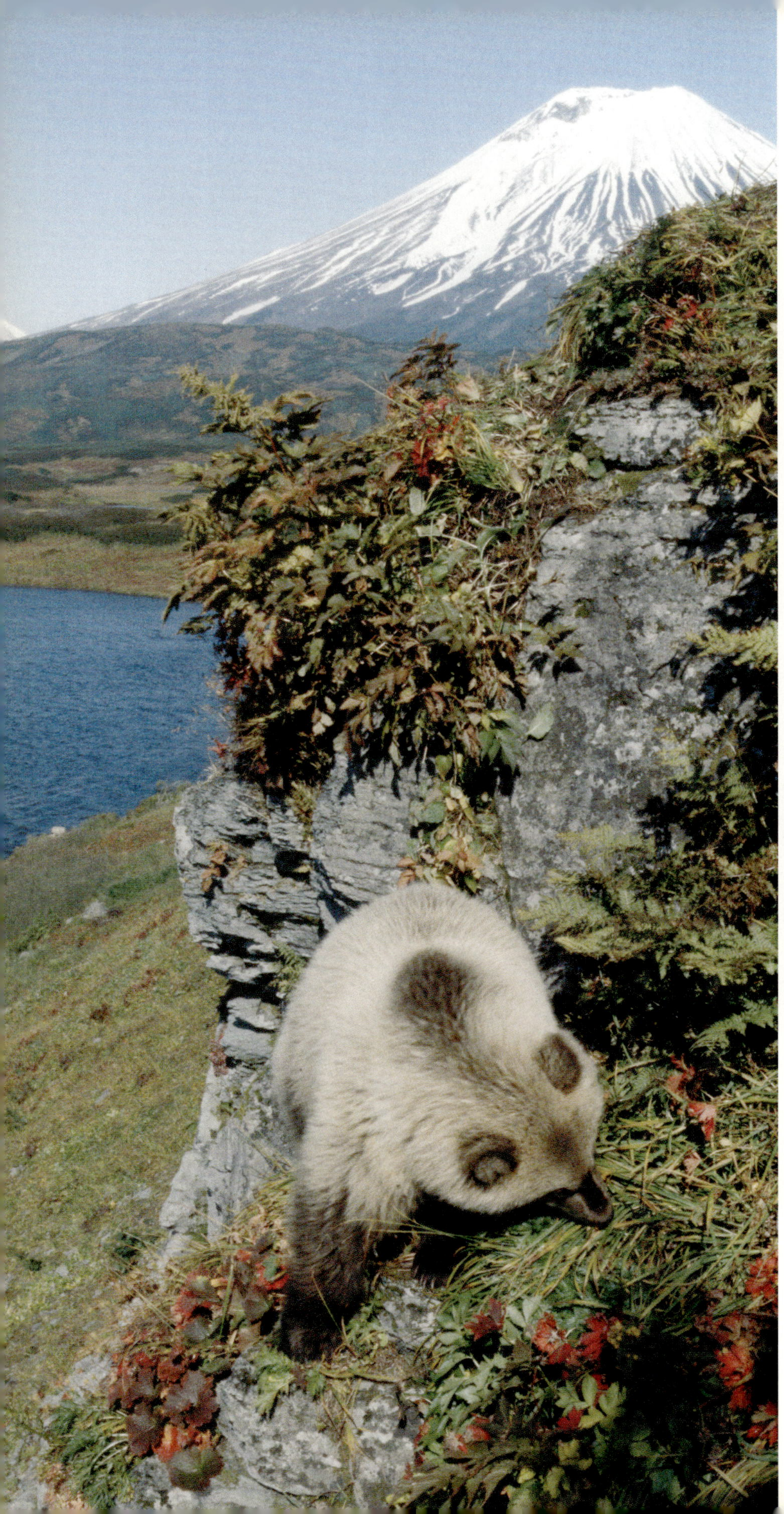

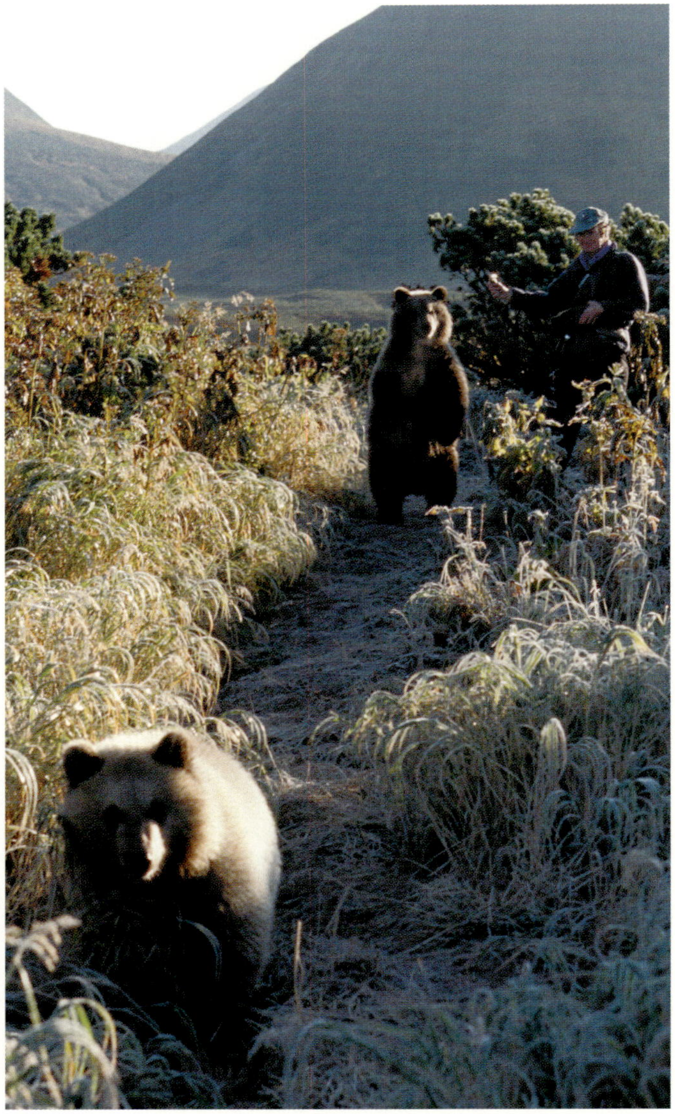

In order to study their ways of communicating, Maureen recorded the many subtle sounds bears make.

One particular section of lakeshore was a bountiful place to find salmon and also offered a quick route to the grassy cliffs above the lake, where the big bears could not pursue the cubs.

Biscuit and Rosie in early fall.

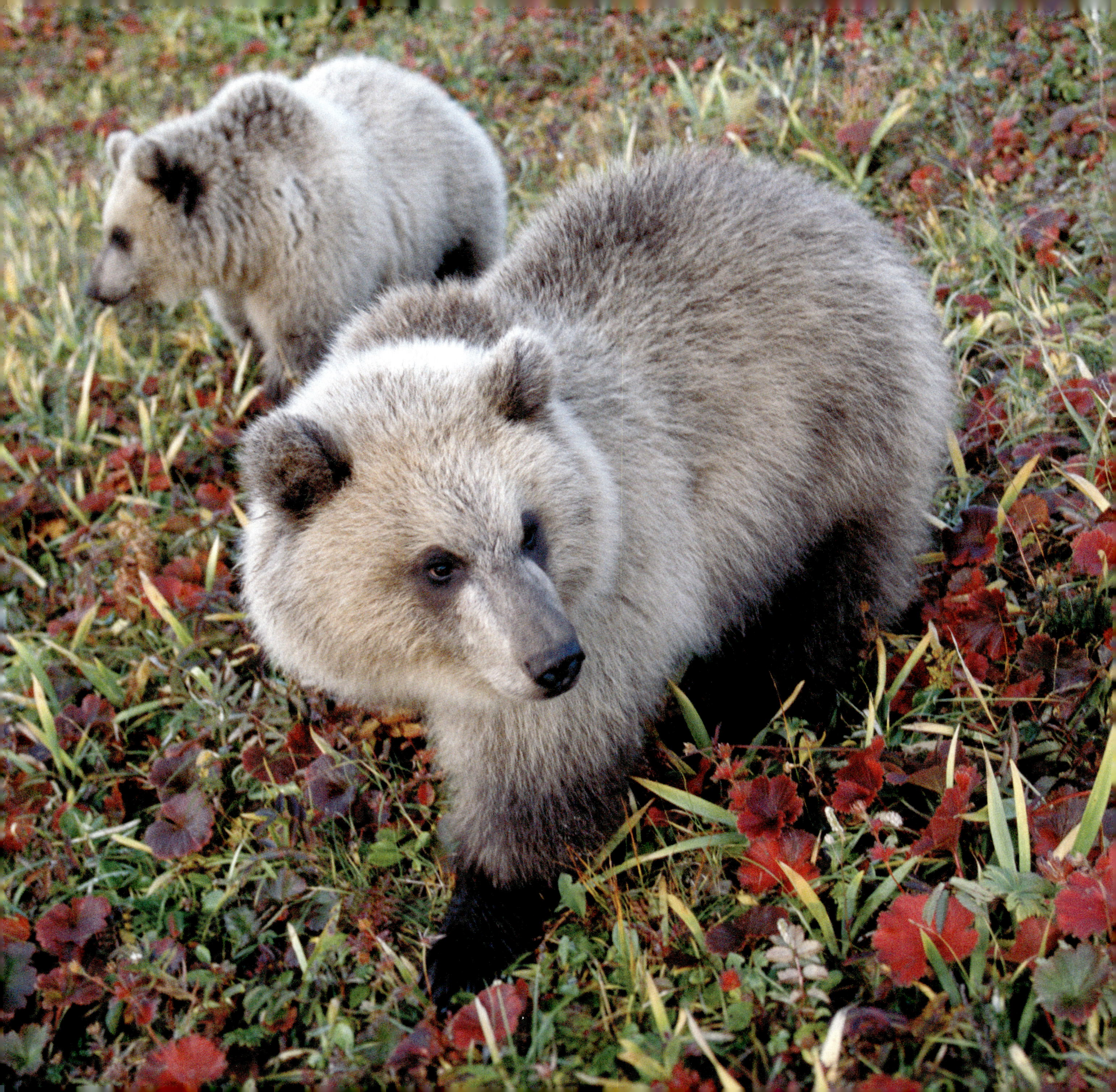

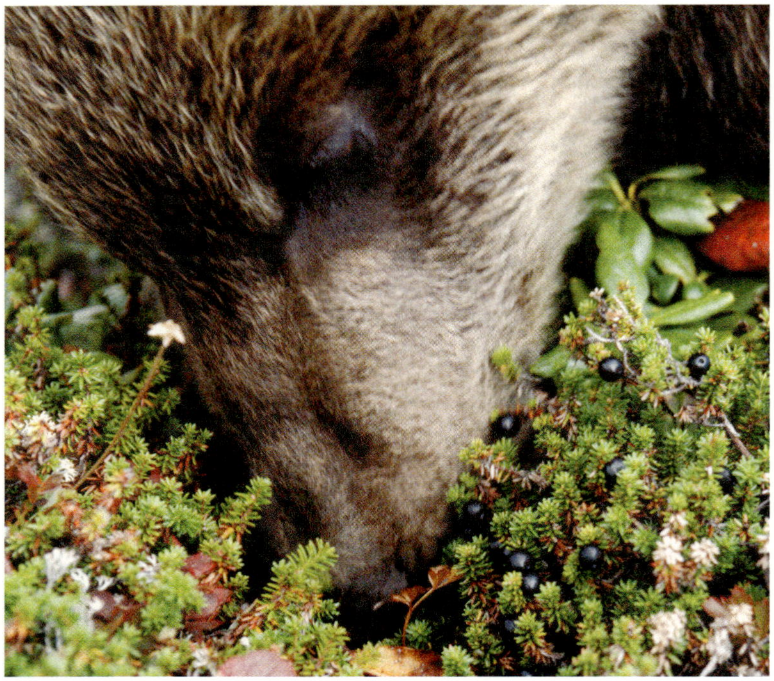

In early September, crowberries were more than just dessert—they were important food.

For bears, the right kind of mud can provide pure bliss—it not only cools down their fur, but keeps biting flies at bay.

Chico.

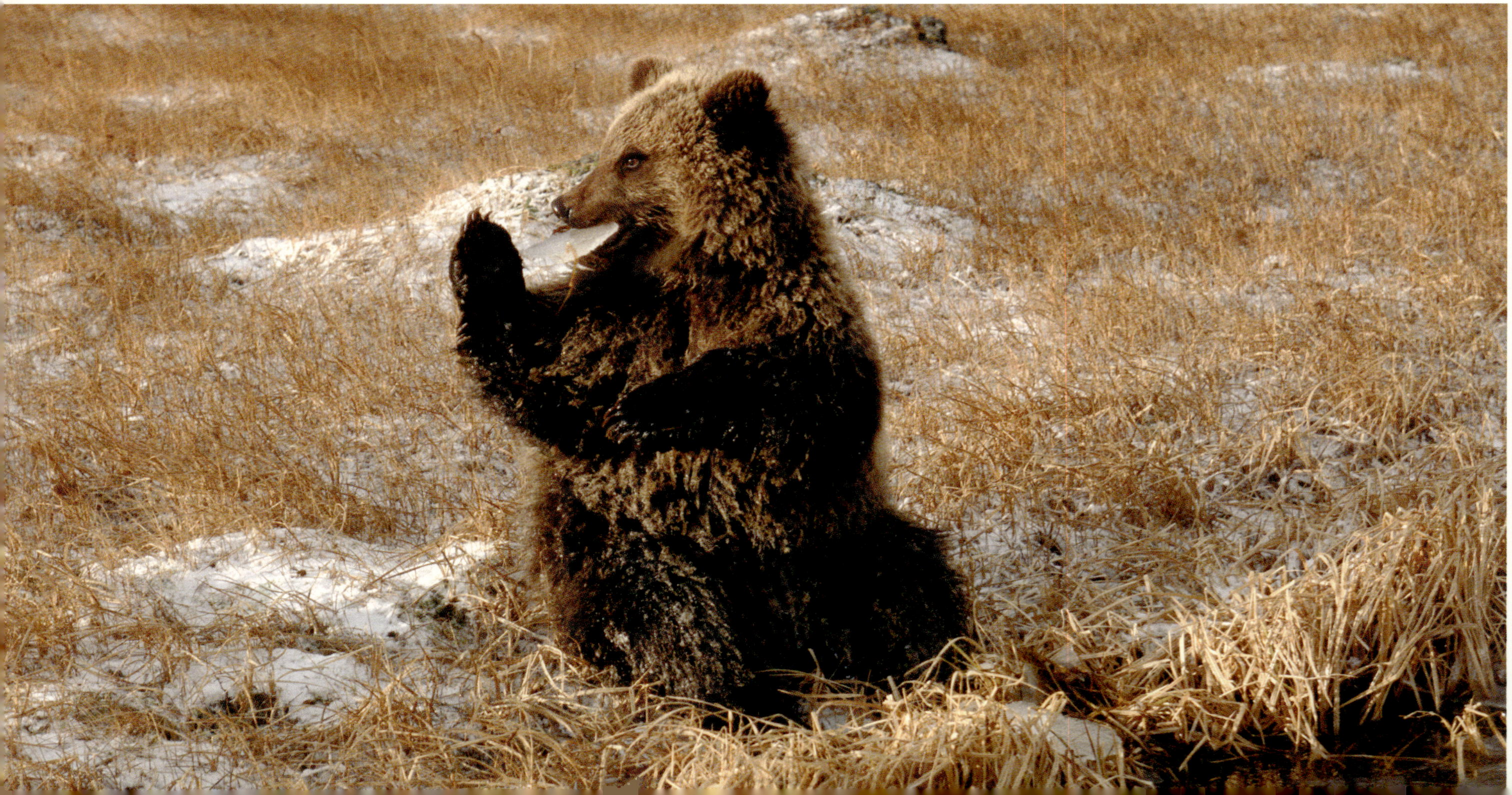

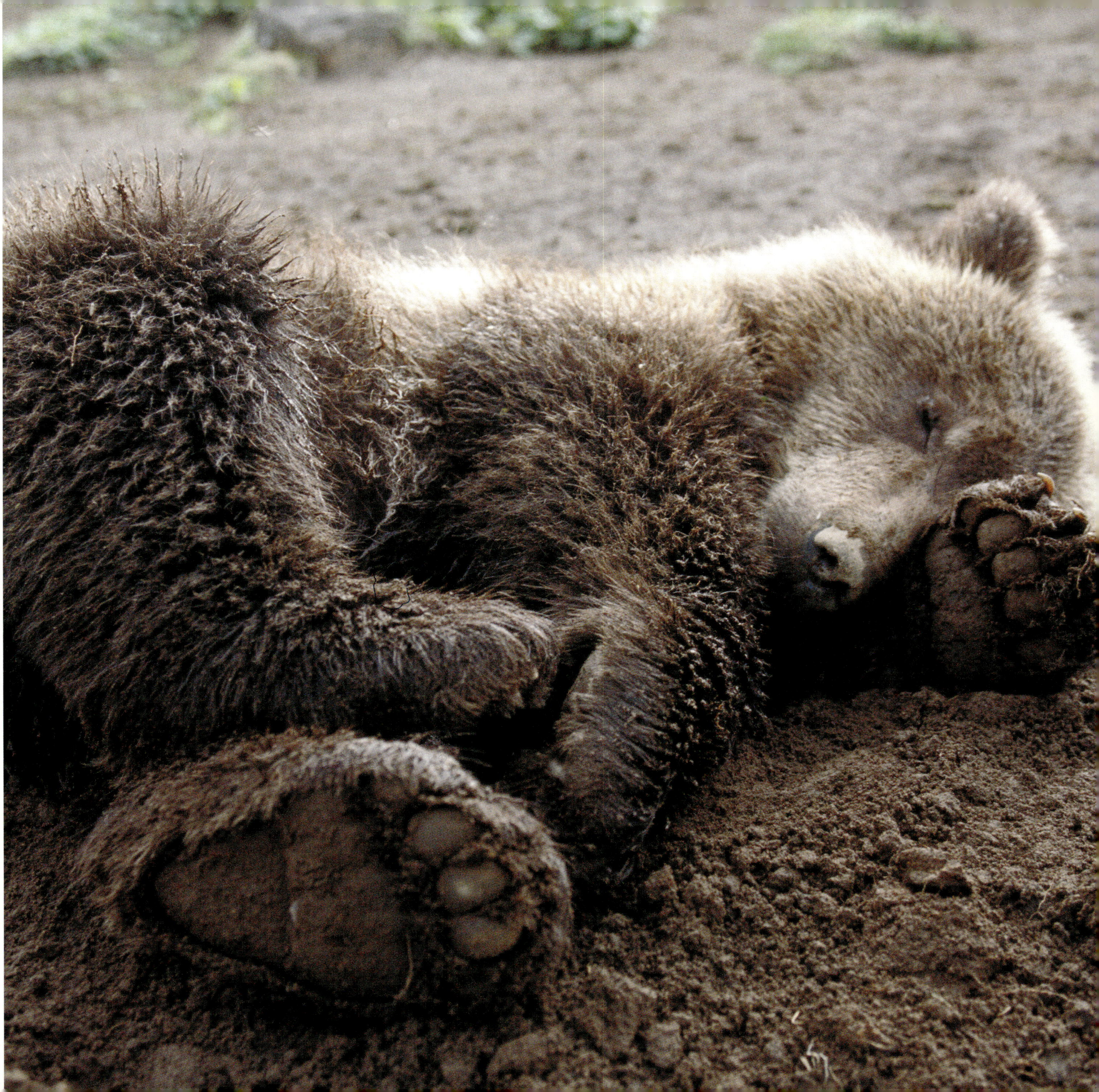

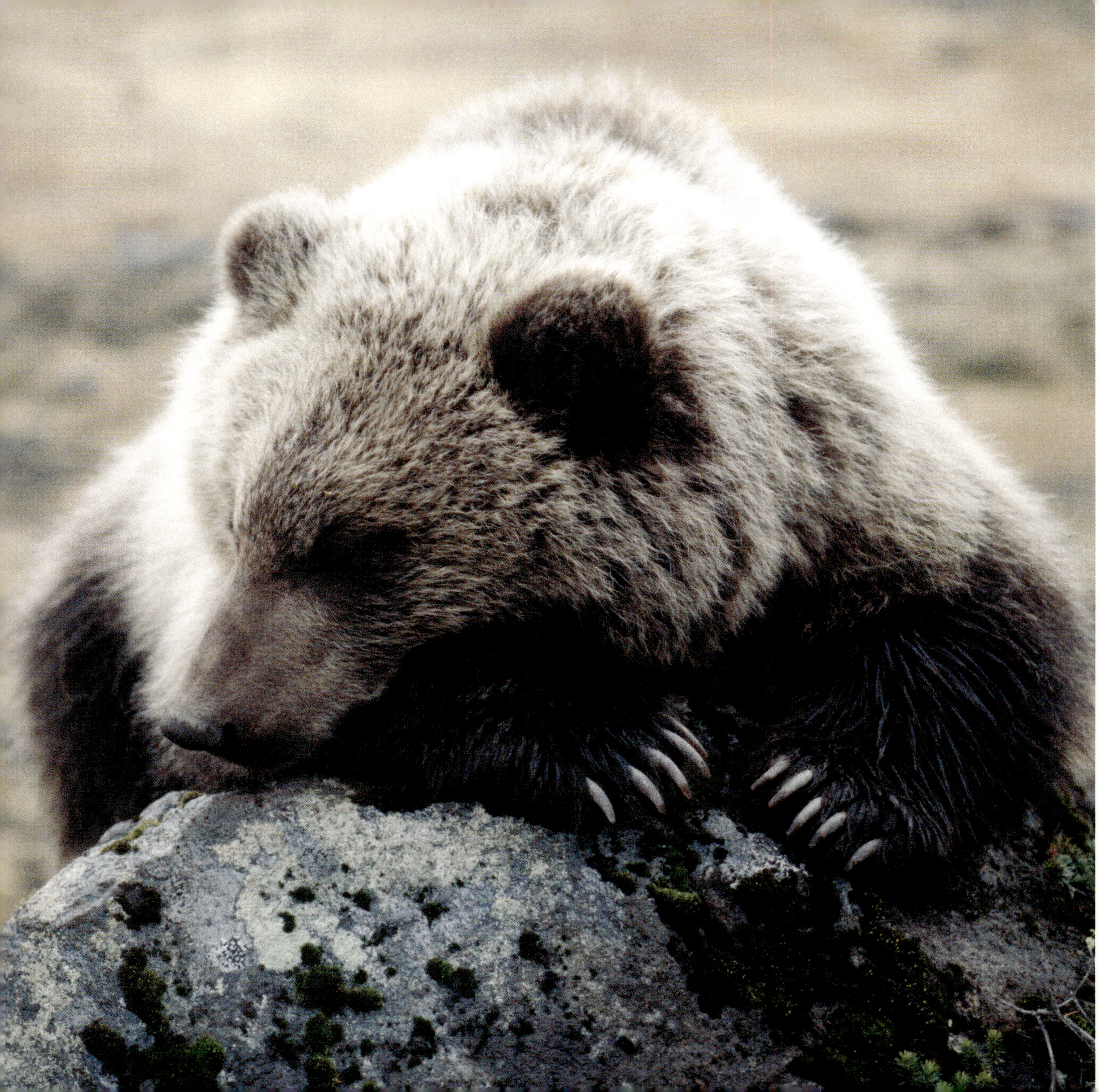

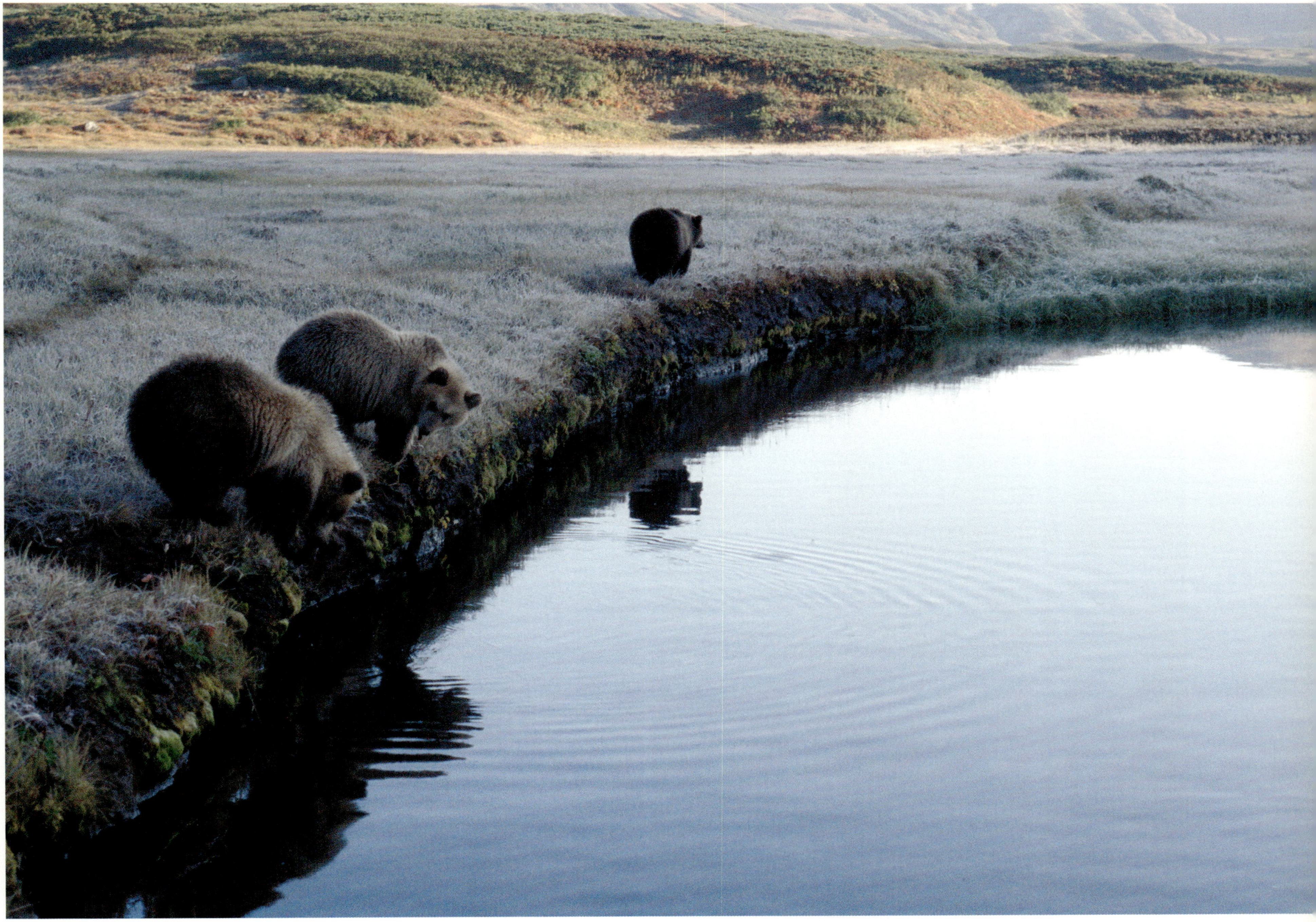

Accustomed to getting up with us for their pre-dawn feedings, the cubs rose earlier than other bears, and always enjoyed having the shore to themselves.

Chico could make herself comfortable anywhere.

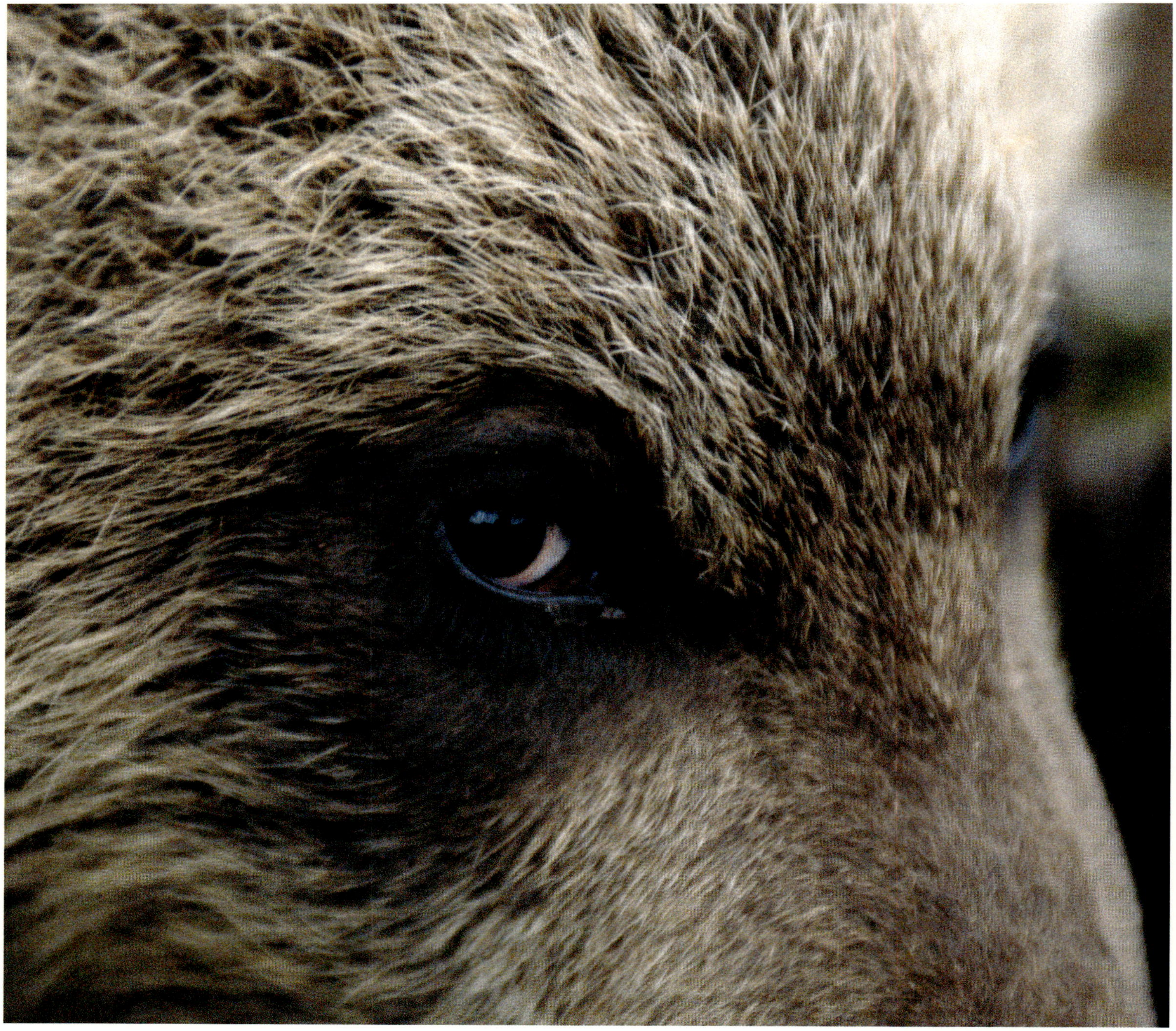

The problem with having a hard and fast rule against looking a bear in the eye is that you miss seeing the intelligence there, and love—and perhaps their kind-hearted pity for your human limitations.

Biscuit on the lookout for danger.

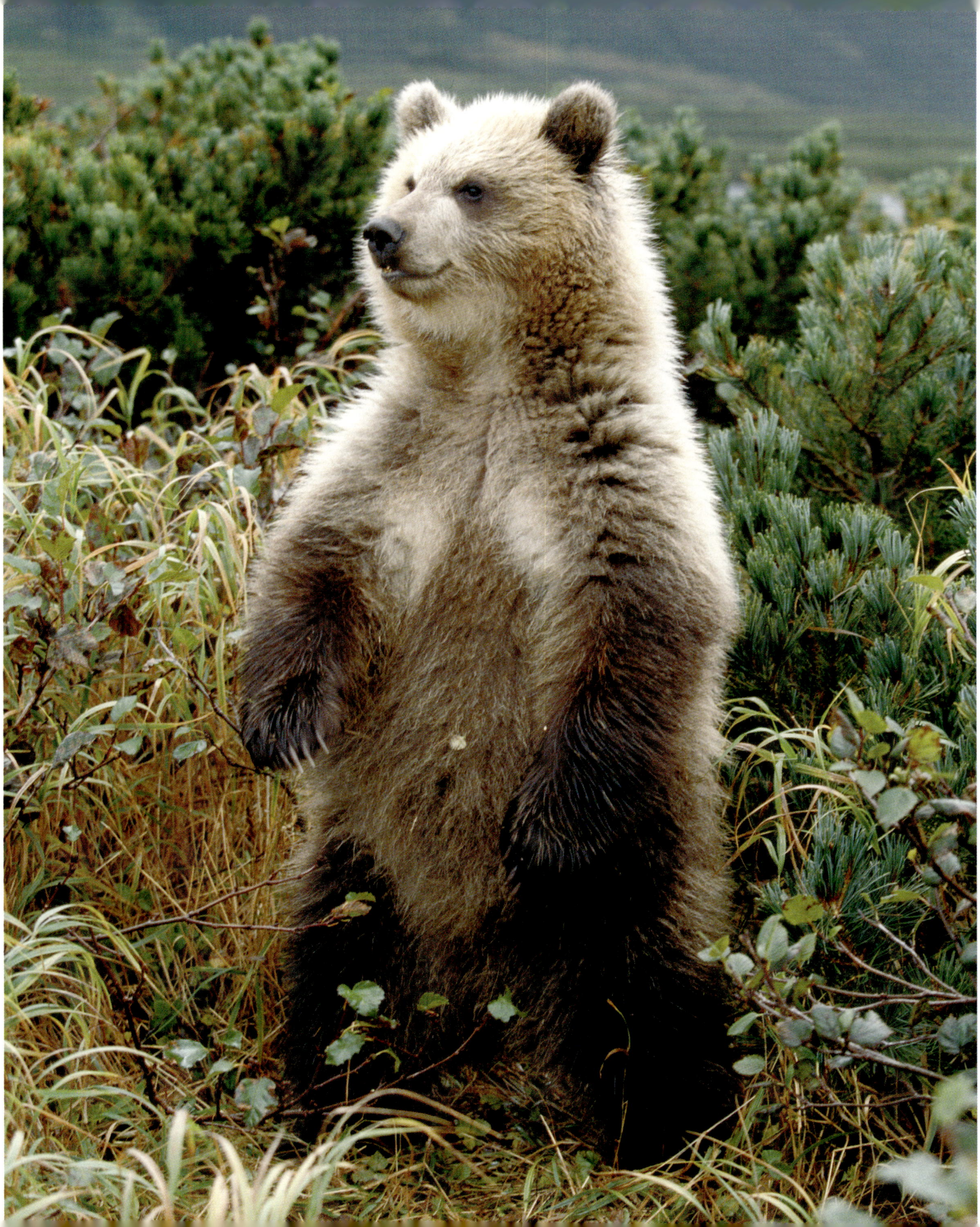

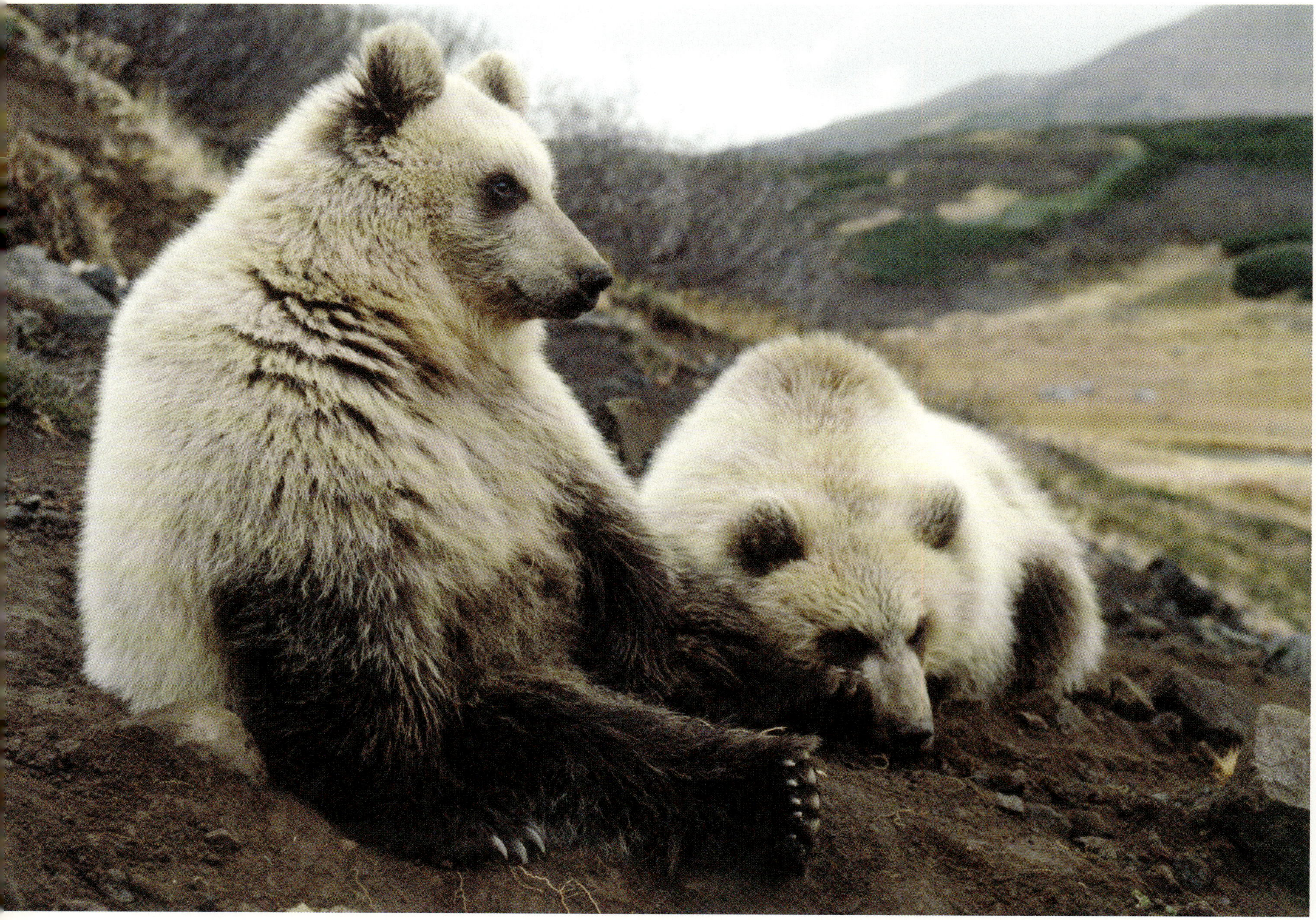

October was a time for lassitude. By then, the cubs had grown from
their spring weight of 10 pounds to a solid 100 pounds, and were almost ready for hibernation.

With snow on the ground and the lake frozen, denning-time was not far off.

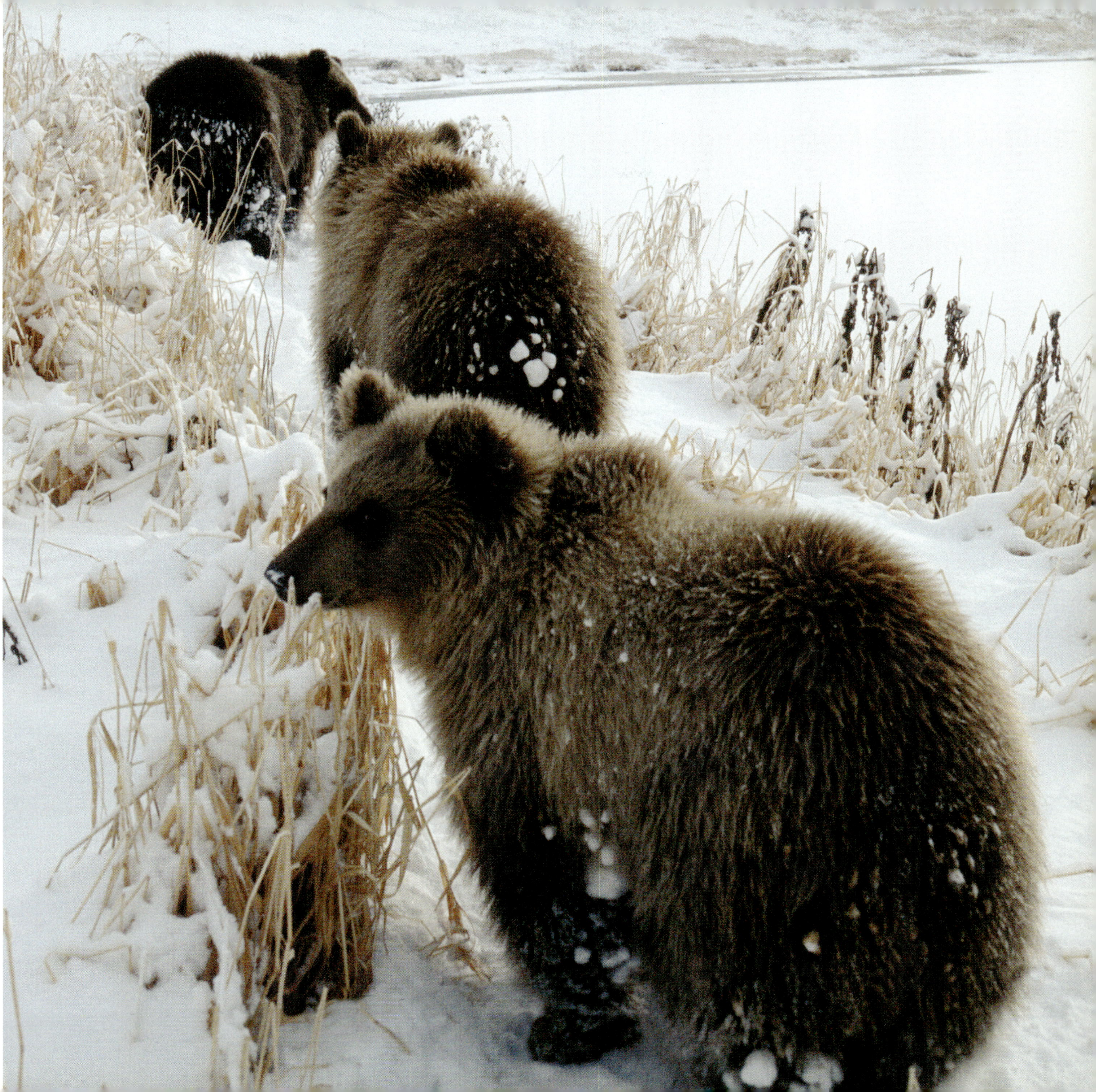

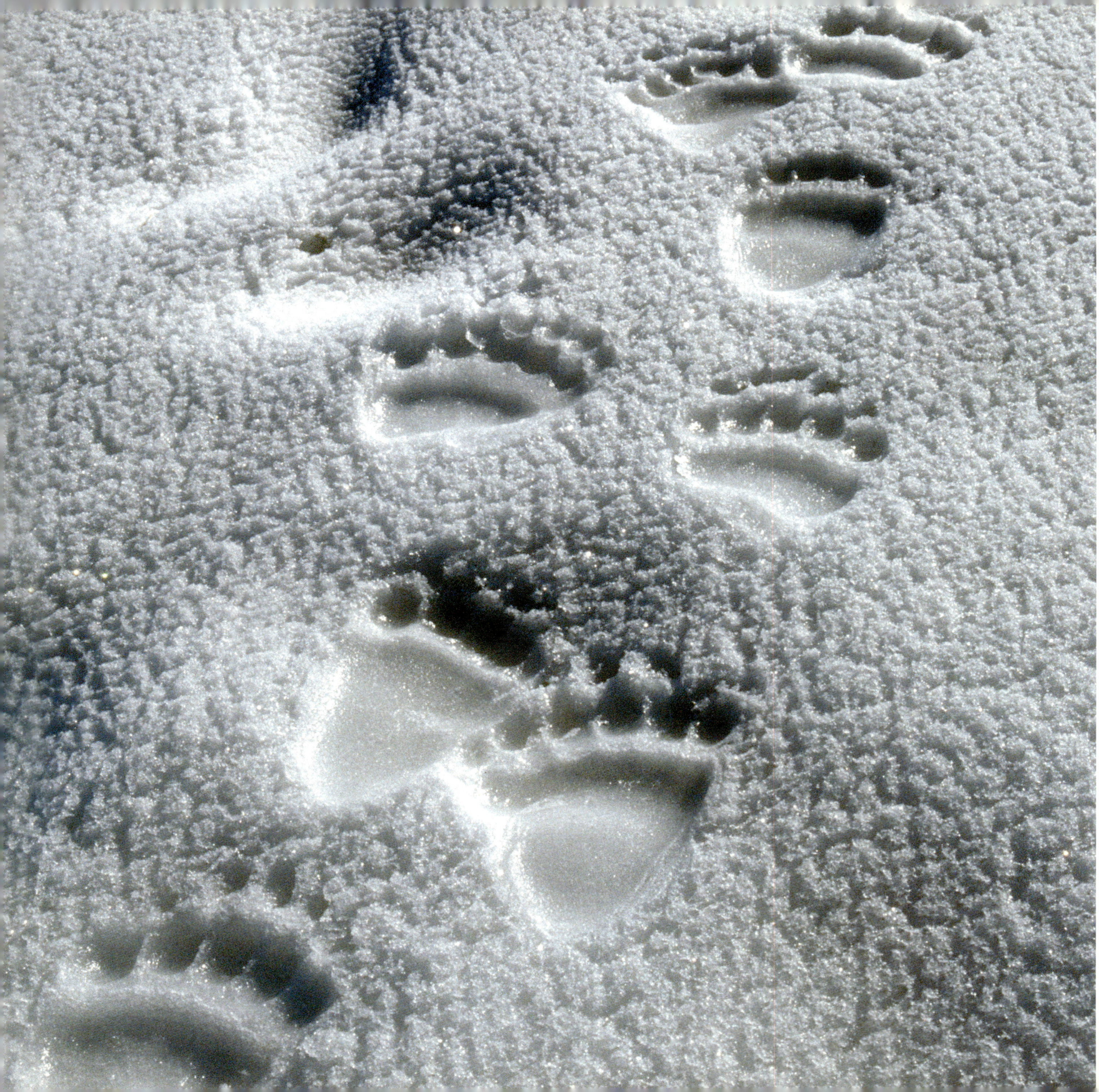

Learning to Be Wild 1998–1999

The mountains surrounding the Kambalnoye basin were still deep in snow when we returned in early May of 1998. It had been a strange winter for us: thousands of miles away from the three extraordinary animals we had grown so attached to, envisioning them snuggled together in a den, and hoping they were safe, comfortable and content.

We had never doubted that the cubs would remember us, but their response to our return was even more than we had hoped for: seeing them for the first time, it was as if we had only been away for a few days. Chico, Biscuit and Rosie ran down the mountain to greet us, bounding and sliding like the fun-loving youngsters we had left behind. All three cubs rubbed their faces in our scent in the snow. But then Chico lay on her back, put her paw up and meshed her claws with Charlie's fingers. So began the second year of trying to understand the makeup of our very special kinship.

We never did find out where our cubs denned that first winter, but they had clearly taken it all in stride, despite having to figure it out on their own. They also had a new air of maturity about them, one that we did not see in other cubs their age, who would still be with their mothers. That snowy May, most of the Kambalnoye females took their cubs to the east coast, where spring was usually a month

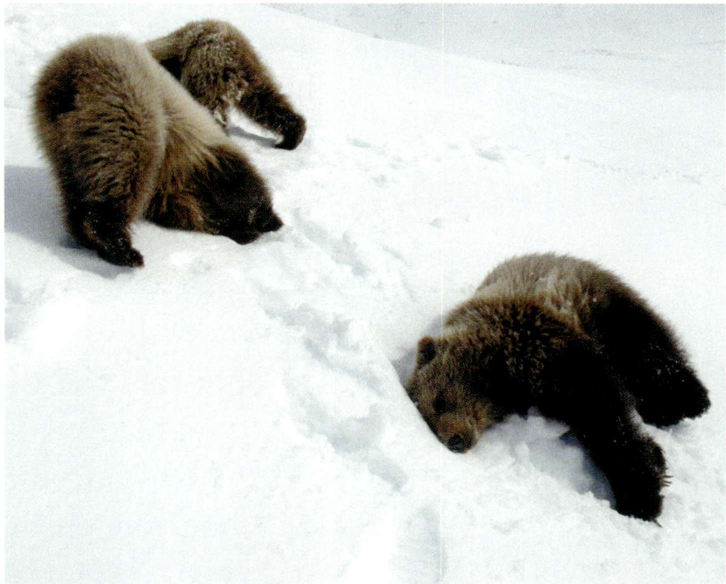

After six months of living on their own, the orphaned cubs immediately rolled around in Charlie's tracks. Judging by their sun-bleached fur, we estimated they had denned for five and a half months and re-emerged three weeks before our arrival.

Three sets of yearling tracks near the cabin were the first signs we had that the cubs had survived the winter.

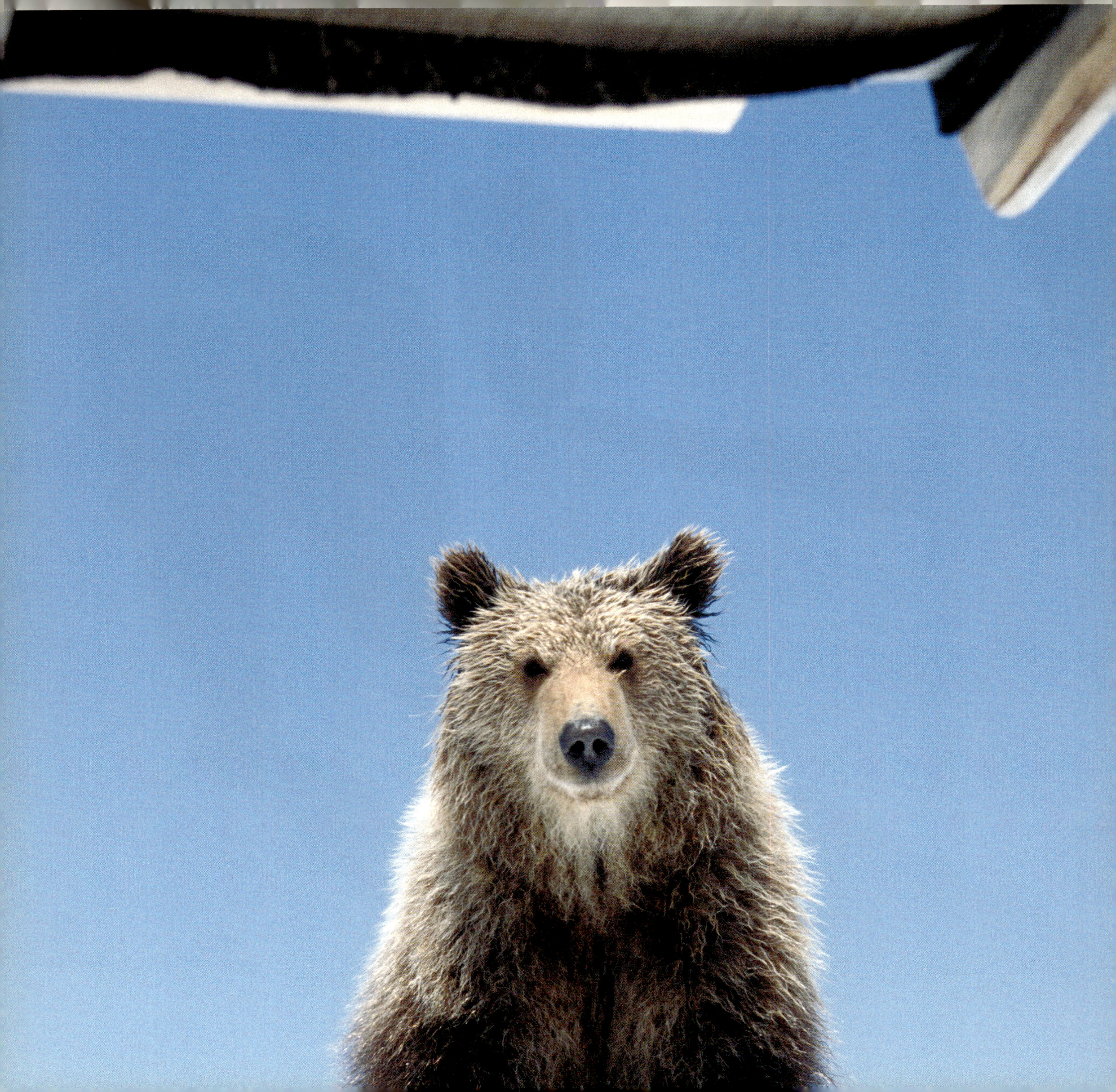

sounded like a herd of horses coming through—and stop at the fence. If we made any move towards getting ready to come, they would wait. If not, they would pound off again and disappear.

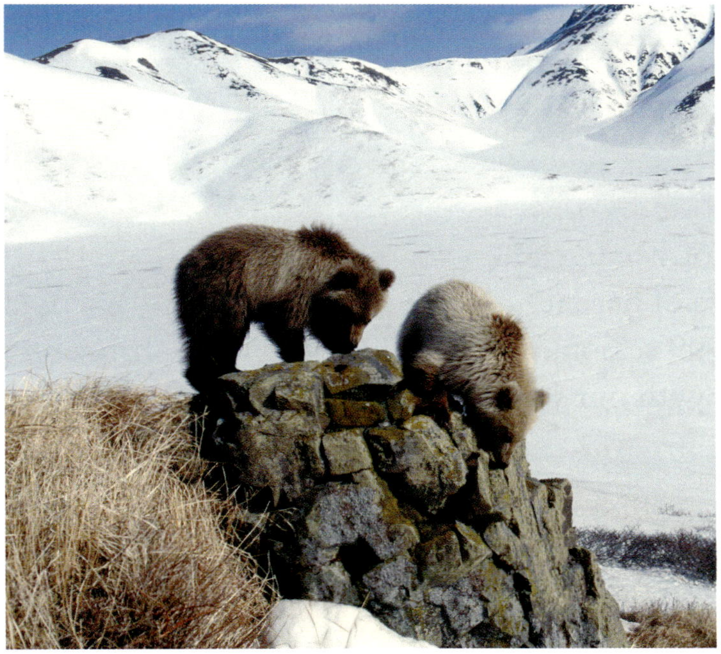

Accompanying them was always an awe-inspiring expedition into the world they now regarded as theirs. We travelled with them not as substitute parents, but as close observers of how wild bears lived. They were not afraid of humans, which defies conventional notions of wildness, but such restrictive definitions are best reserved for people who need to see themselves as separate from the natural world. In terms of freedom and self-sufficiency, our cubs had taken their rightful places in the Kamchatkan wild.

Of course, we were also still exploring the nature of our shared trust, and Chico still loved to have the mosquitoes brushed away from around her eyes while she napped. The praise she received for a great catch of a leaping trout or salmon seemed to cement our bond with her, because it indicated our interest in what she was doing. Understanding her reactions meant understanding the most important and remarkably simple key to having a way with animals: recognizing what we share in intelligence, feelings and emotions.

Every other year, pink salmon spawn upstream from the cabin, in Char Creek. The cubs' second season in Kamchatka, in 1998, coincided with this bounty of protein and fat. It gave them the opportunity to hone their fishing skills and to fatten up in preparation for their second winter. Before the cubs denned that year, however, Rosie must have made a terrible mistake—one that

The bears had little to eat in the spring, and we were surprised by how they could survive on their fat from the previous year. Supplemented with vegetation as it became available, this fat would keep them going until salmon showed up in mid-August.

No privacy, even in the privy.

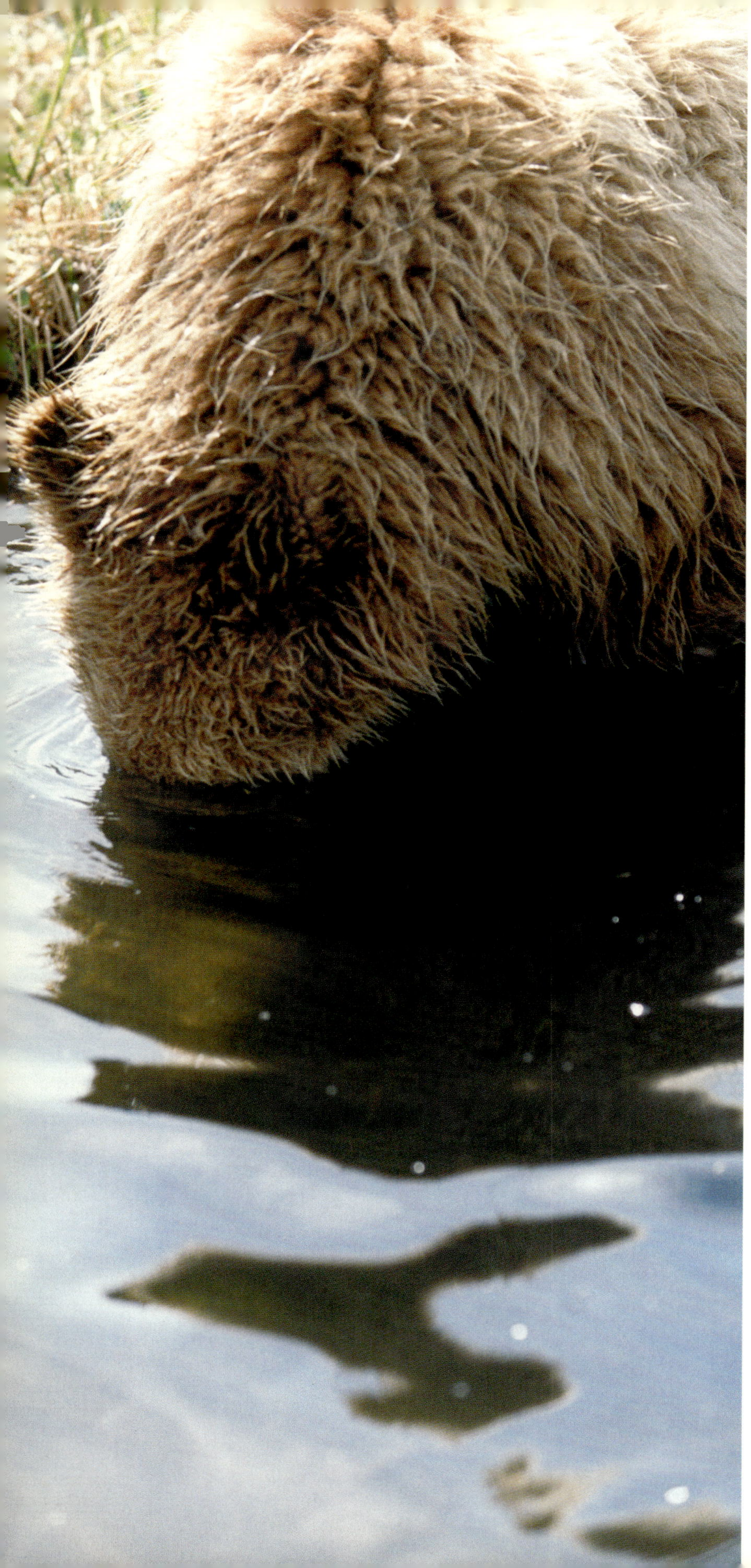

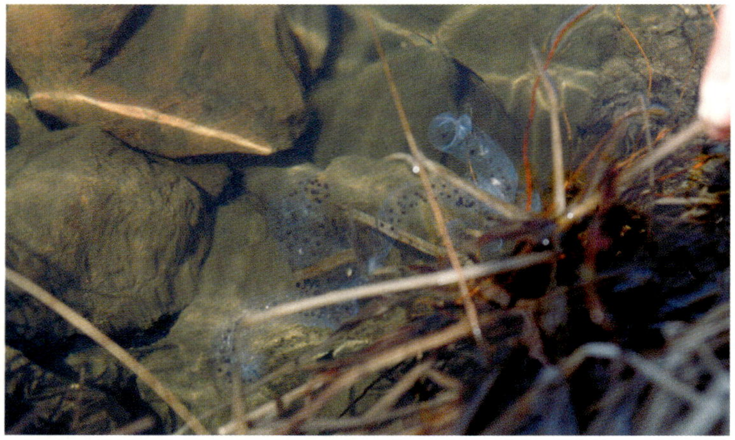

In late June, salamanders lay their eggs on stems of grass along the edges of the small lakes north of the cabin.

Unfortunately for the salamanders, Biscuit developed quite a taste for the eggs.

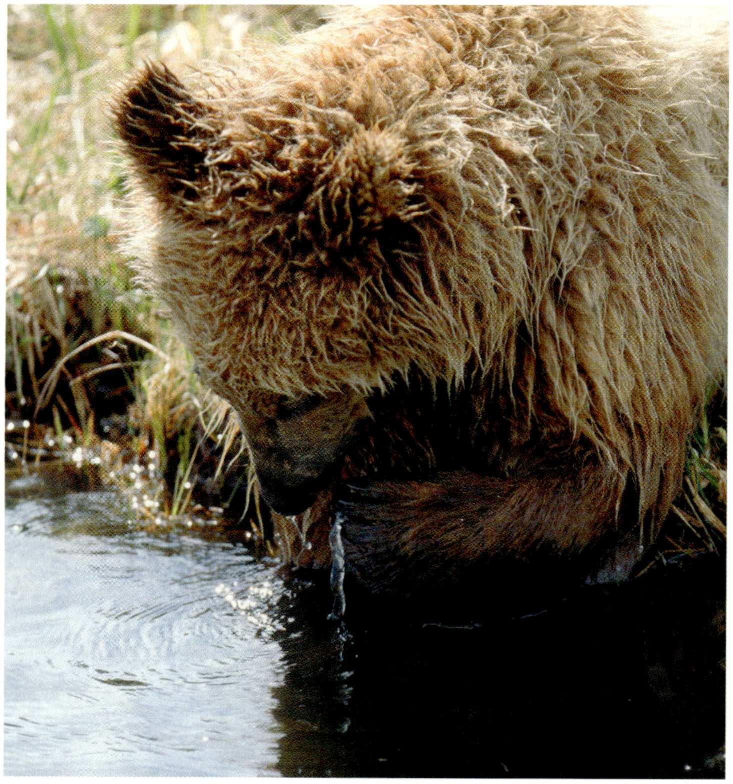

Rosie caught on quickly.

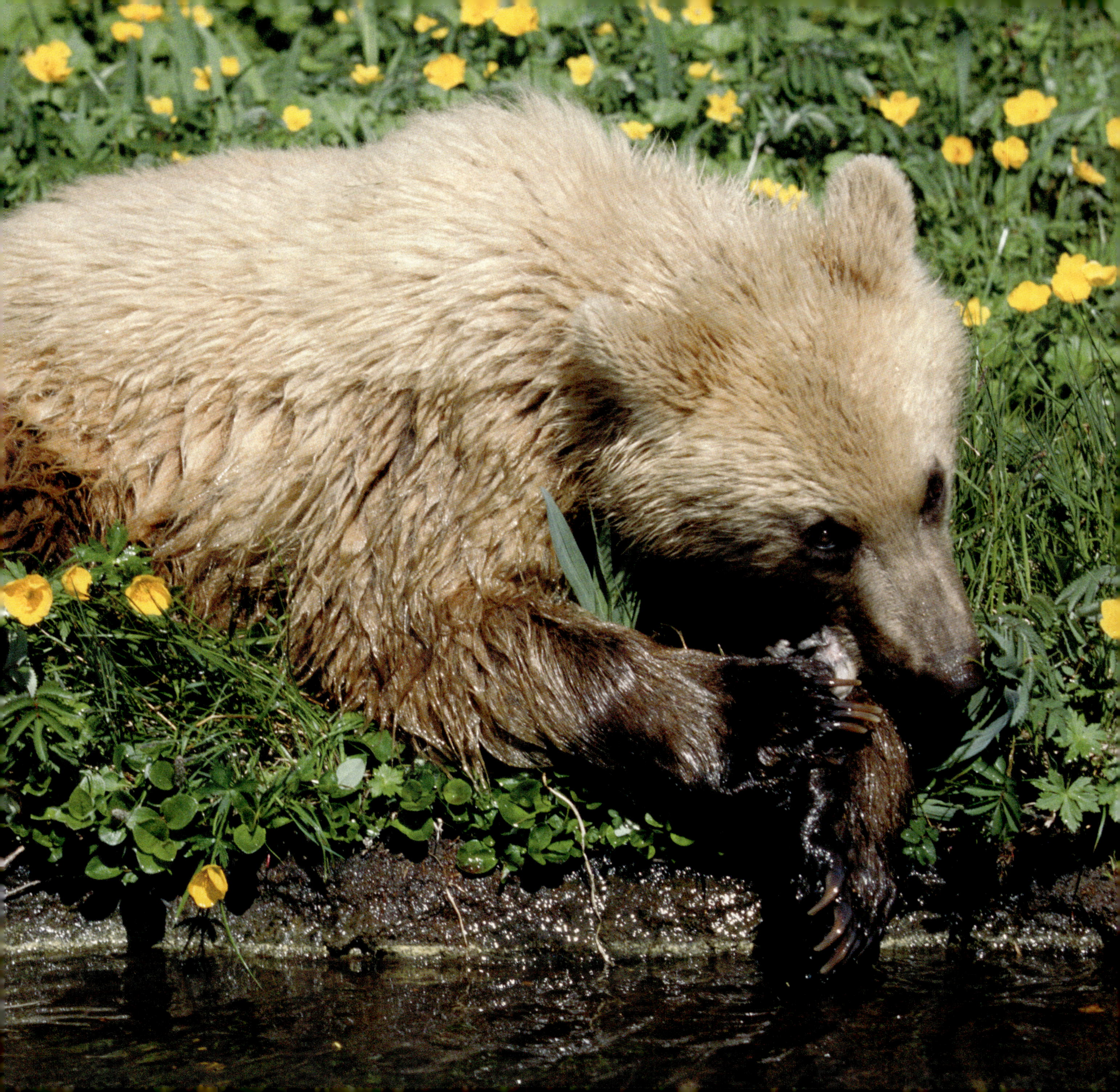

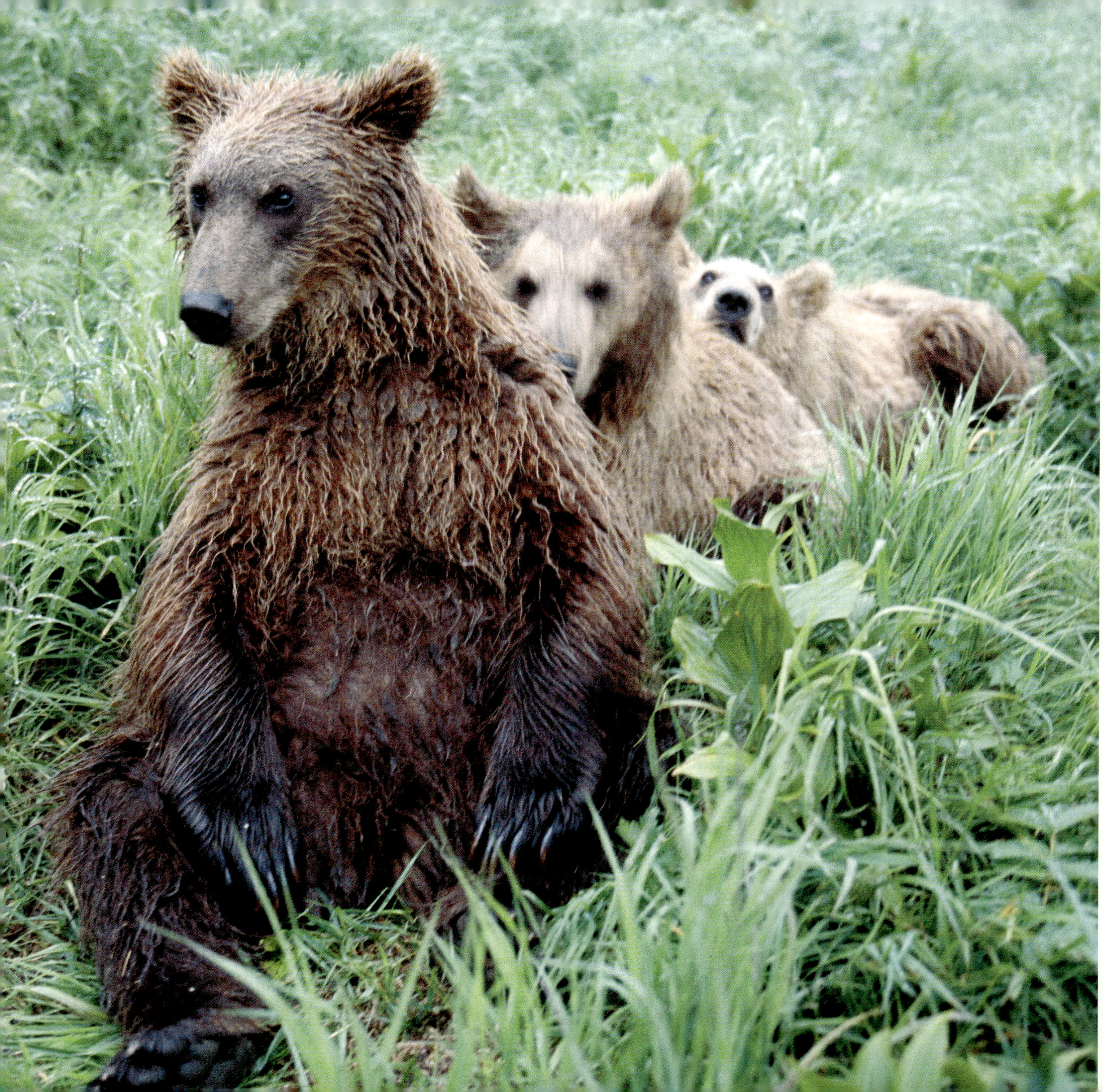

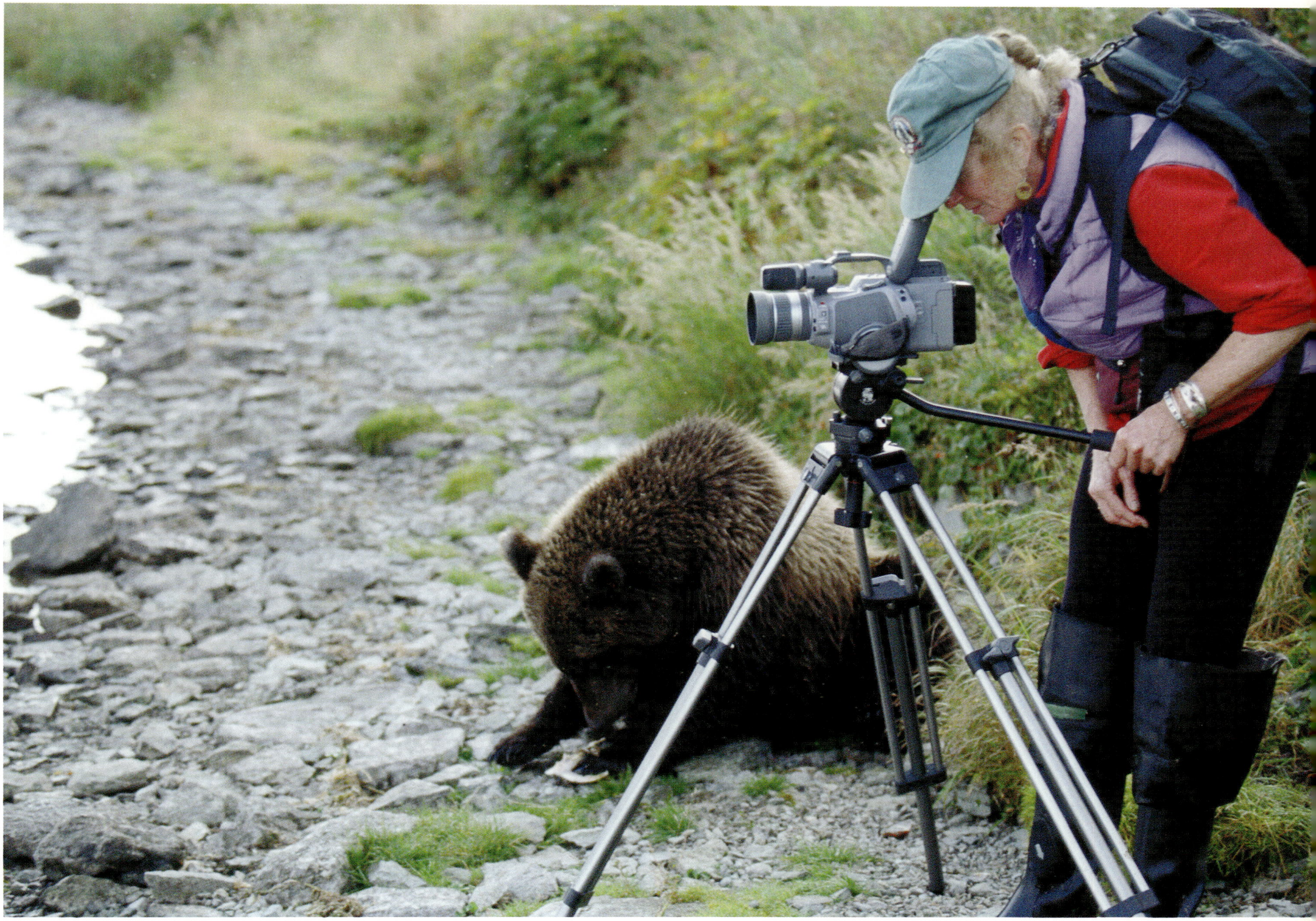

Maureen films mist lifting off the lake, seemingly oblivious to the grizzly eating a salmon four feet to her right. Mornings along the lakeshore could be wonderfully nonchalant.

From an early age, Chico came across as a ham.

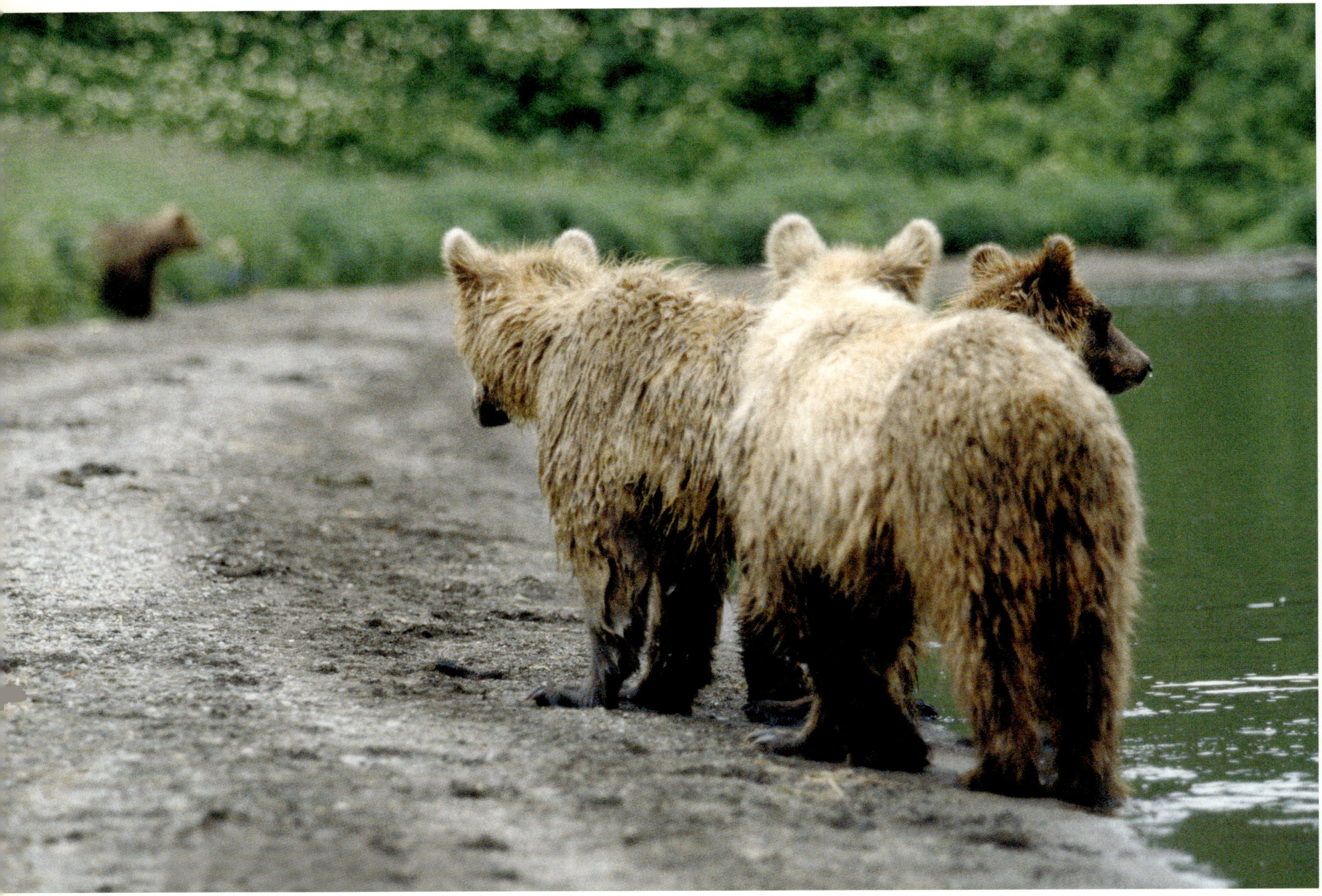

The cubs eventually learned how to judge other bears' intentions towards them.

By our second year, the cubs were displaying increasing degrees of independence. We would often hear them gallop up to the cabin and stop. If we picked up our gear, they would wait for us to come and spend the day with them. If we made no move to get up, they would head out to explore on their own.

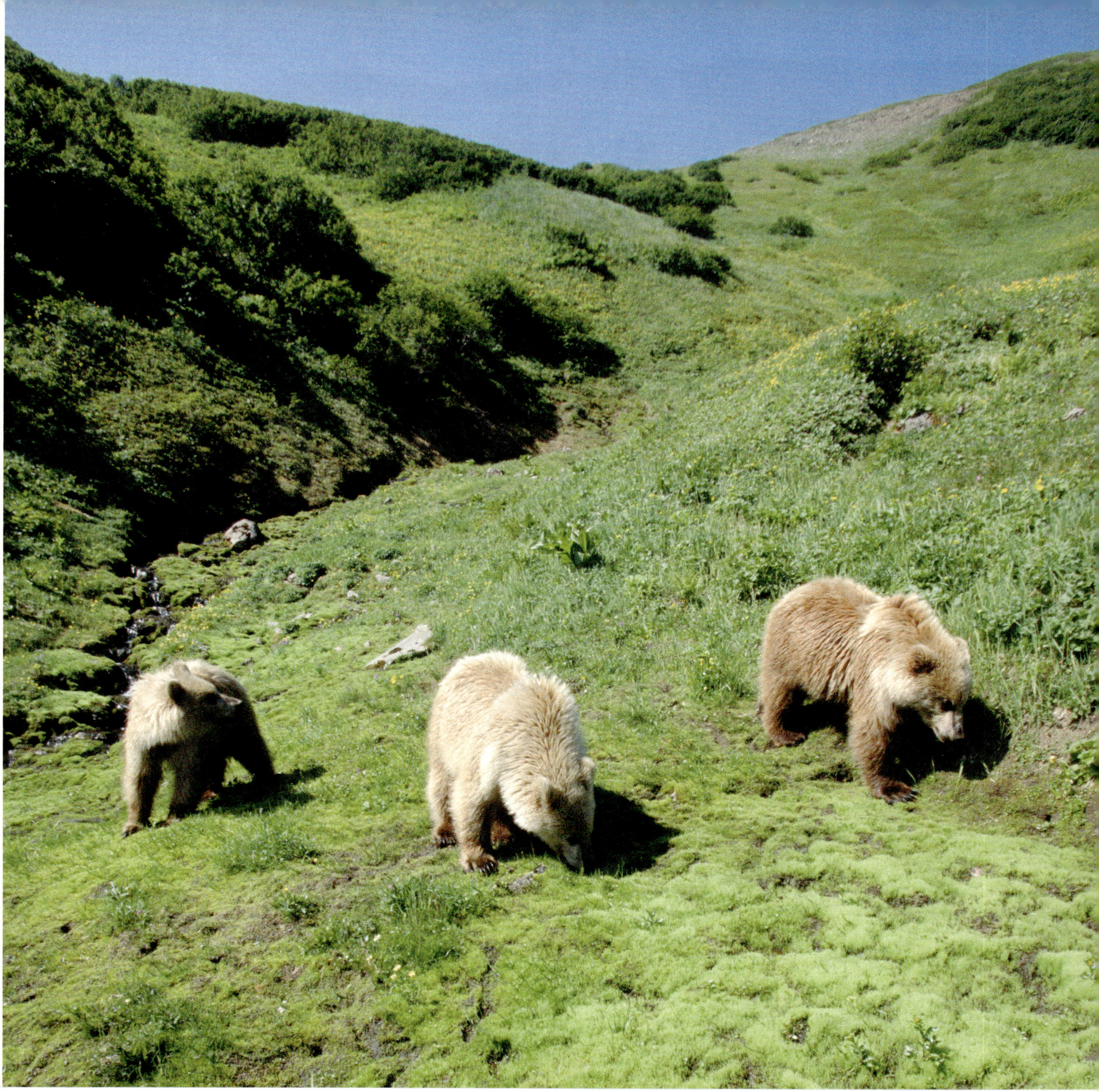

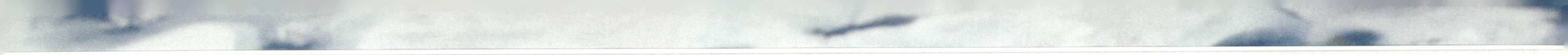

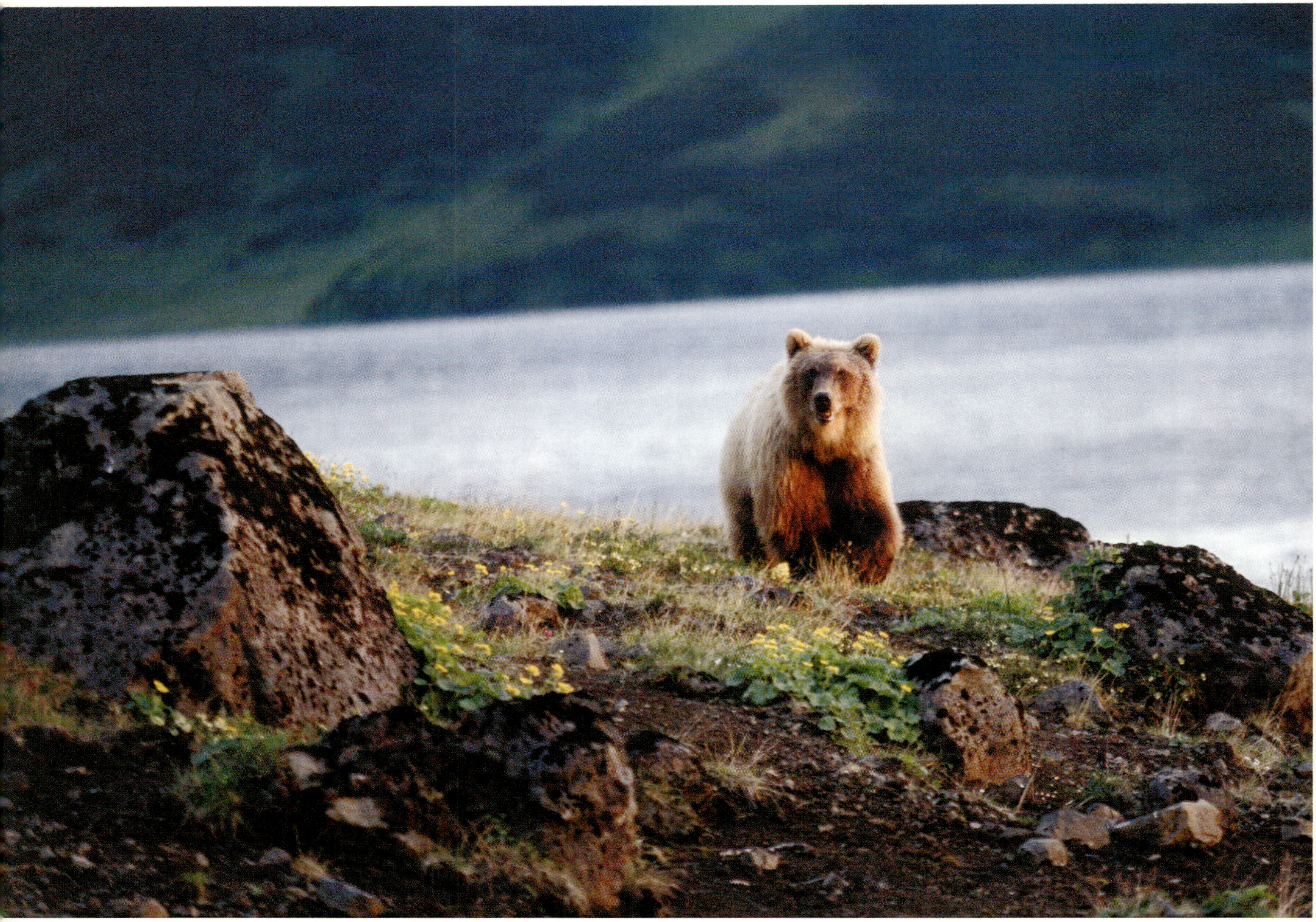

Chico at the lakeshore, late summer.

It required us looking through binoculars to see what Chico and Biscuit could smell easily: a bear on the opposite shore, a thousand yards away.

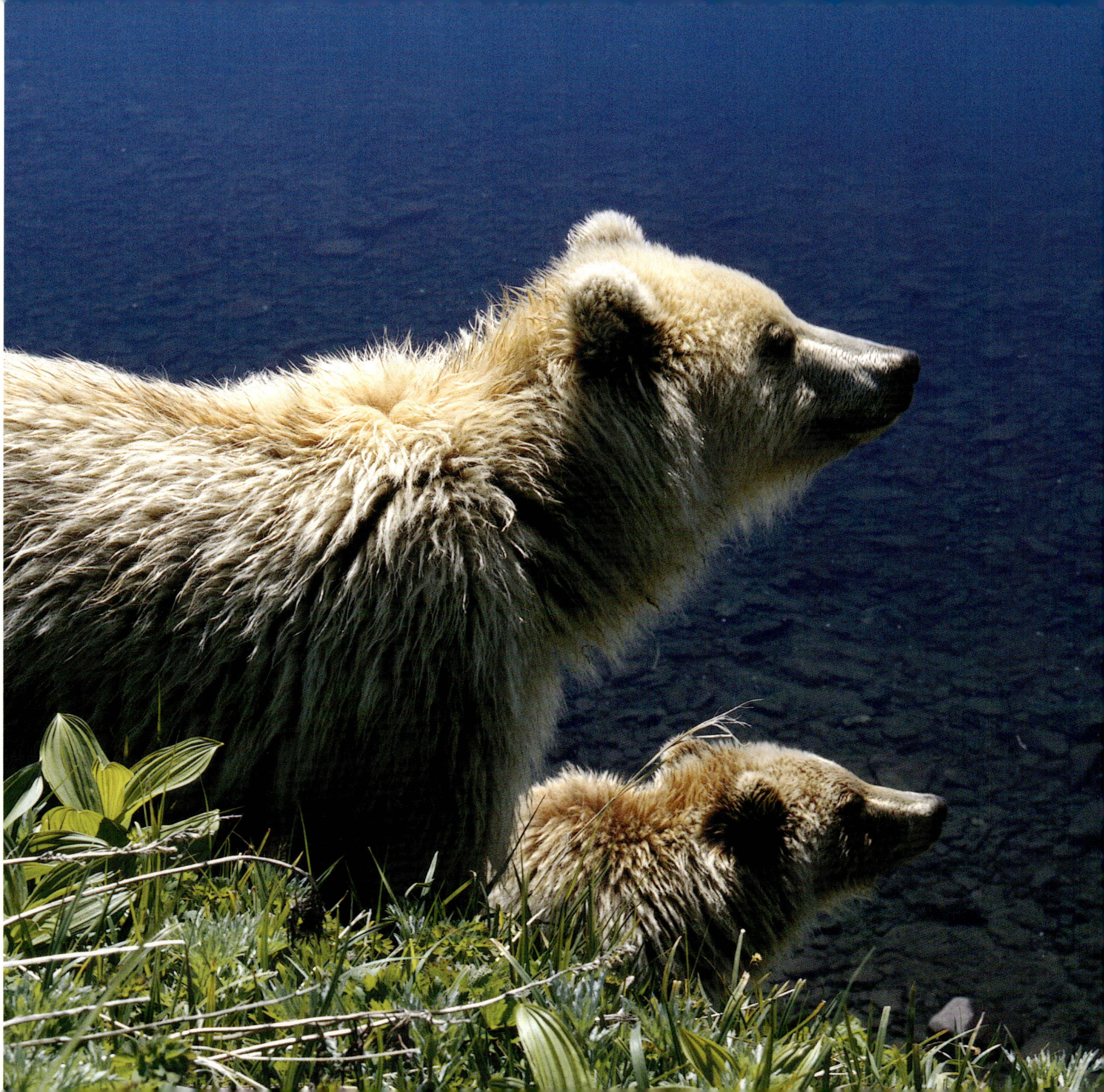

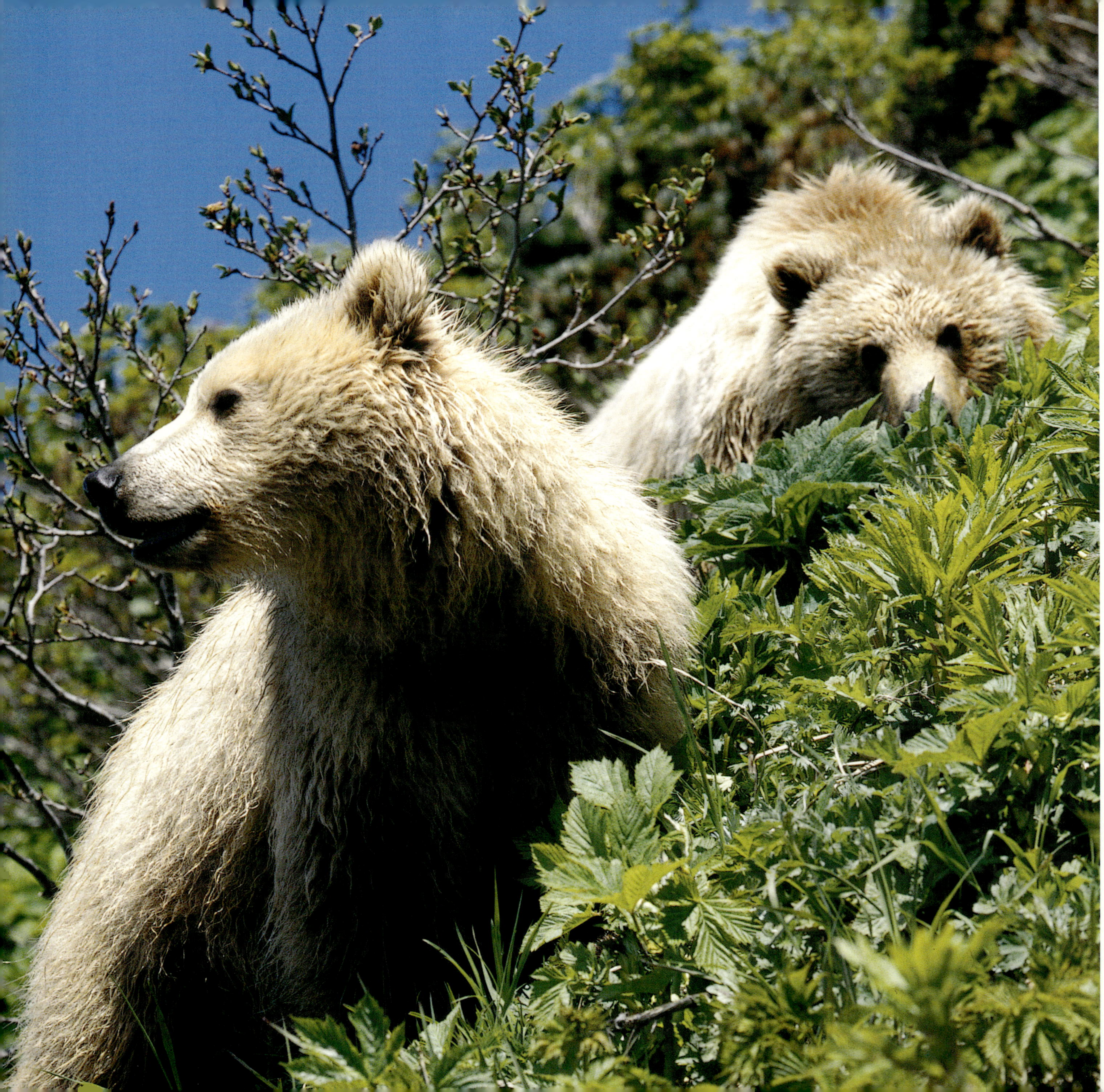

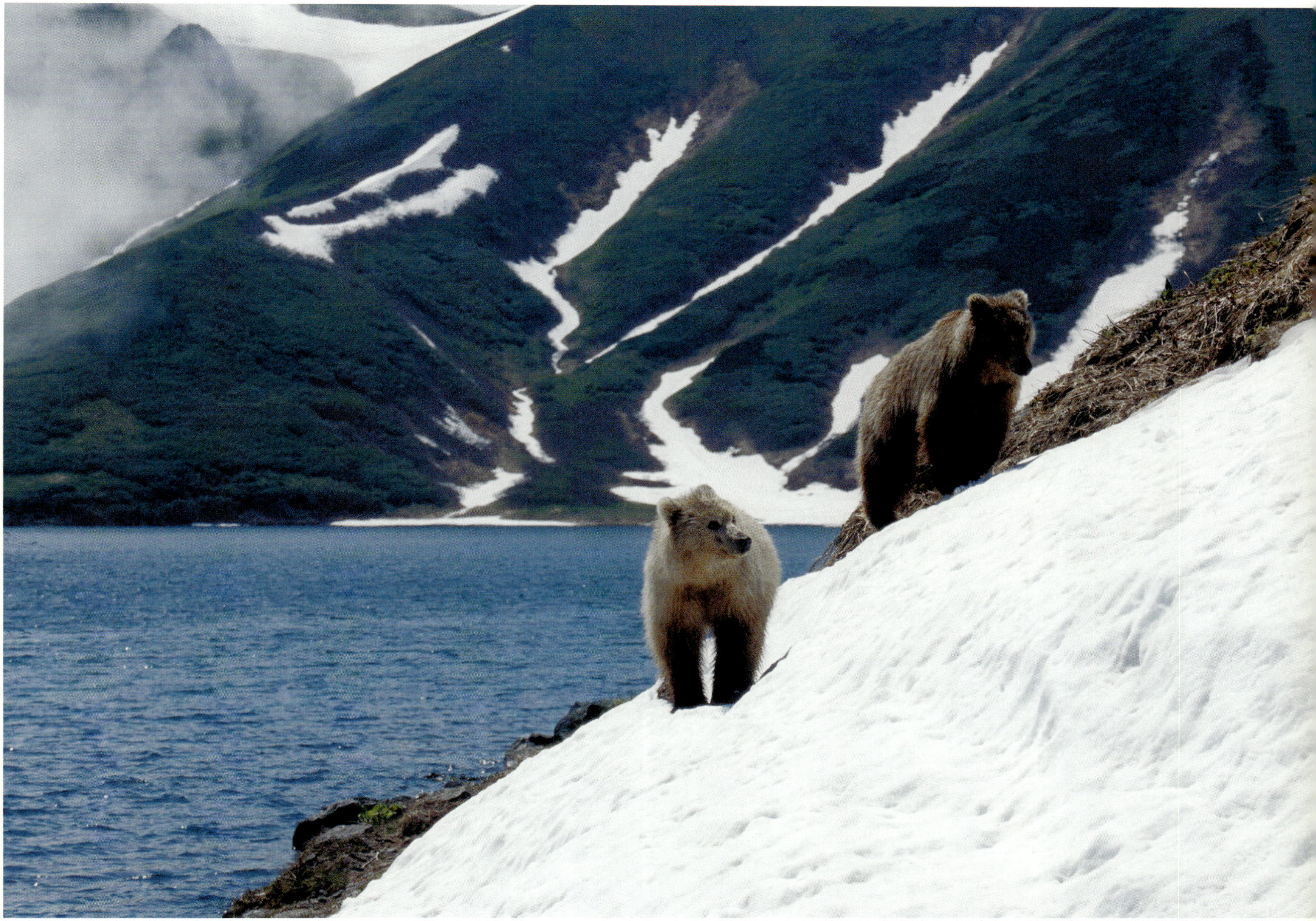

Patches of snow frame the lush greenery of Kambalnoye basin well into July.

Early summer is a time of quiet contentedness, before the urgency of having to get fat for hibernation sets in. By August, bears take on serious dispositions.

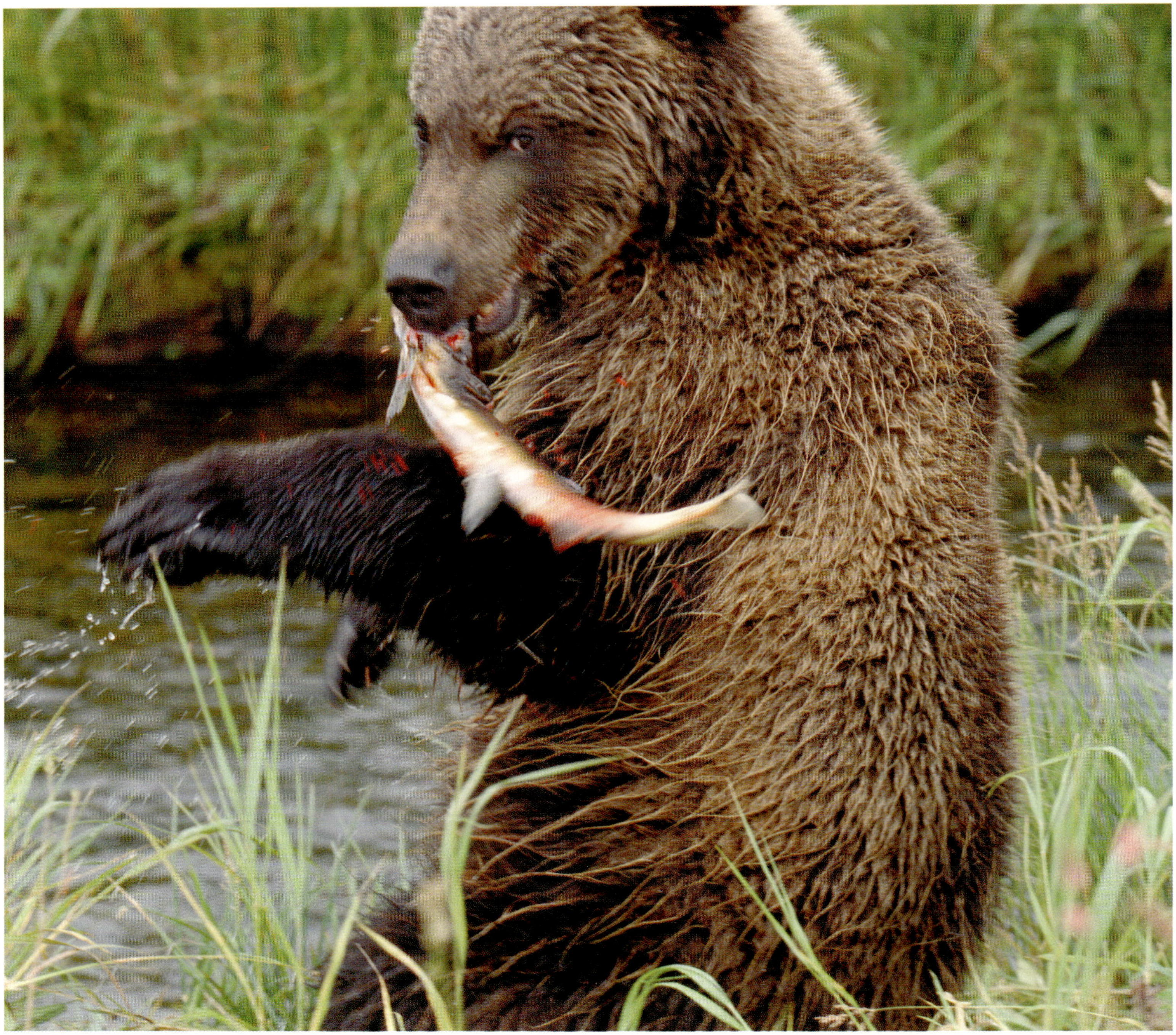

Chico glances back at us, looking for praise of her spectacular catch of a pink salmon.

The first of many salmon to be amazed—too late—by Biscuit's fishing prowess.
By the second fall the cubs displayed remarkable skill, and were even able to fish the river.

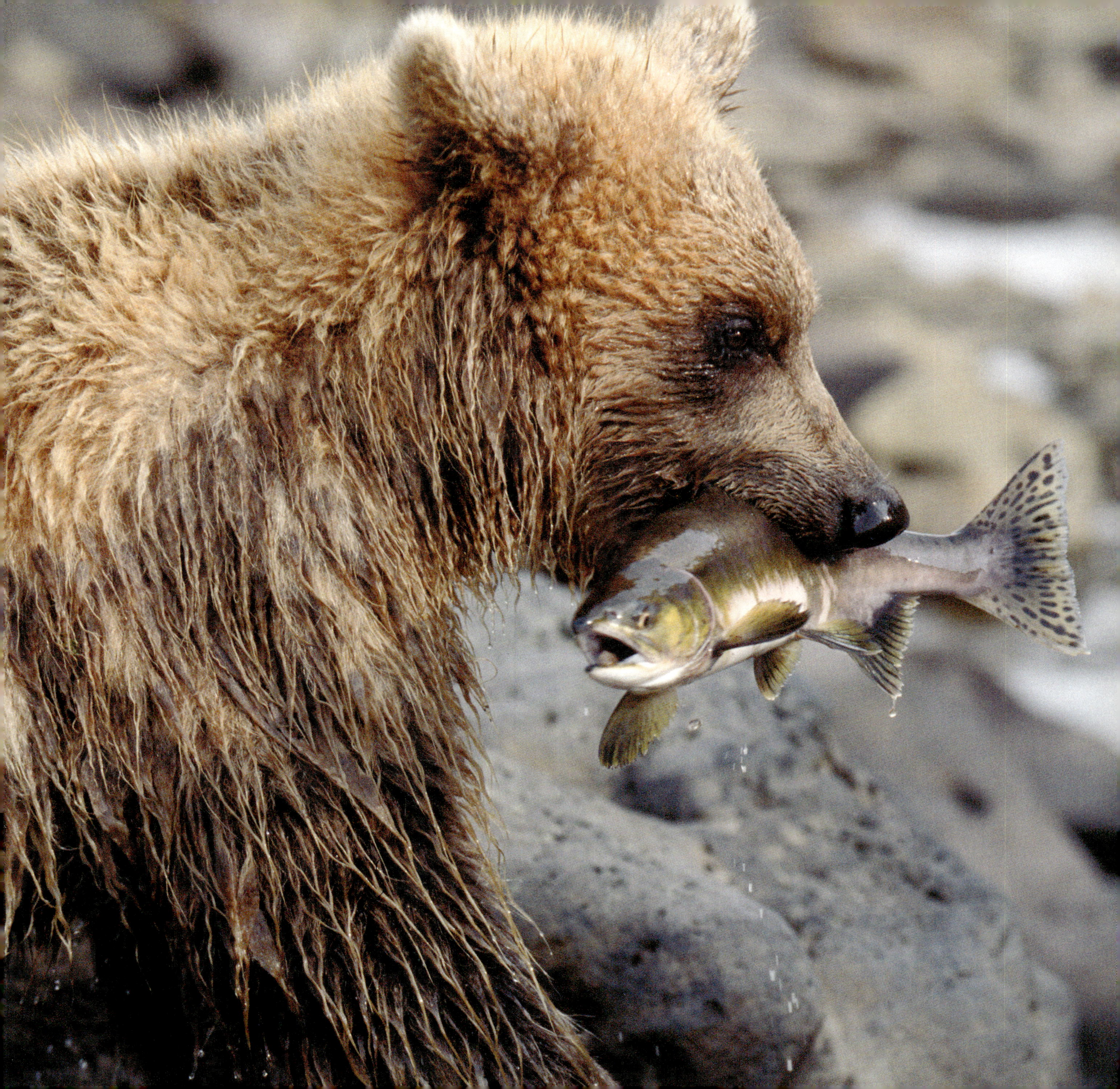

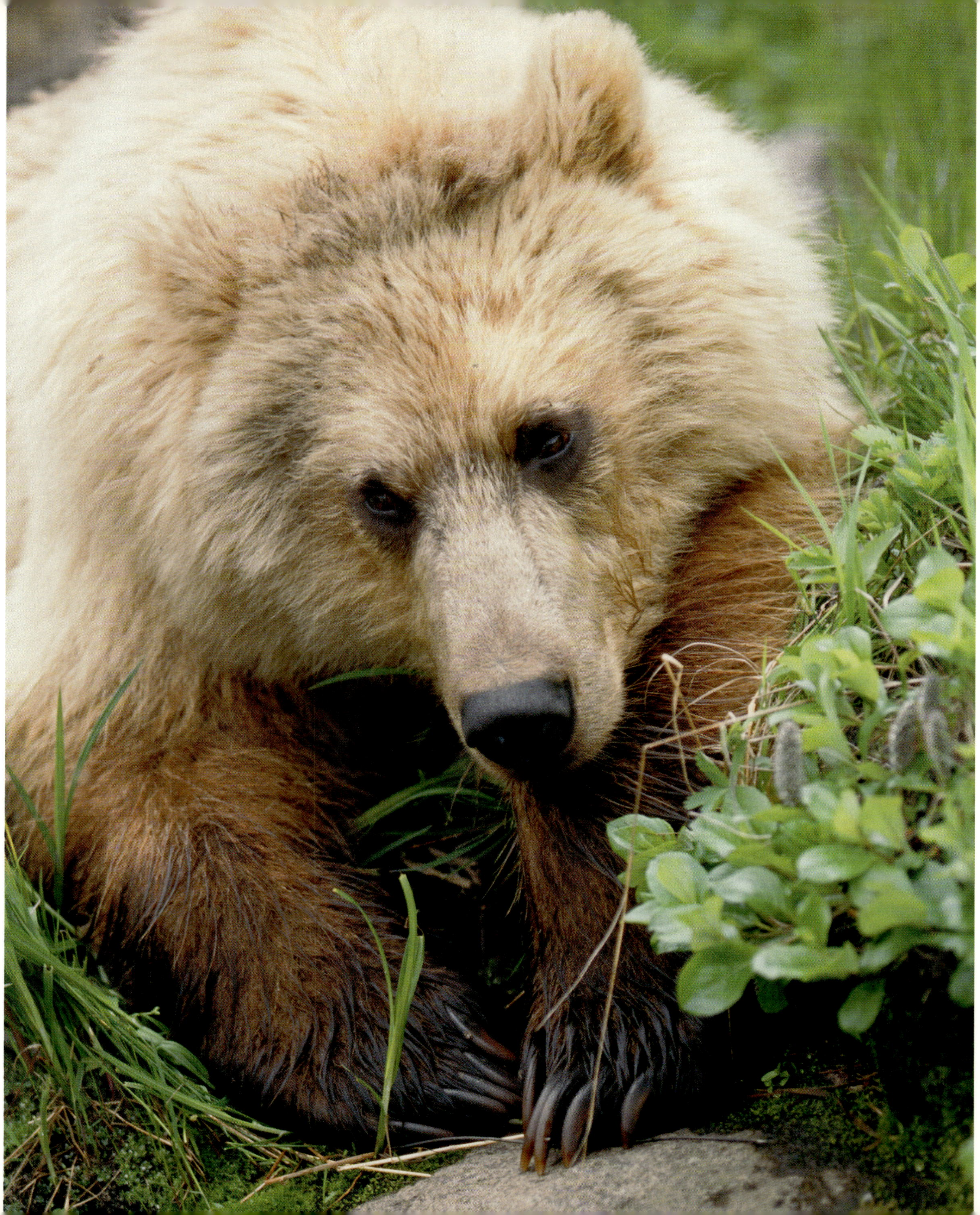

Biscuit, at two years and seven months of age.

Edenic existence is an attainable goal for those who understand the appropriate courtesies of living in the wilderness—most importantly kindness, attention, and respect.

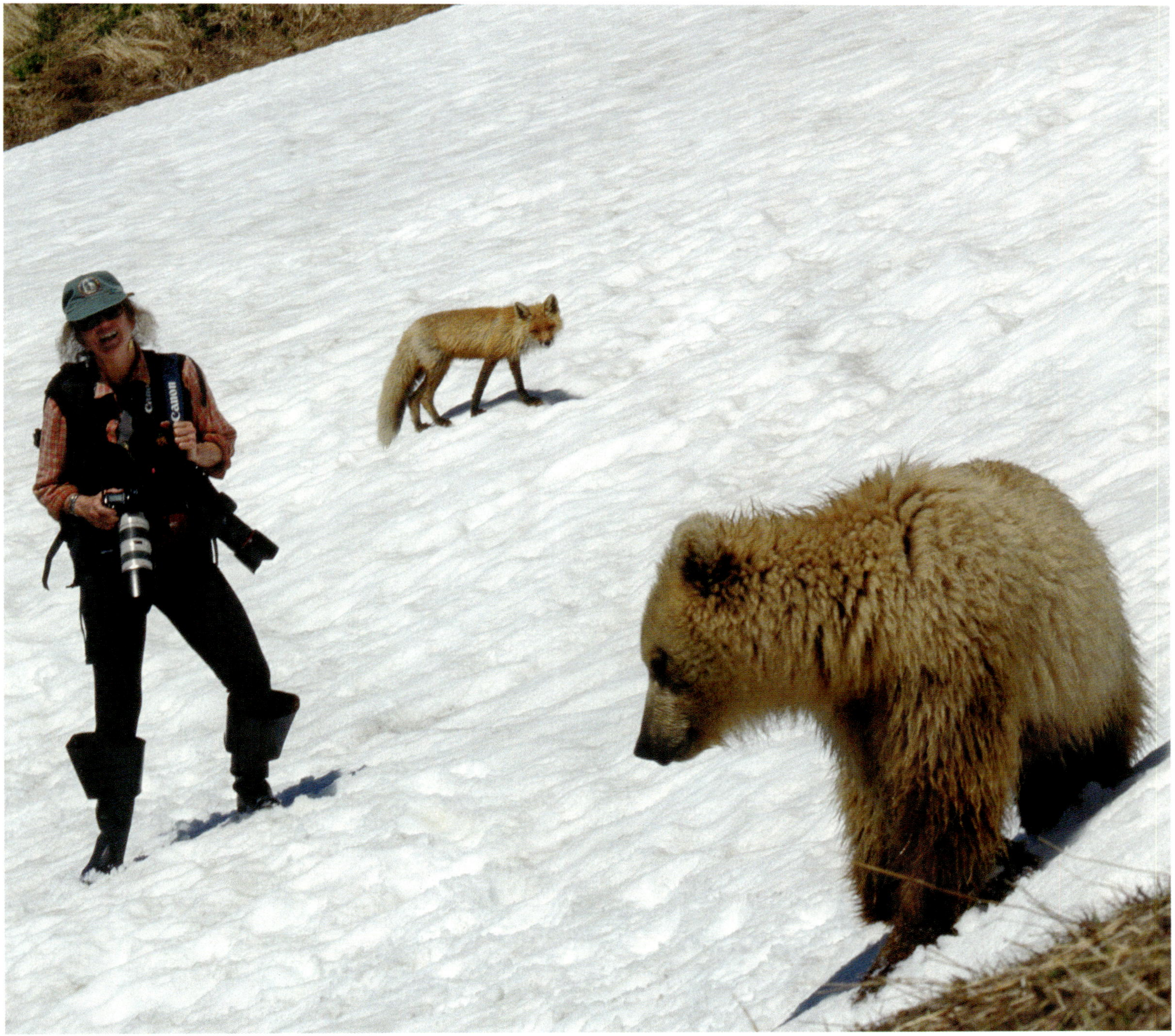

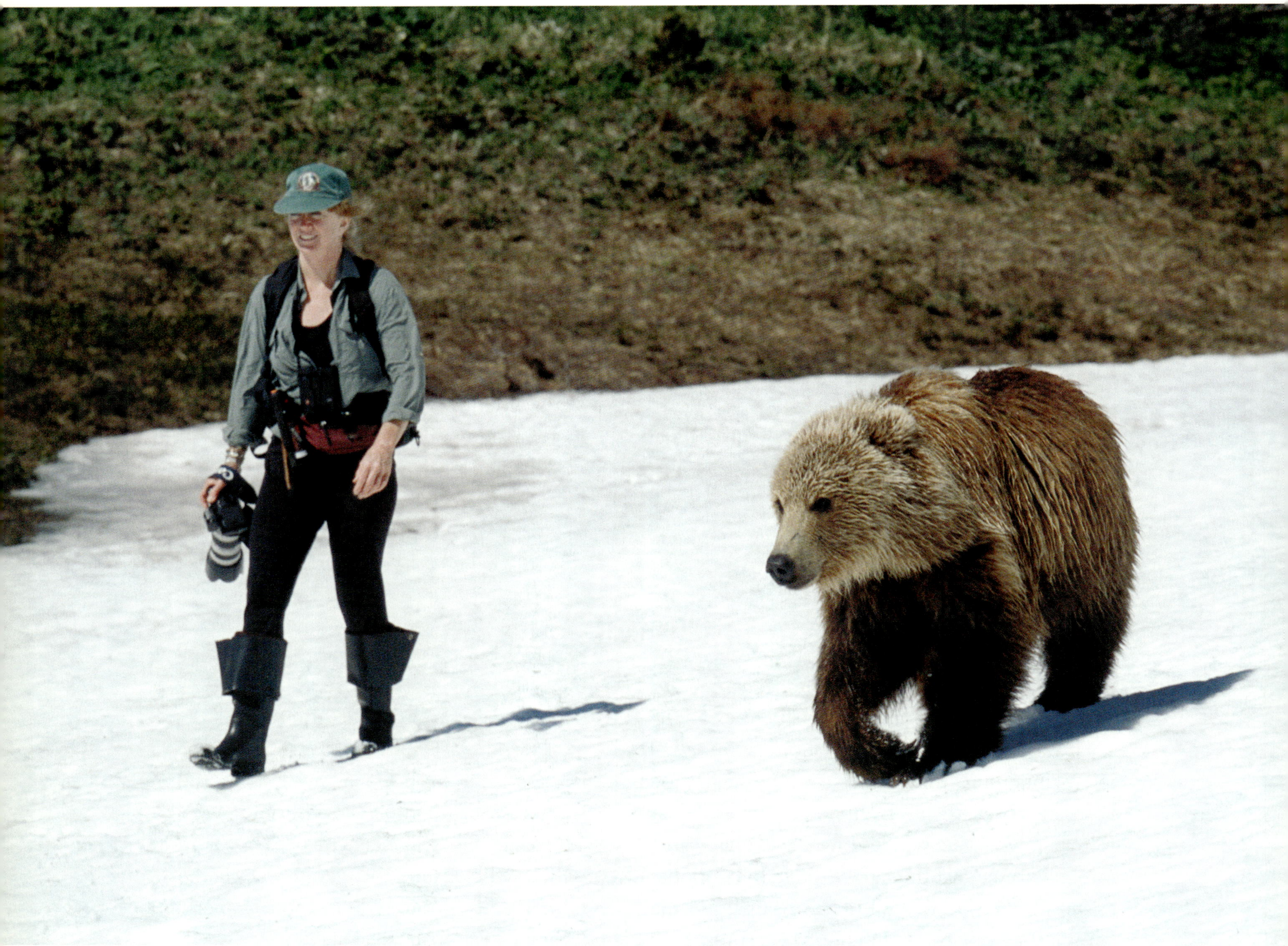

As the years passed, walking with the bears became even more of an impressive undertaking, due to their size.

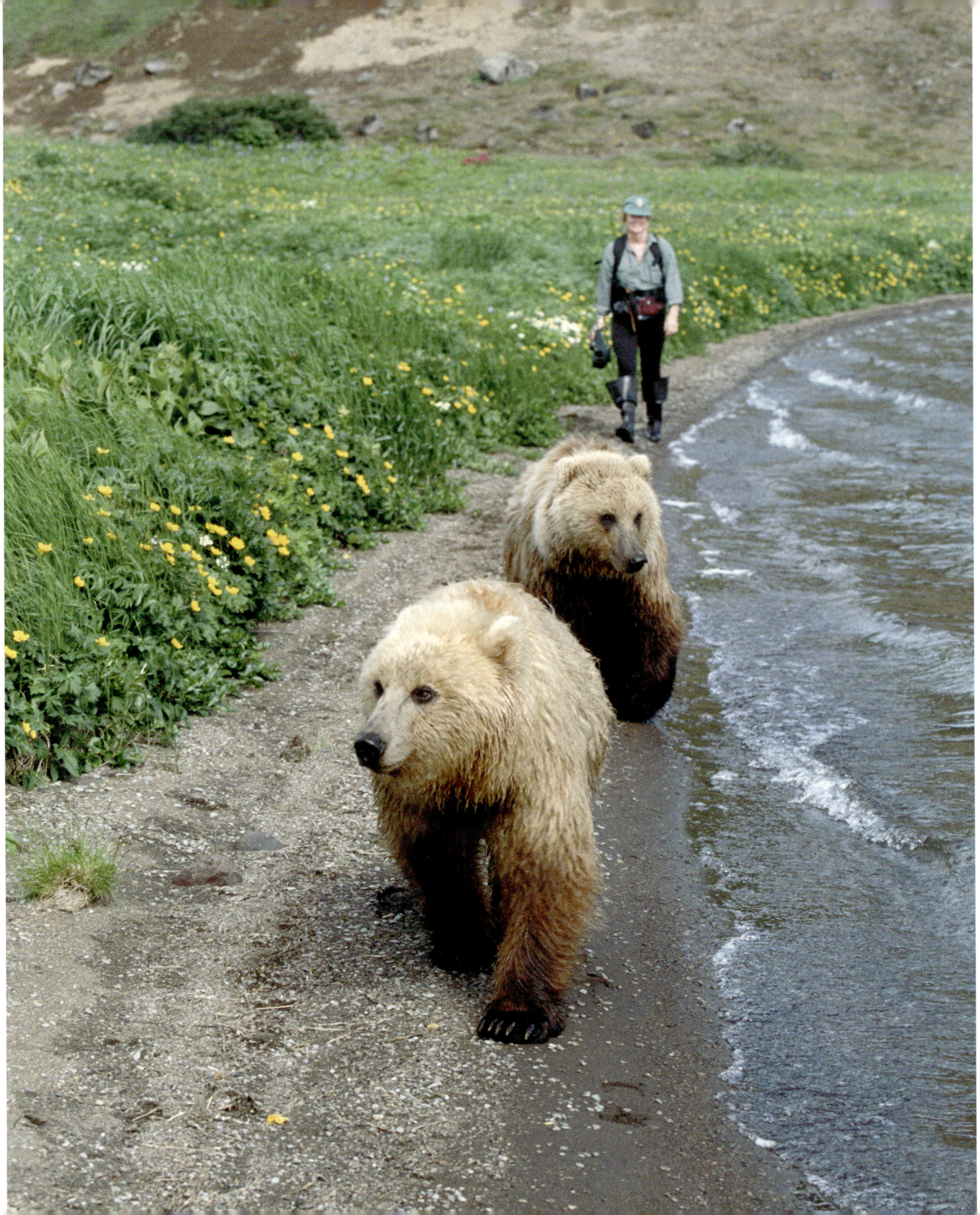

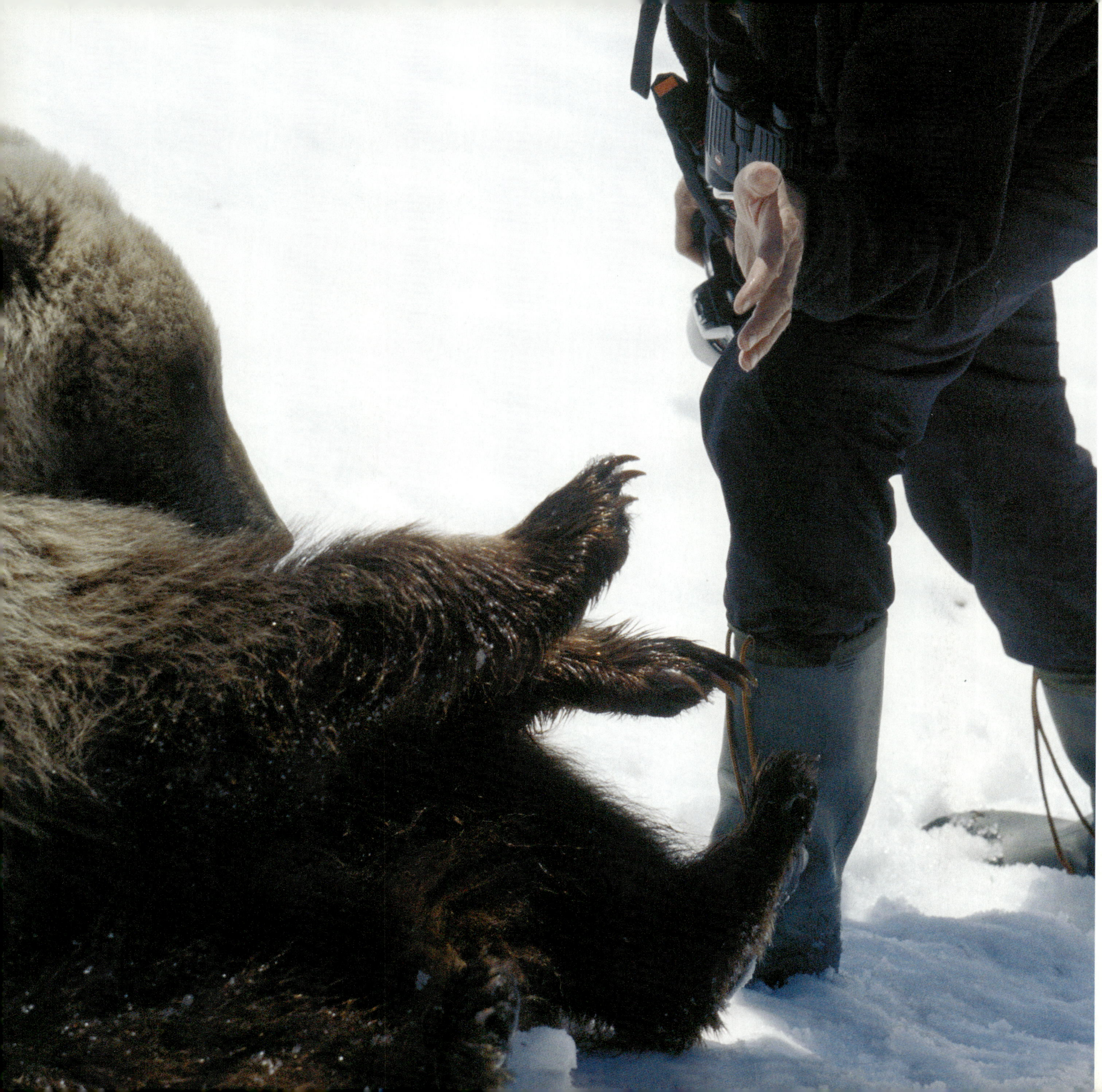

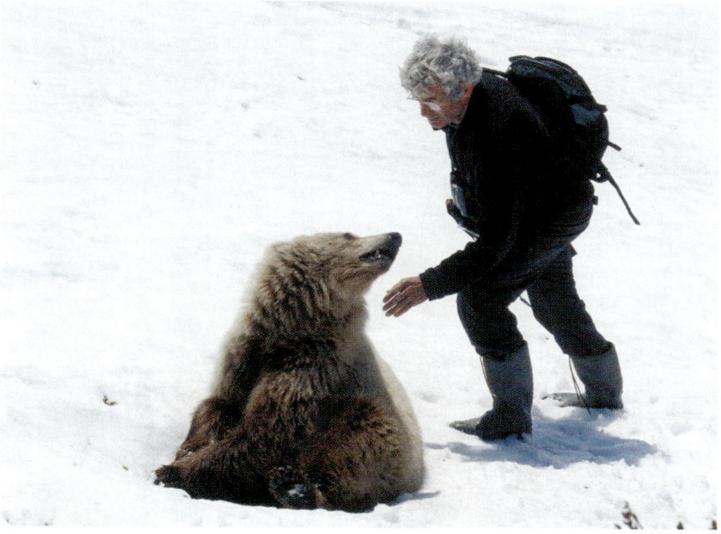

Each spring, after not having seen each other all winter, Chico and Charlie had their special greeting.

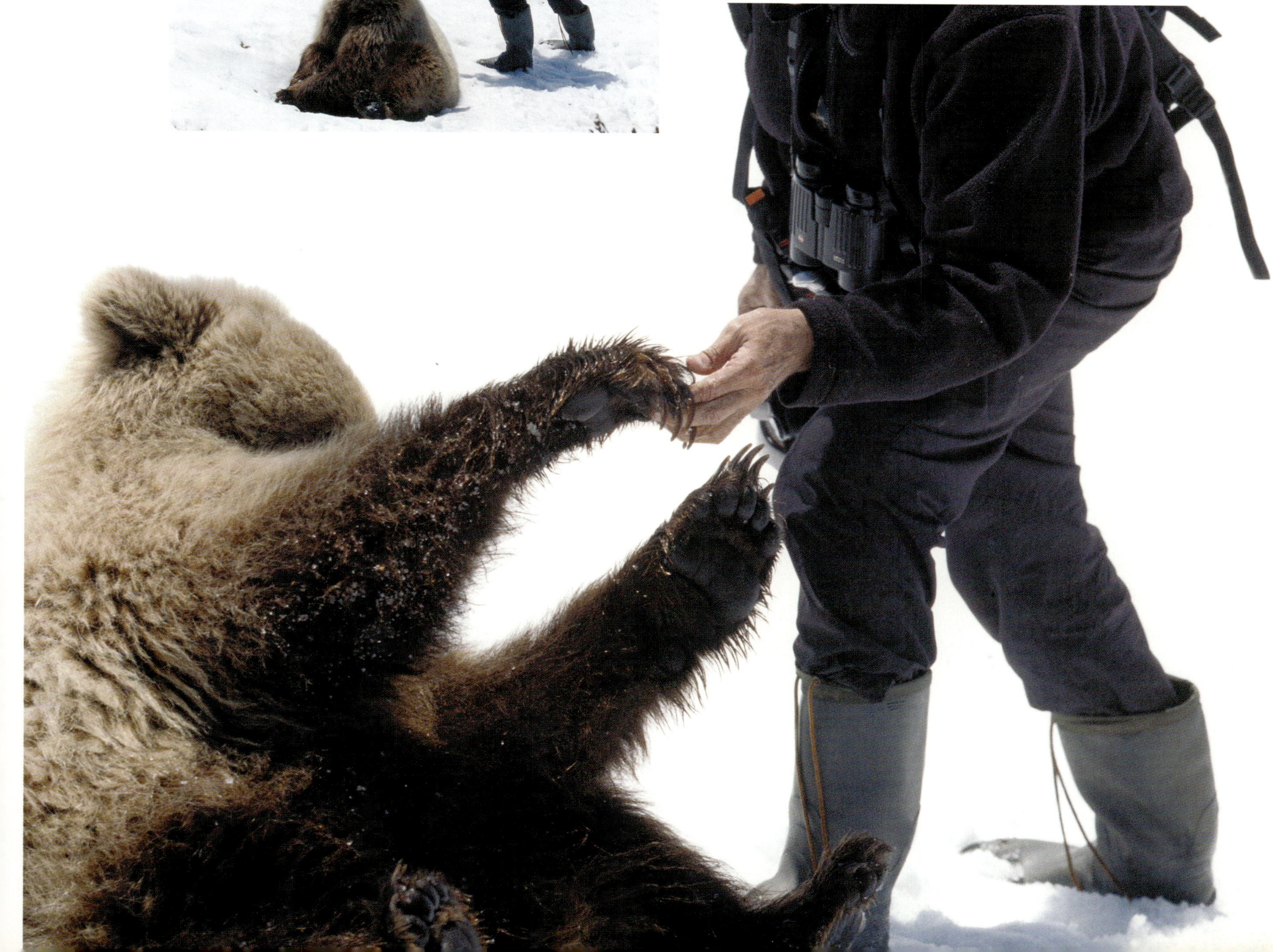

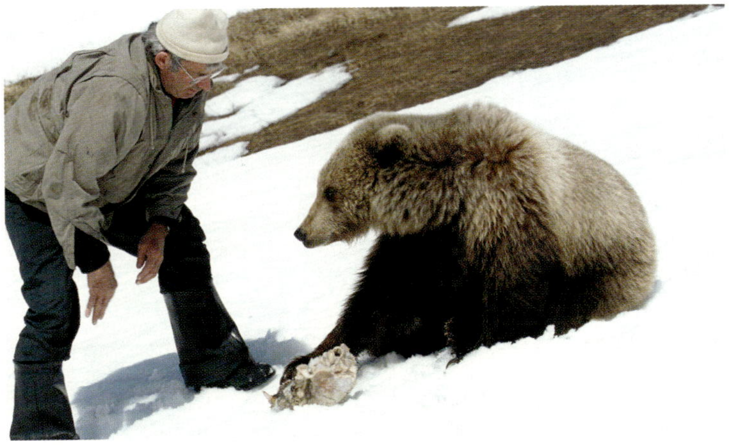

Snow often made Biscuit feel playful. She would leap into the water, leap out again, then run around us in circles—just as the cubs had done so many times in our first year.

Worried that poachers might be in the area, Charlie wanted to check for bullet holes in the bear skull Chico had found. At first Chico was protective of her find, but then she decided to look the other way. Once Charlie confirmed there weren't any holes, he gave back the skull.

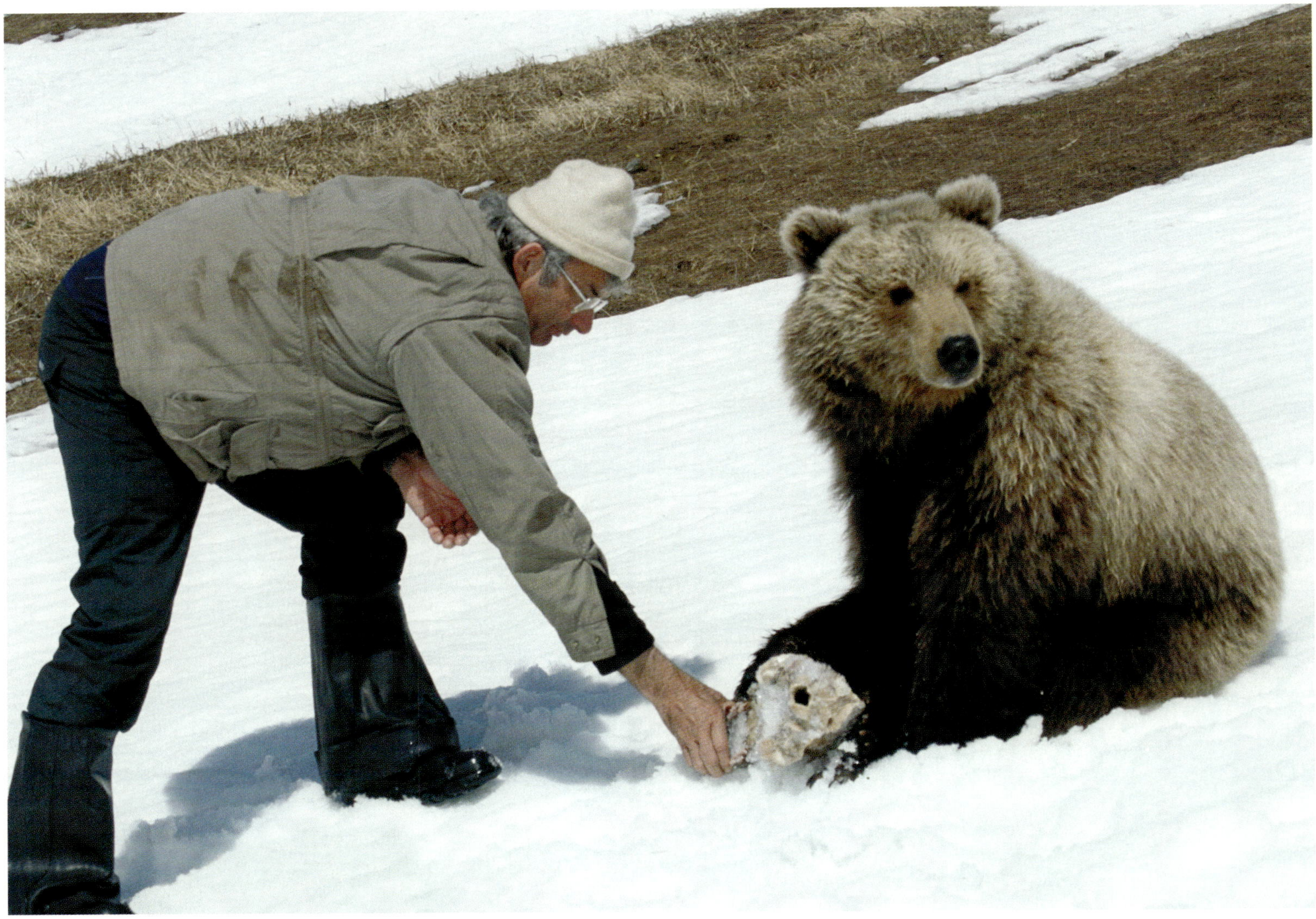

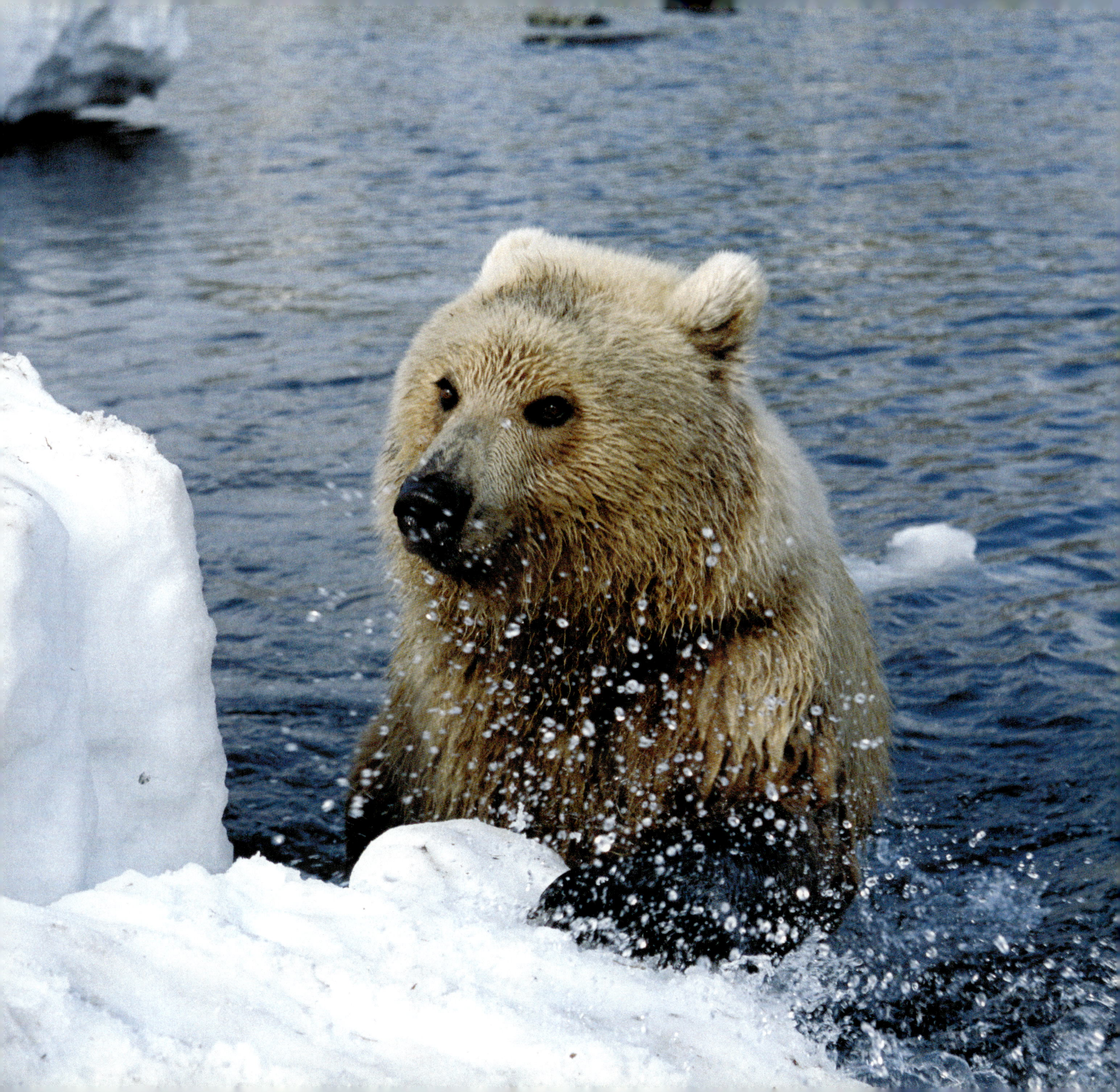

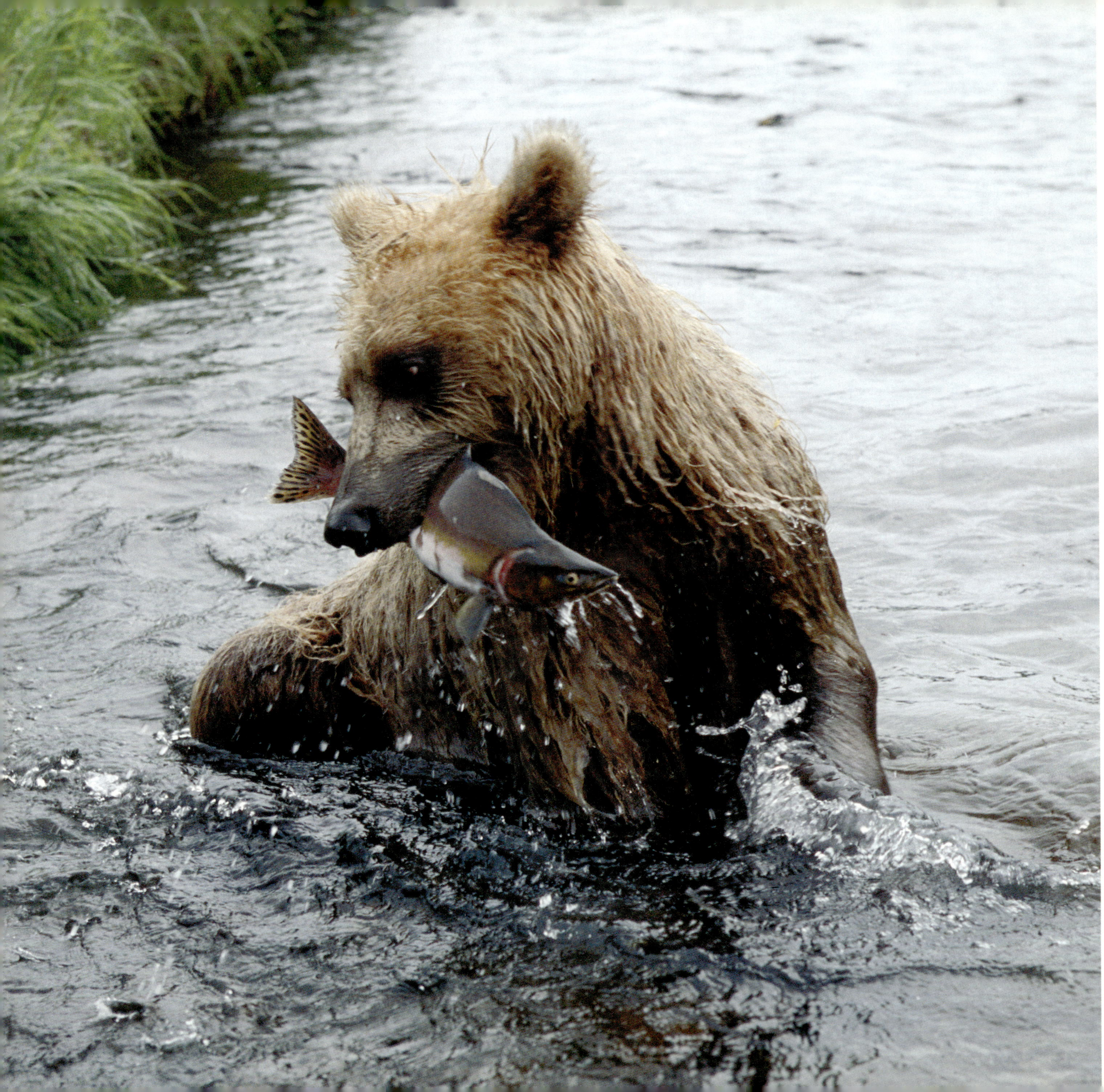

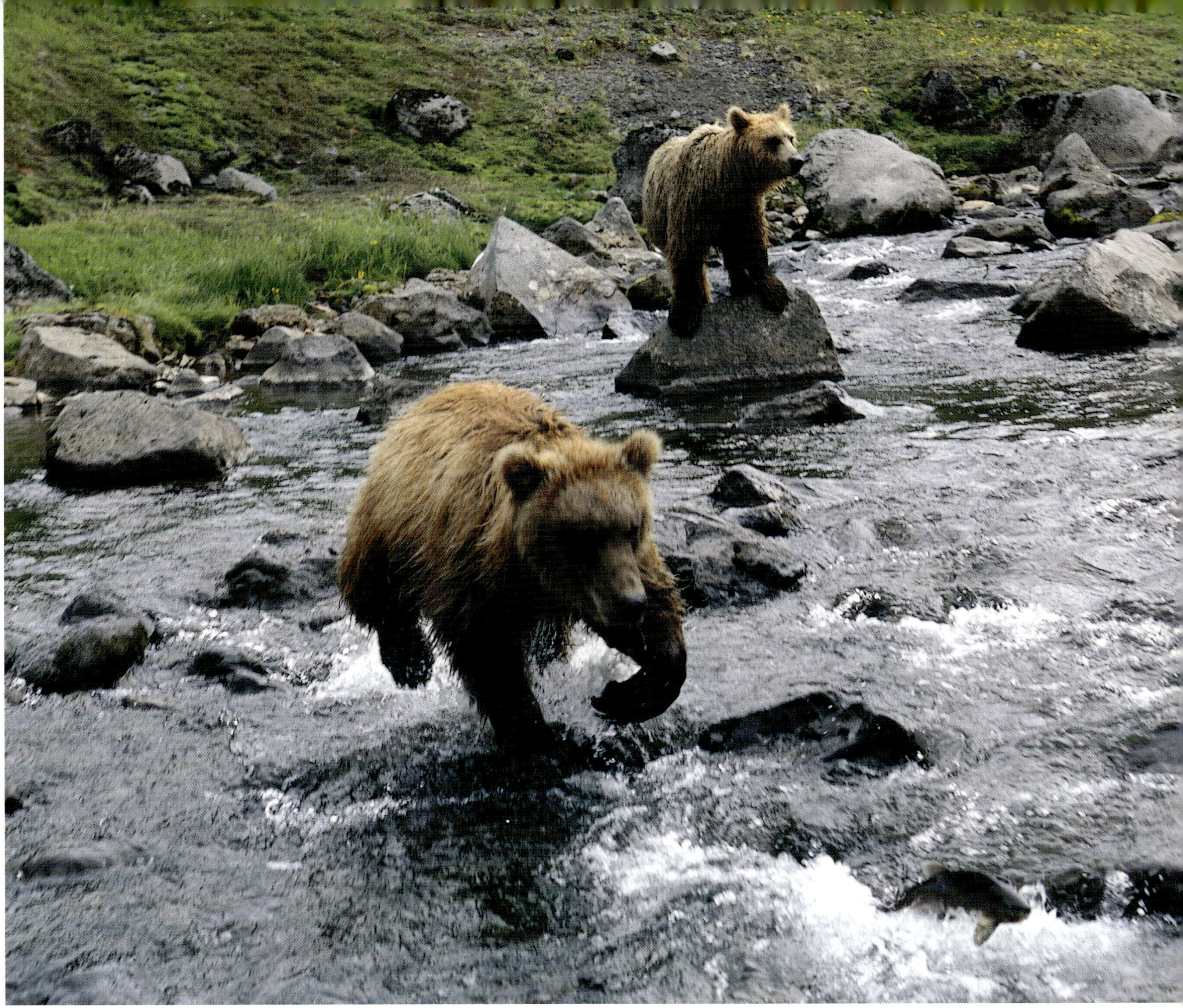

Our bears' favourite place to pursue pink salmon was a place we called Char Creek, which ran through a beautiful canyon north of our cabin. Pink salmon spawned in Char Creek only in years with even numbers.

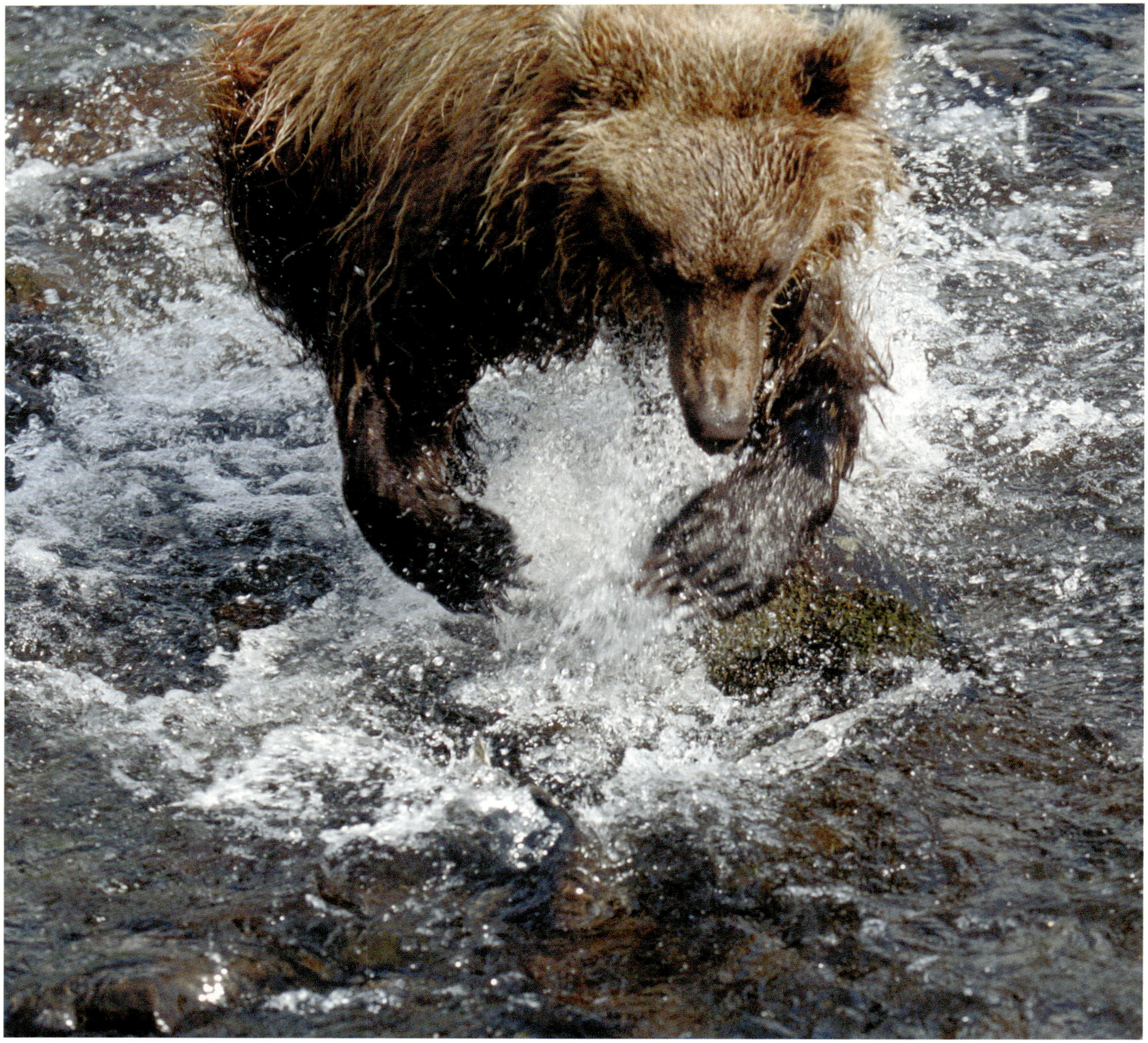

The final leap.

Biscuit's turn to show off.

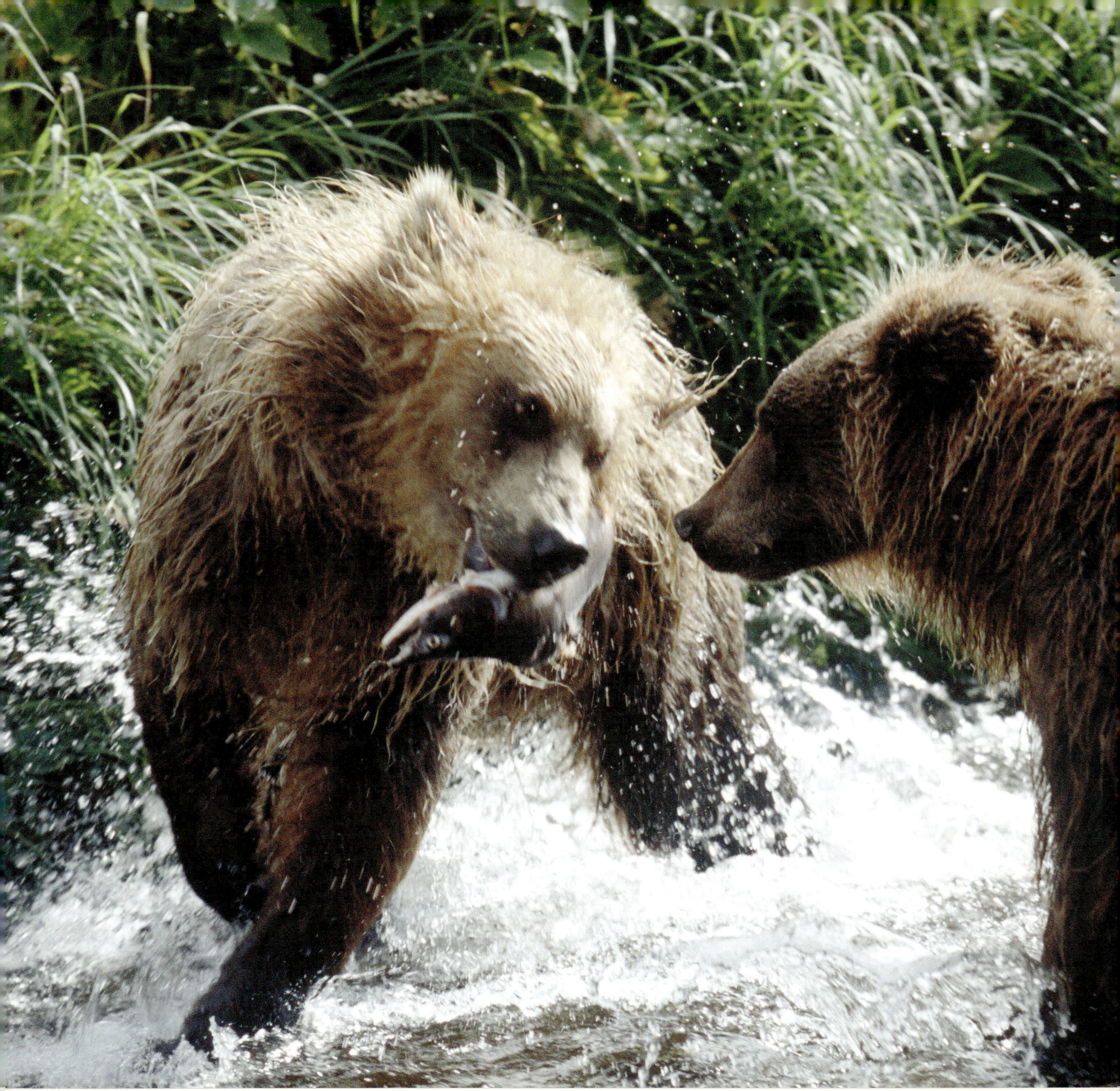

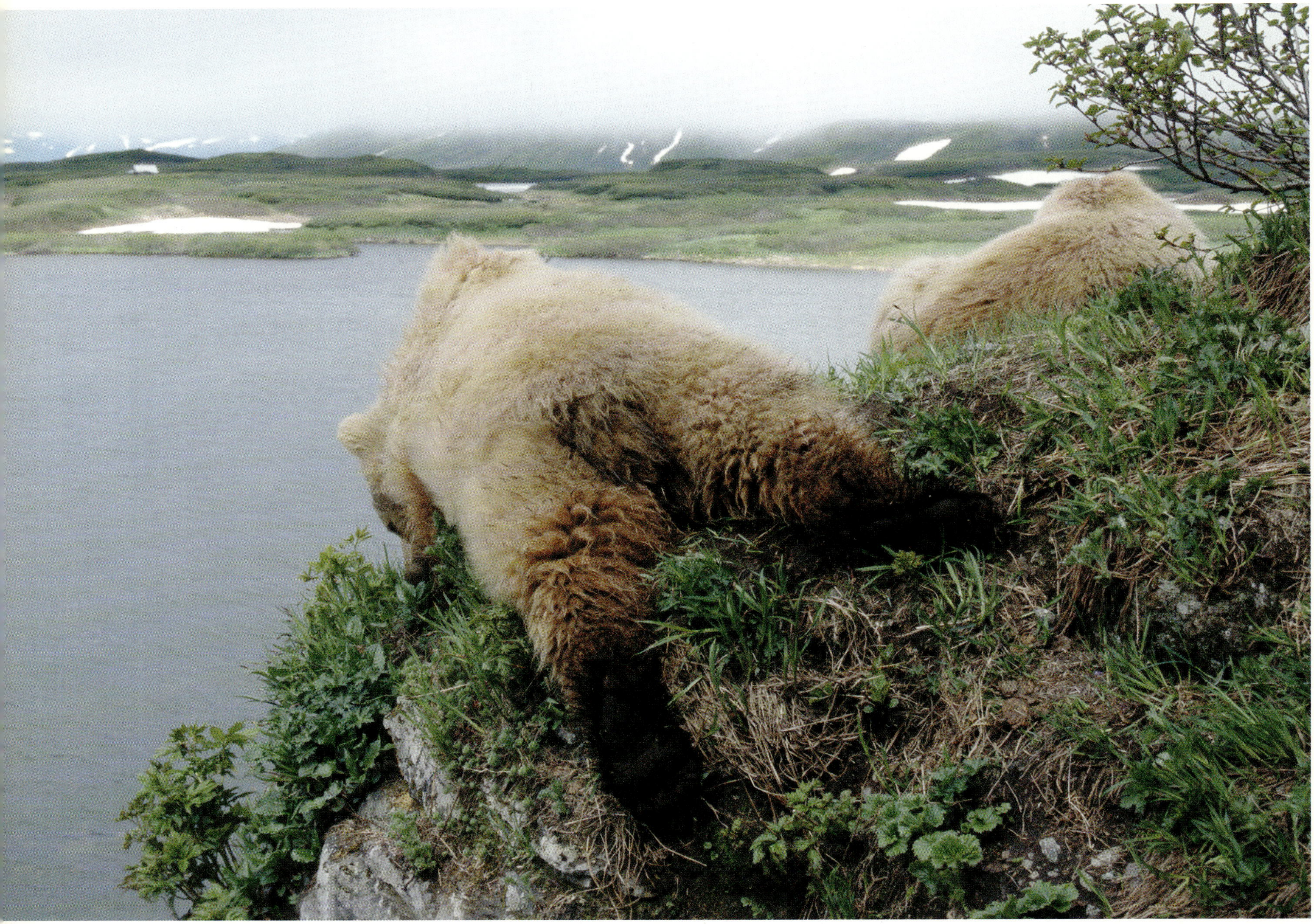

Chico and Biscuit matured quickly, but until they became fully confident
around other bears, the cliff above Bear Skull Bay was their well-protected hangout.

Biscuit's face frequently changes with her feelings. Here she's about to be pounced upon by Chico.

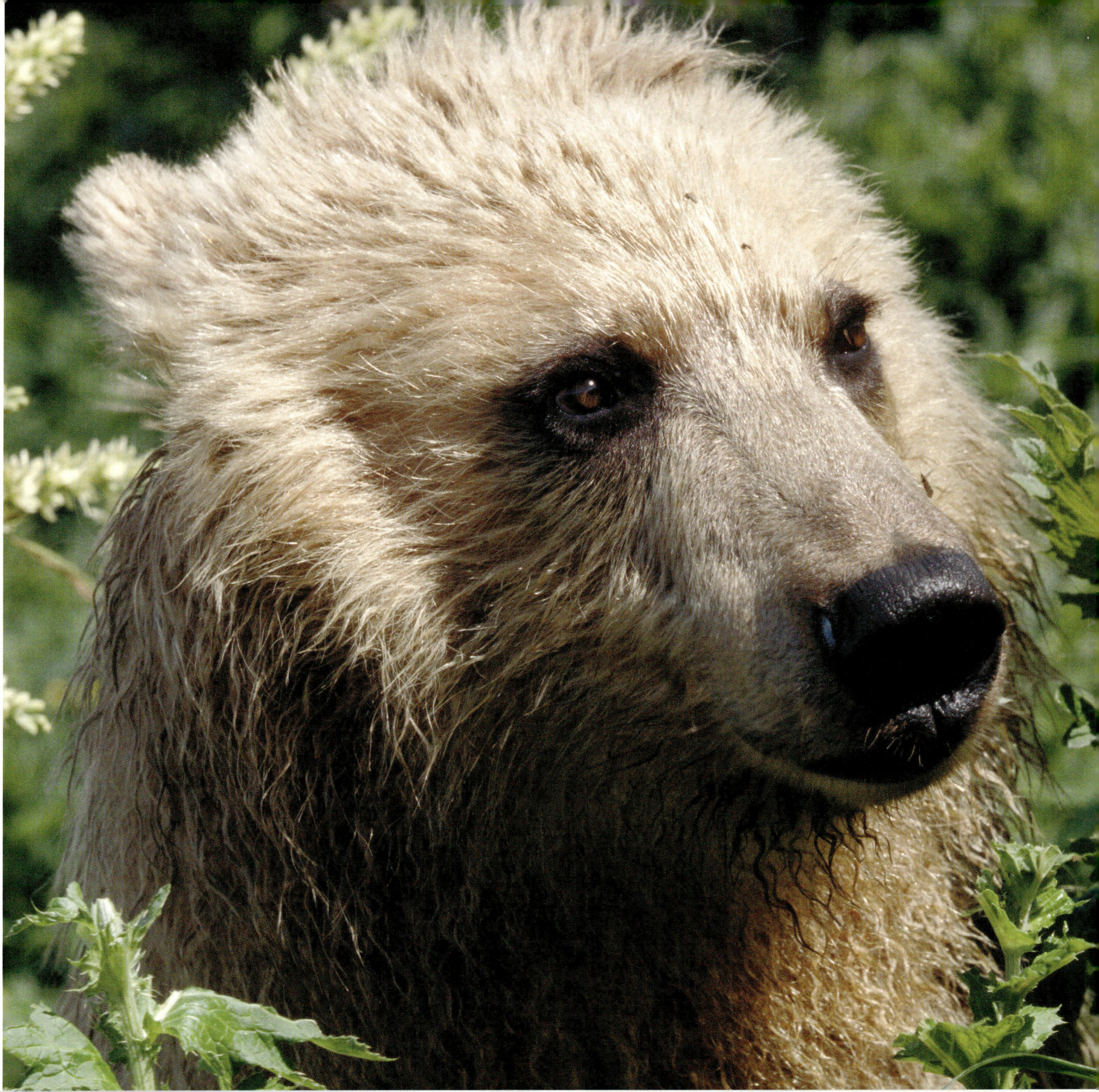

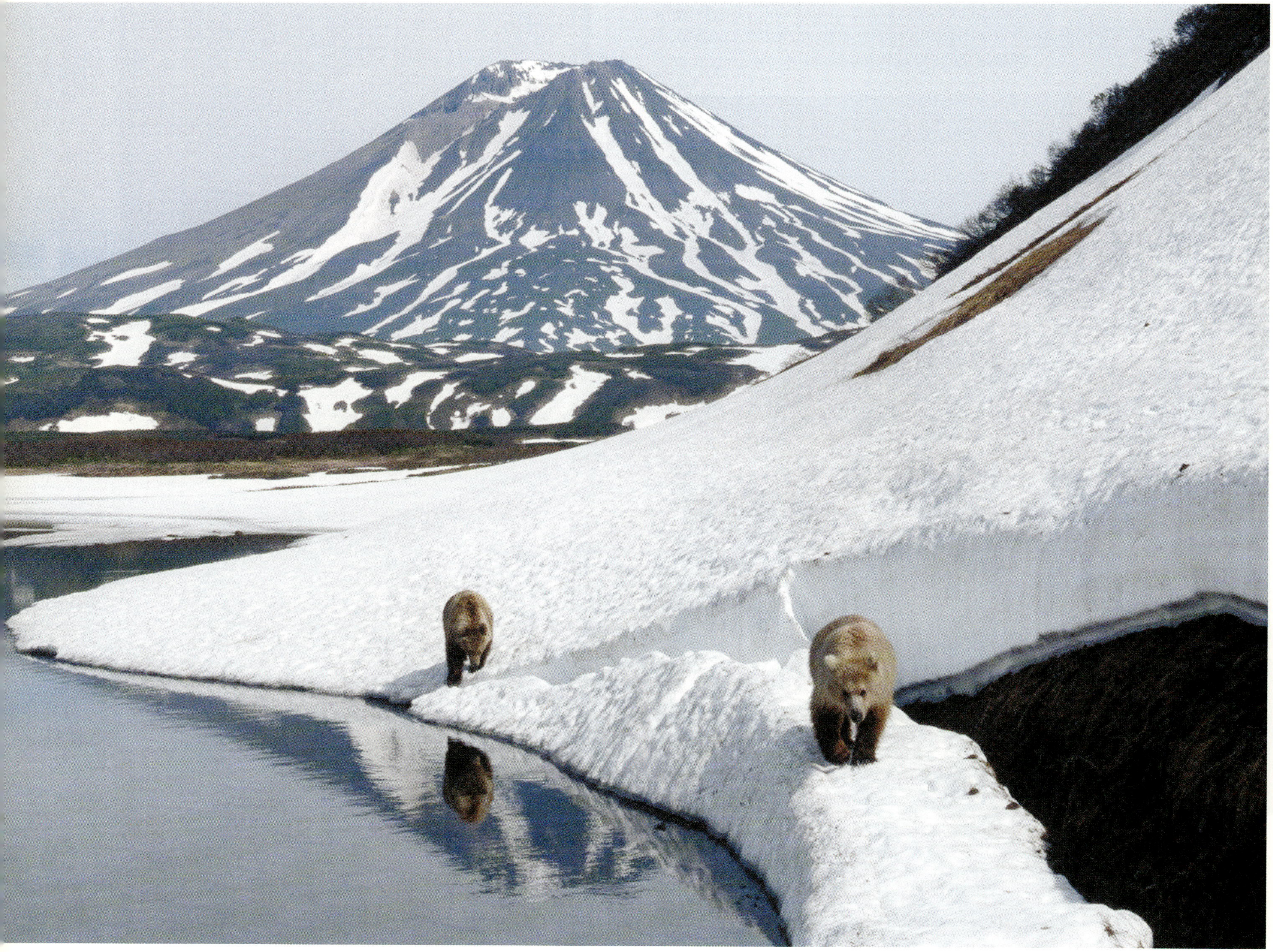

Our last photograph of Chico (right), still the darker of the two,
before she departed the Kambalnoye Lake basin for parts unknown.

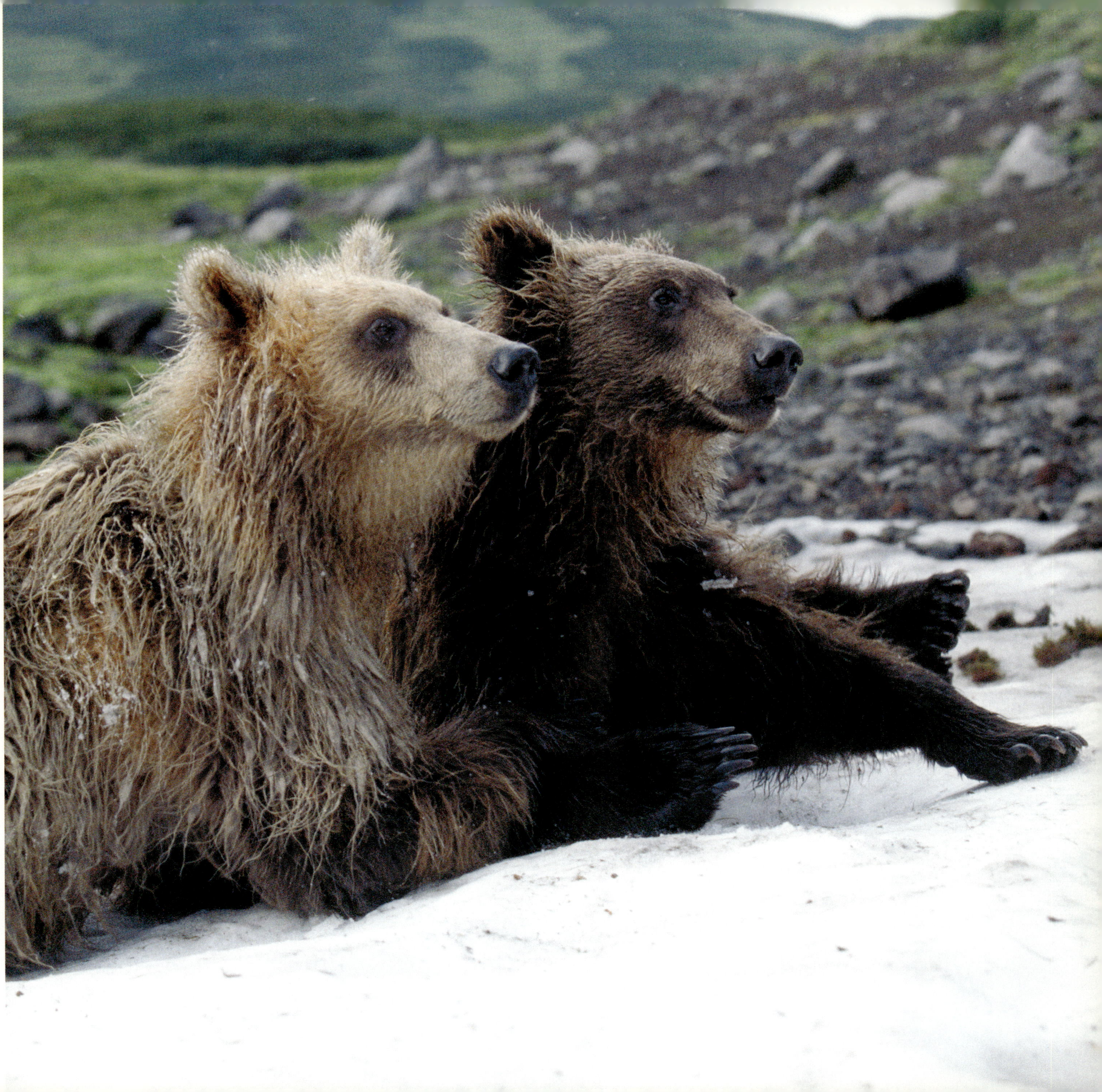

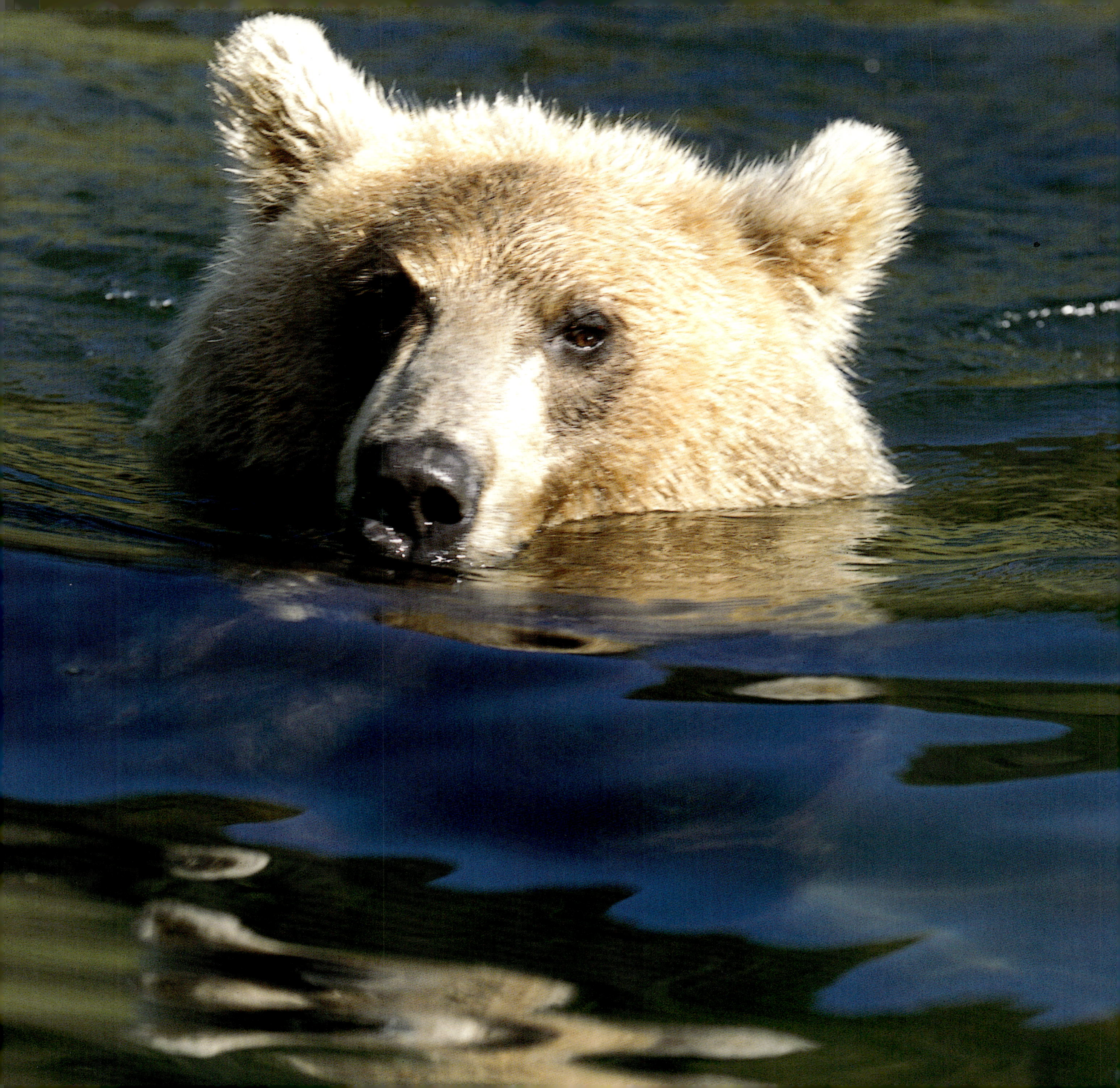

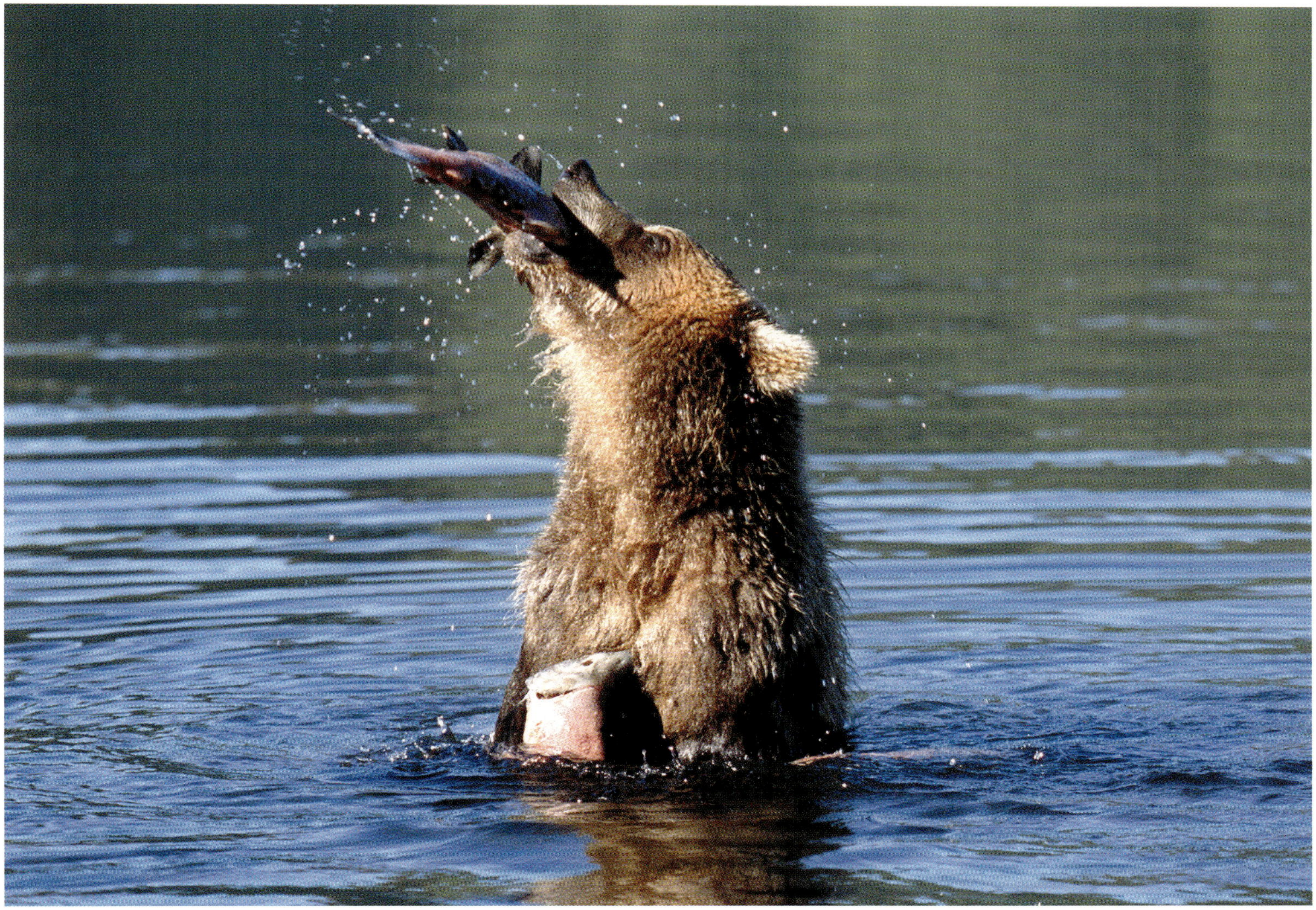

Salmon would spawn, die, and sink to the bottom of the shallow bay. Biscuit gathered them up with her feet. She would bring the fish to the surface, toss them into the air, then catch and eat them.

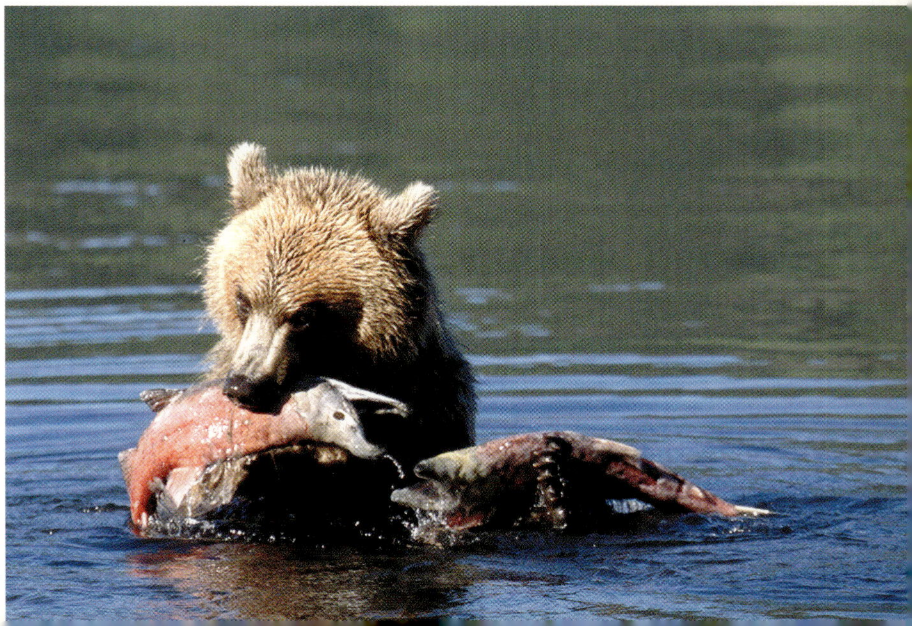

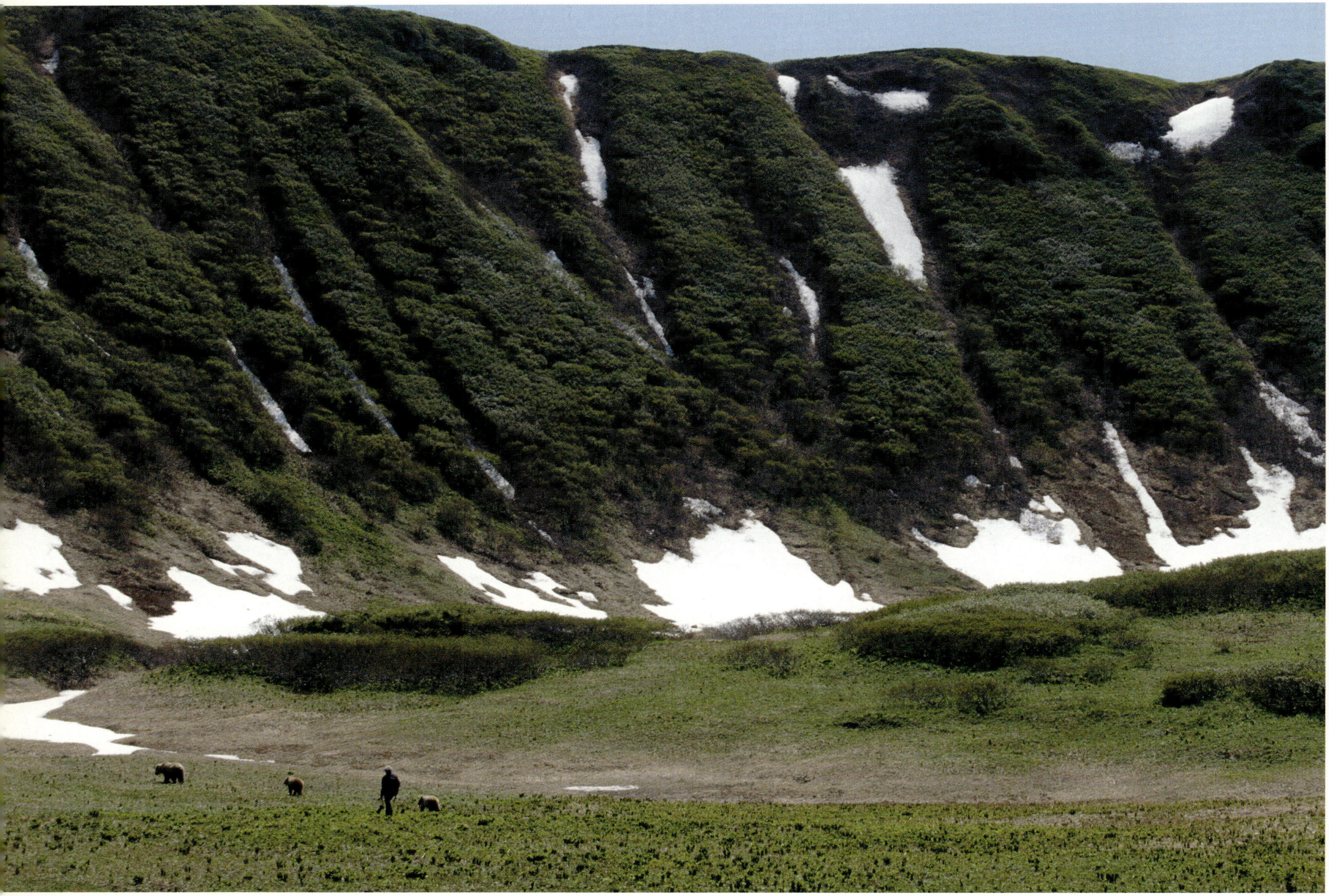

Charlie takes a stroll with Brandy and her two yearlings, Gin and Tonic. One of the most important things the bears of Kambalnoye Lake have taught us is that humans don't have to be misfits in the bear world—that you can fit in as long as you don't make a nuisance of yourself.

Brandy, Gin and Tonic.

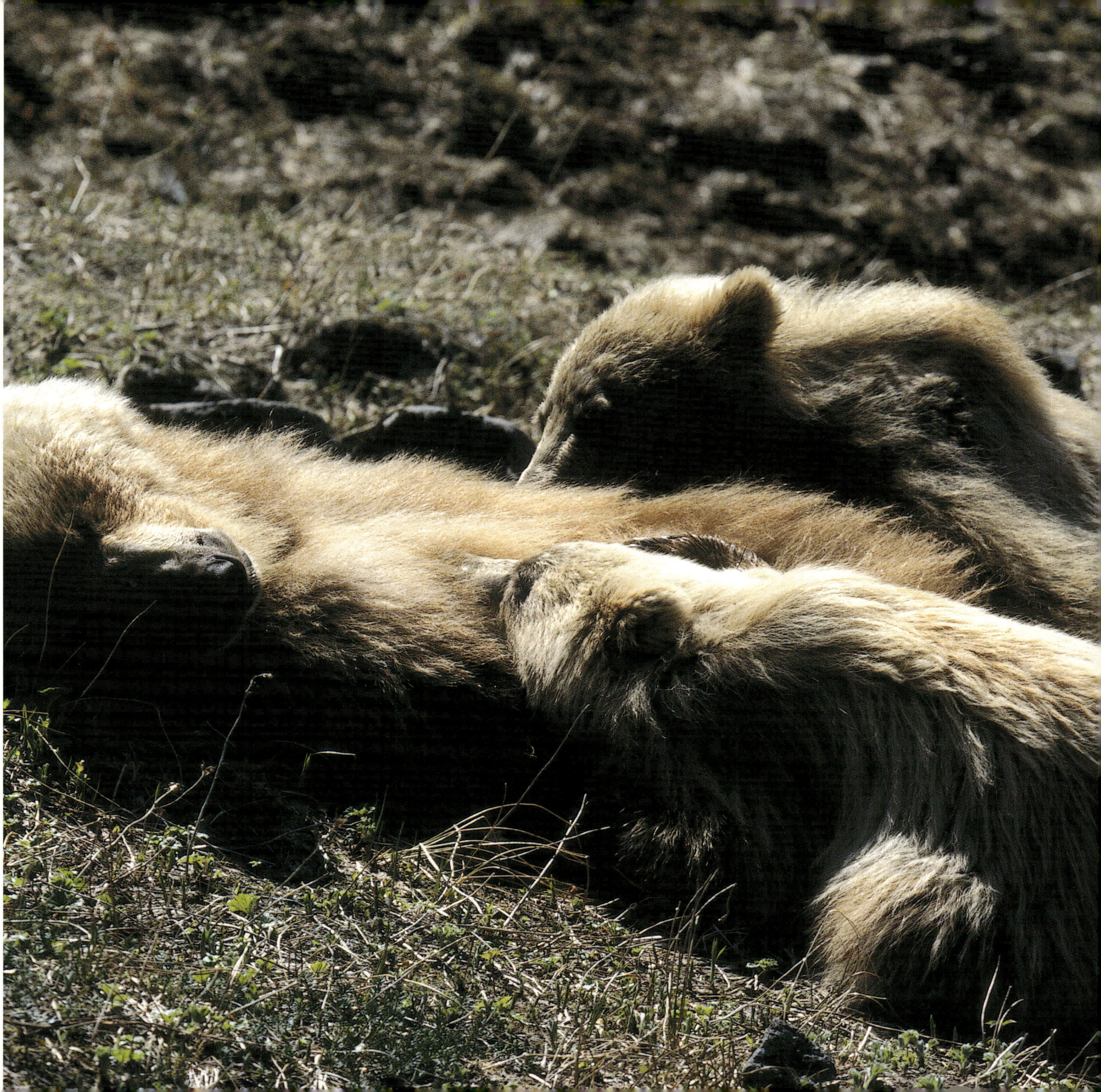

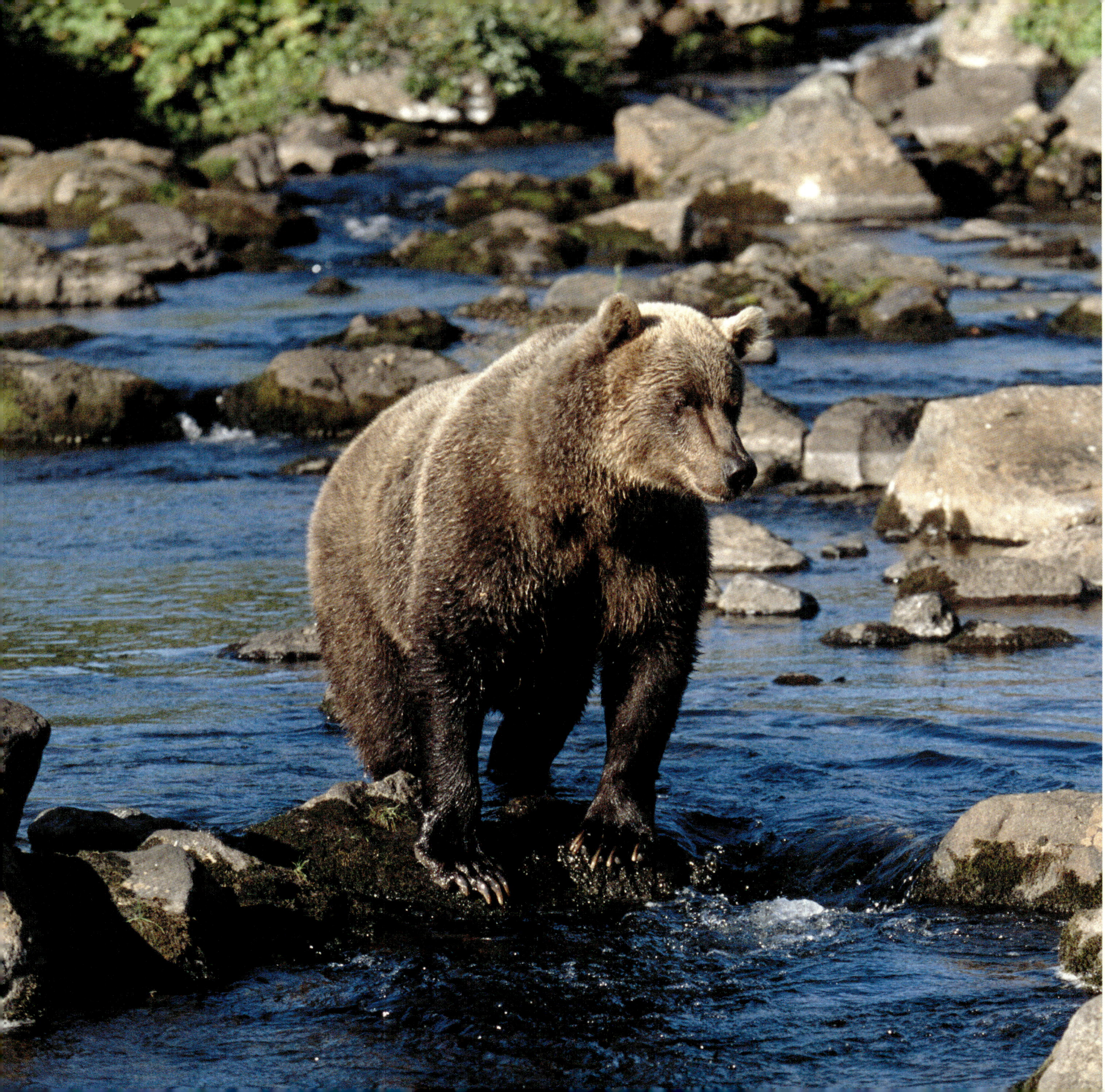

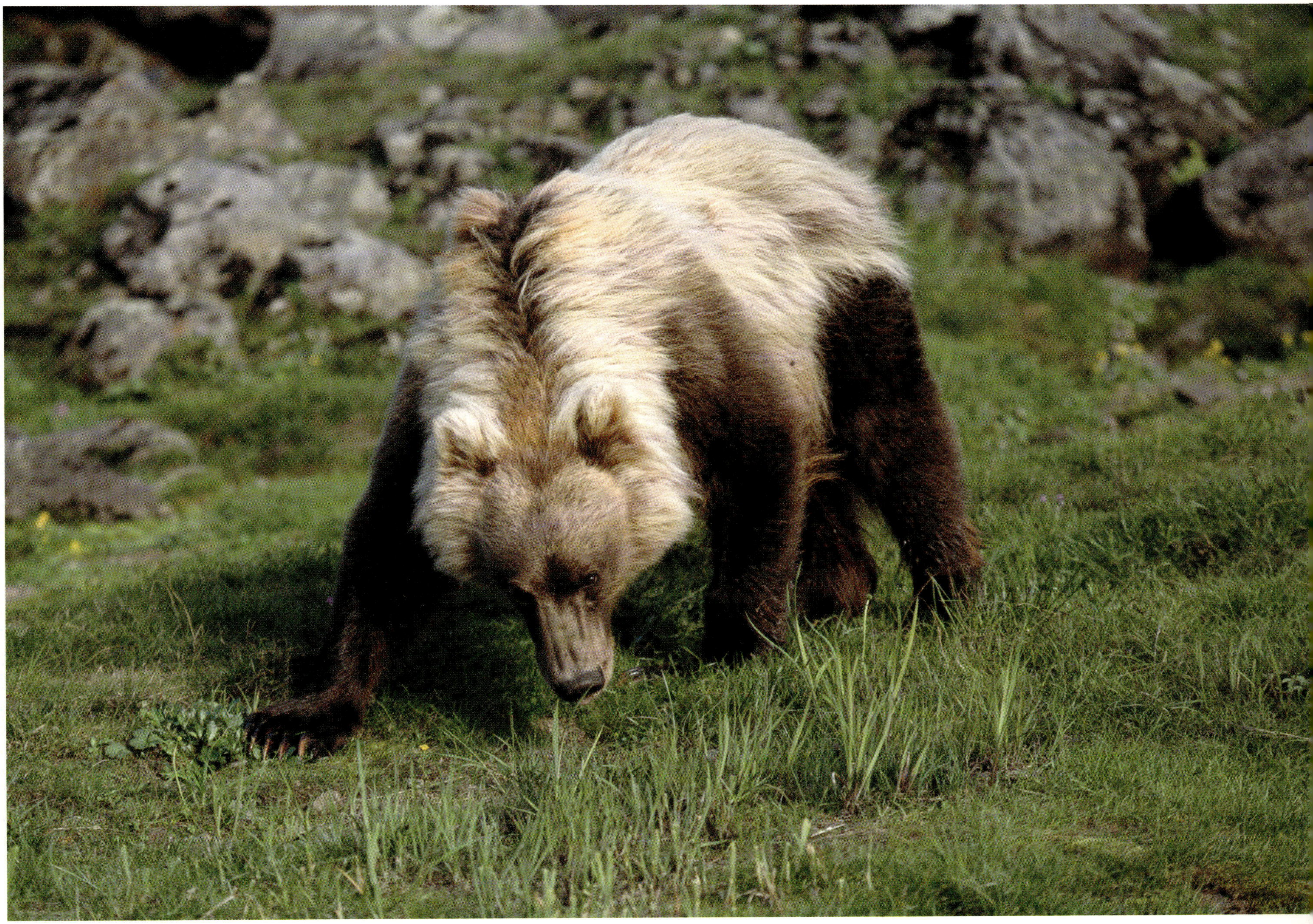

Gin at age three, a year after he was weaned.

Brandy's summer off between cub litters. Not having to nurse,
she focused her attention on the bounty of Char Creek and quickly put on fat.

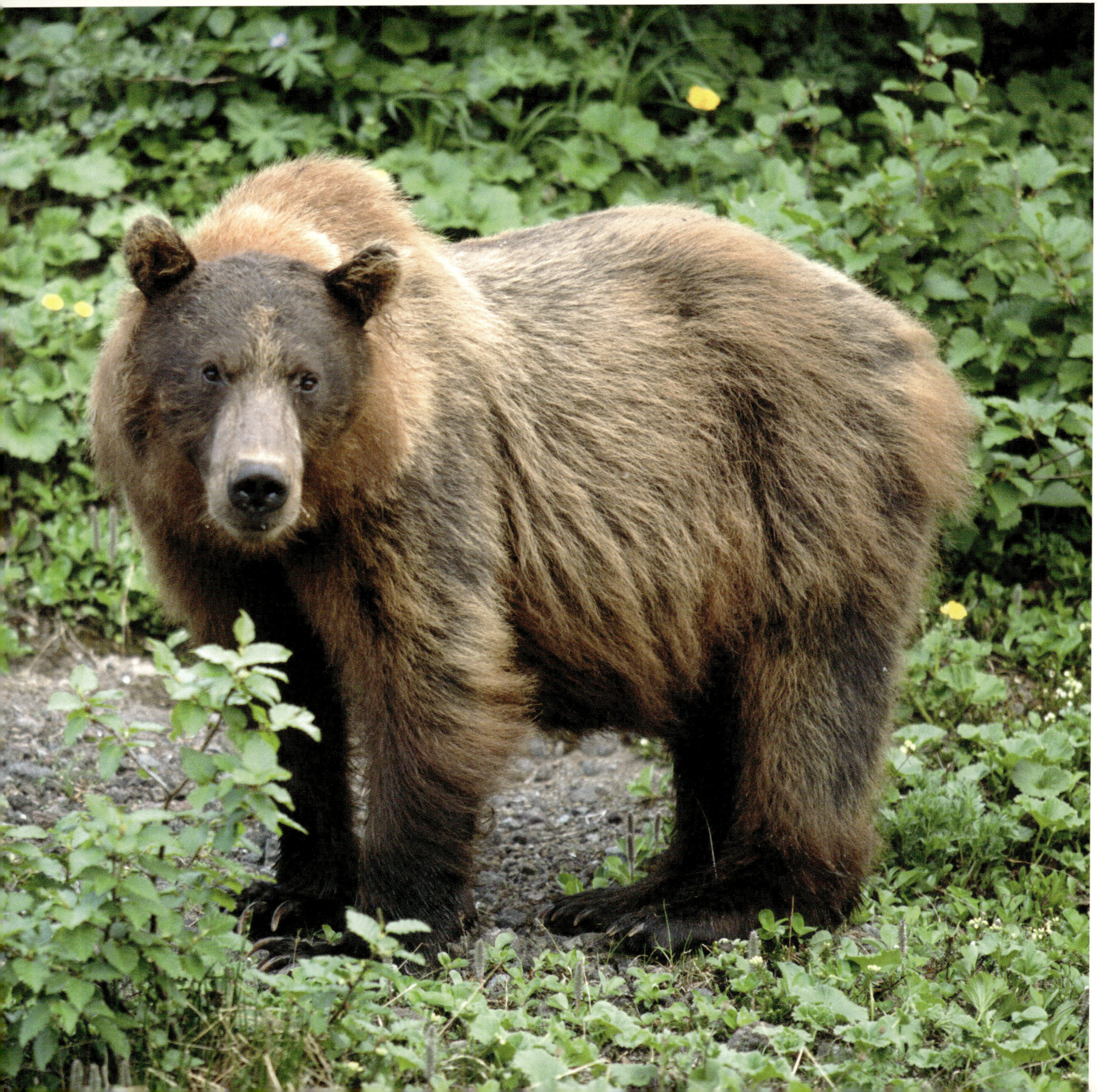

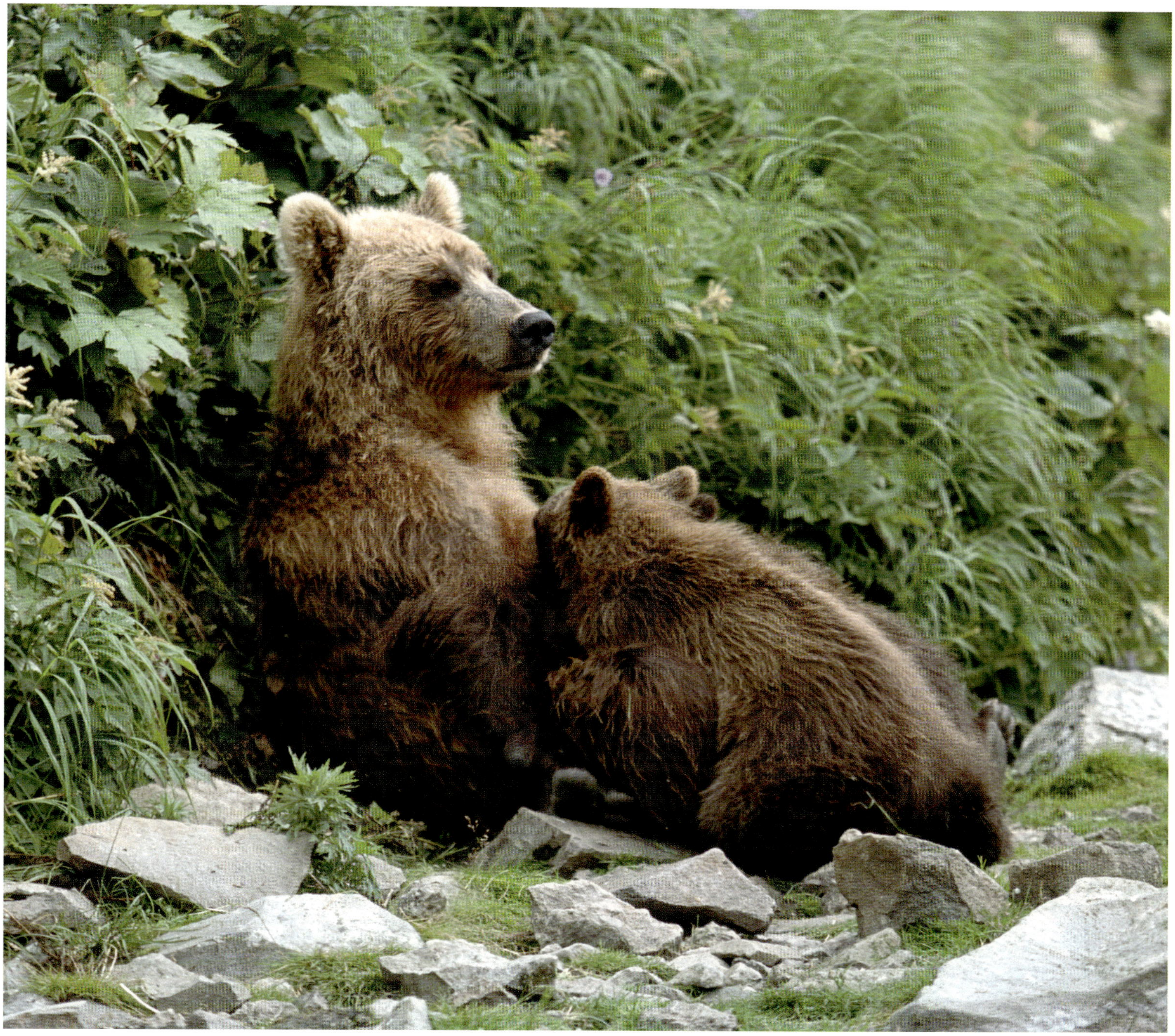

Walking along the lakeshore, we came upon Brandy nursing her second pair of cubs, Lemon and Lime. She was clearly comfortable in our presence, as she allowed us to proceed around her, along the narrow shore. She didn't even look up as we passed by.

Walnut is another of the resident bears we see year after year, but he always waits until the middle of August to show up.

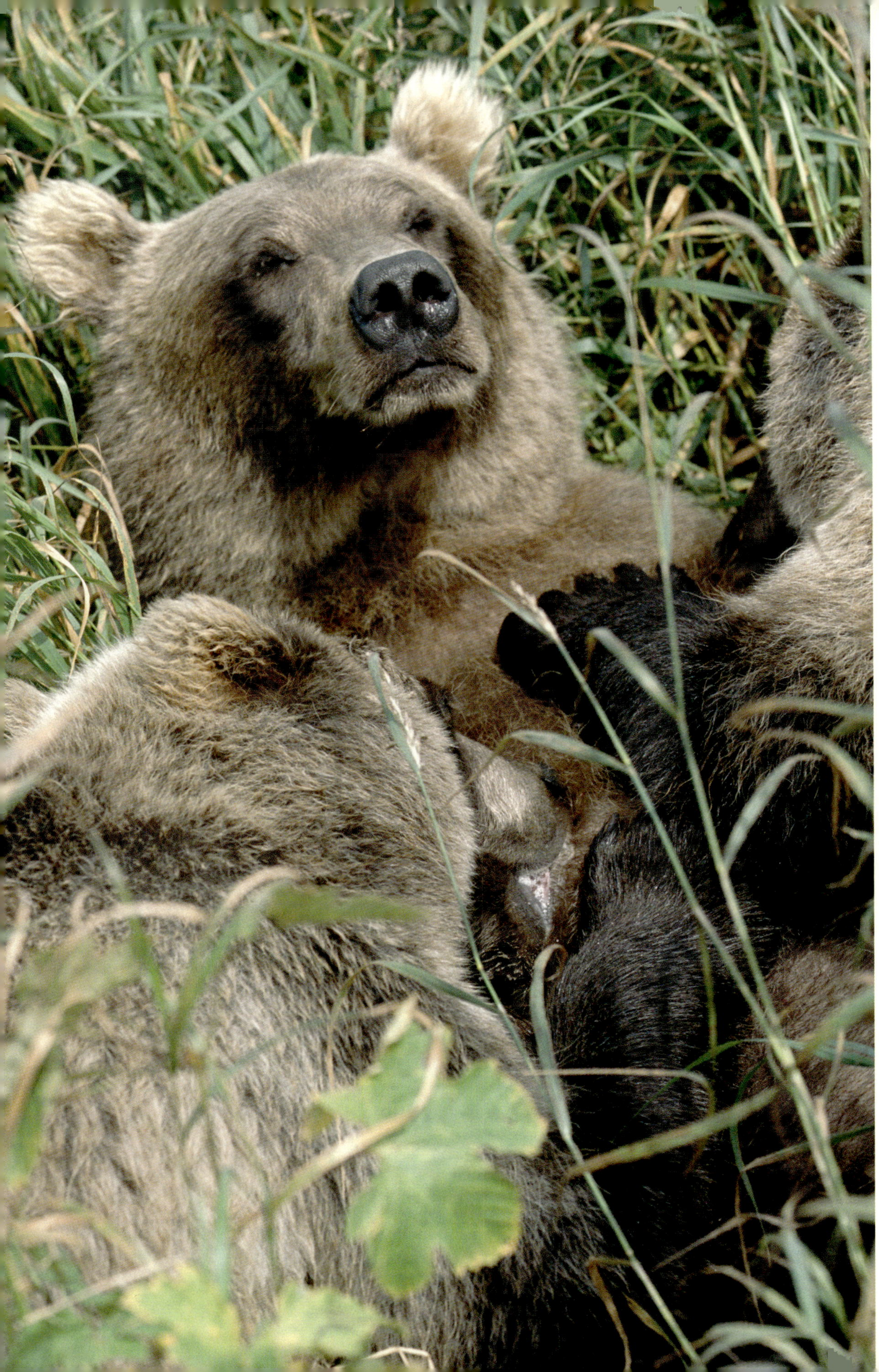

Brandy didn't even mind letting us have a close-up of her suckling her cubs.

Brandy occasionally startled us with a sudden loud hiss if we got in her way, but her roaring ferociousness with other bears made our hair stand on end.

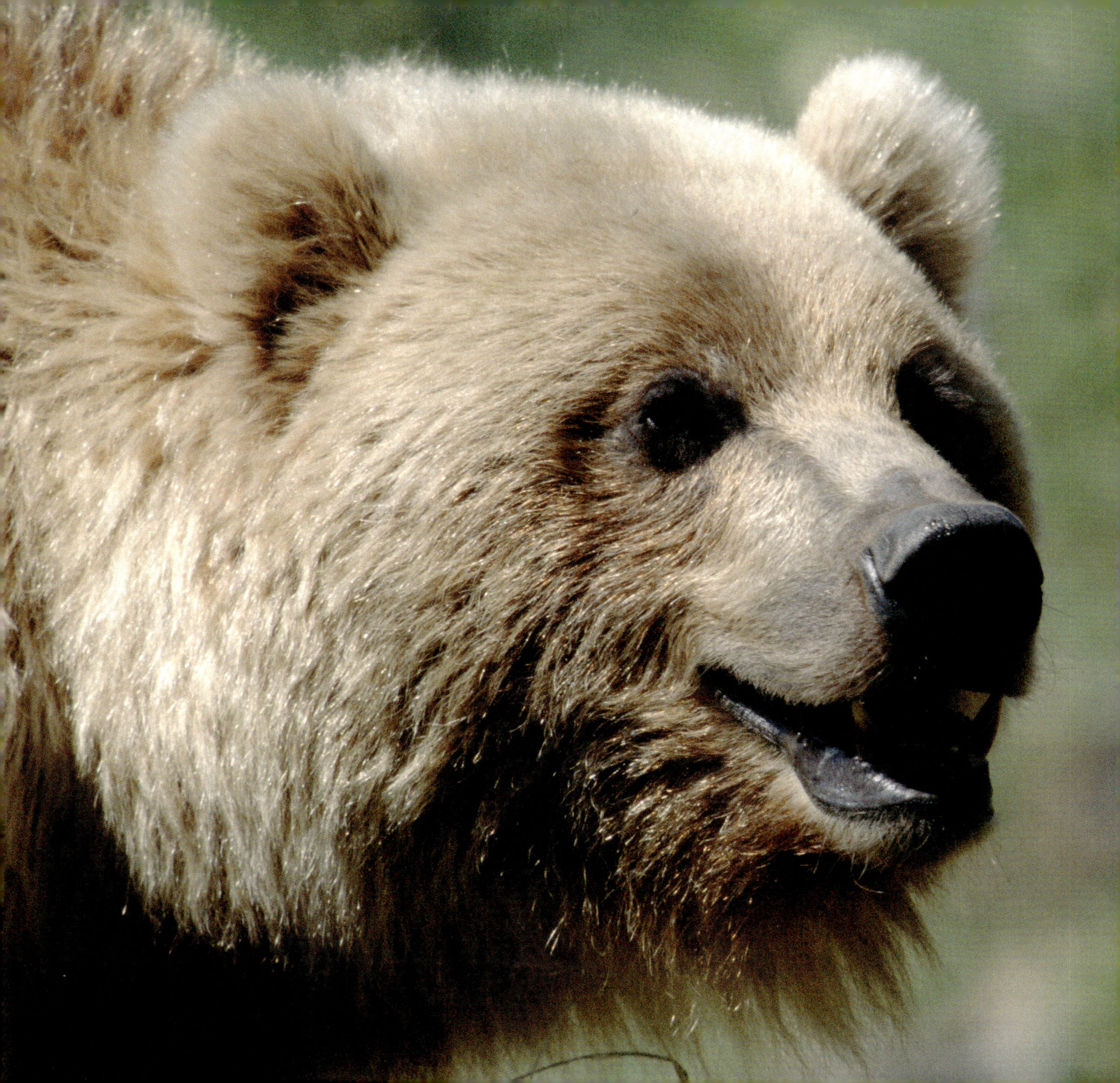

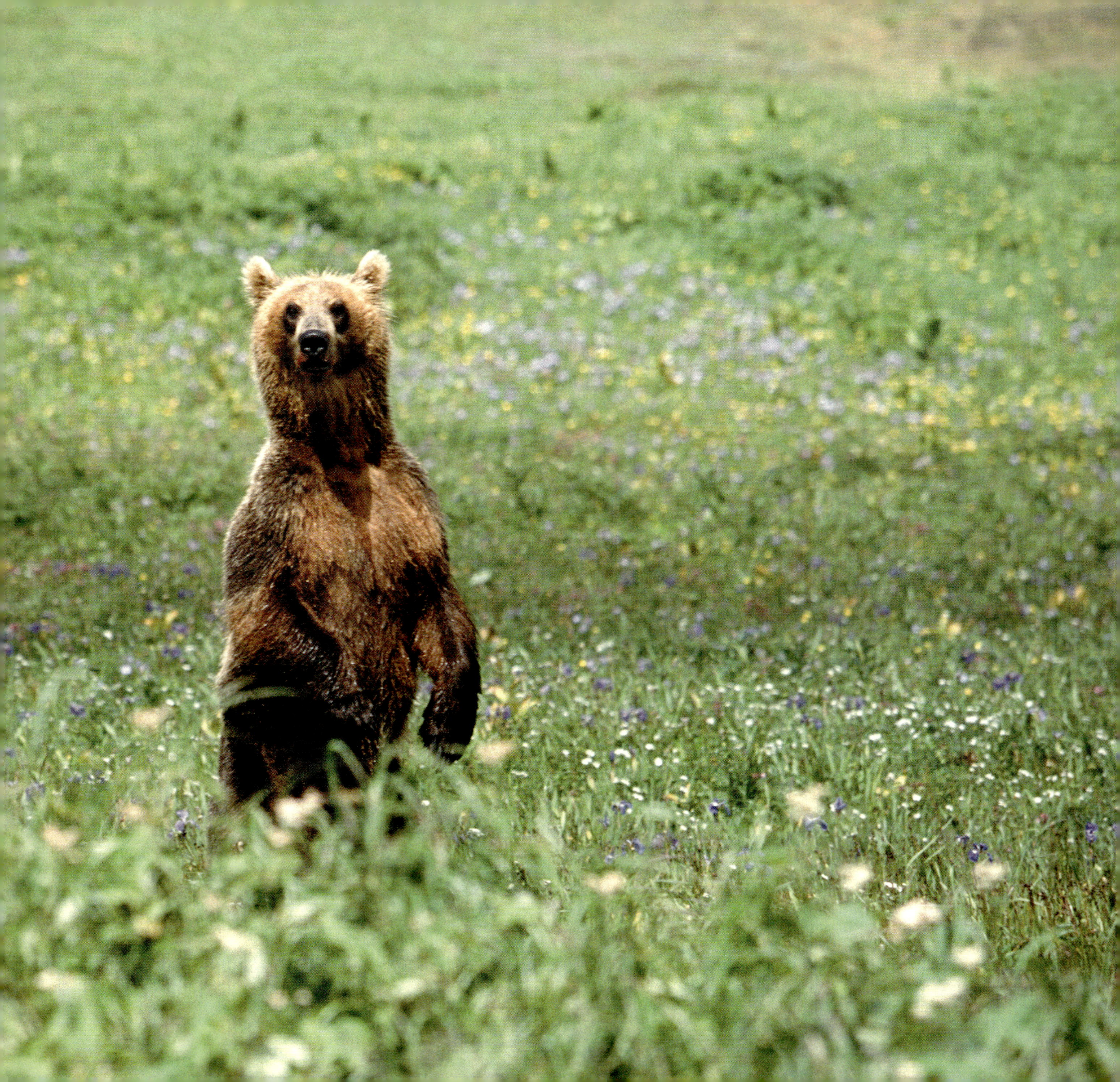

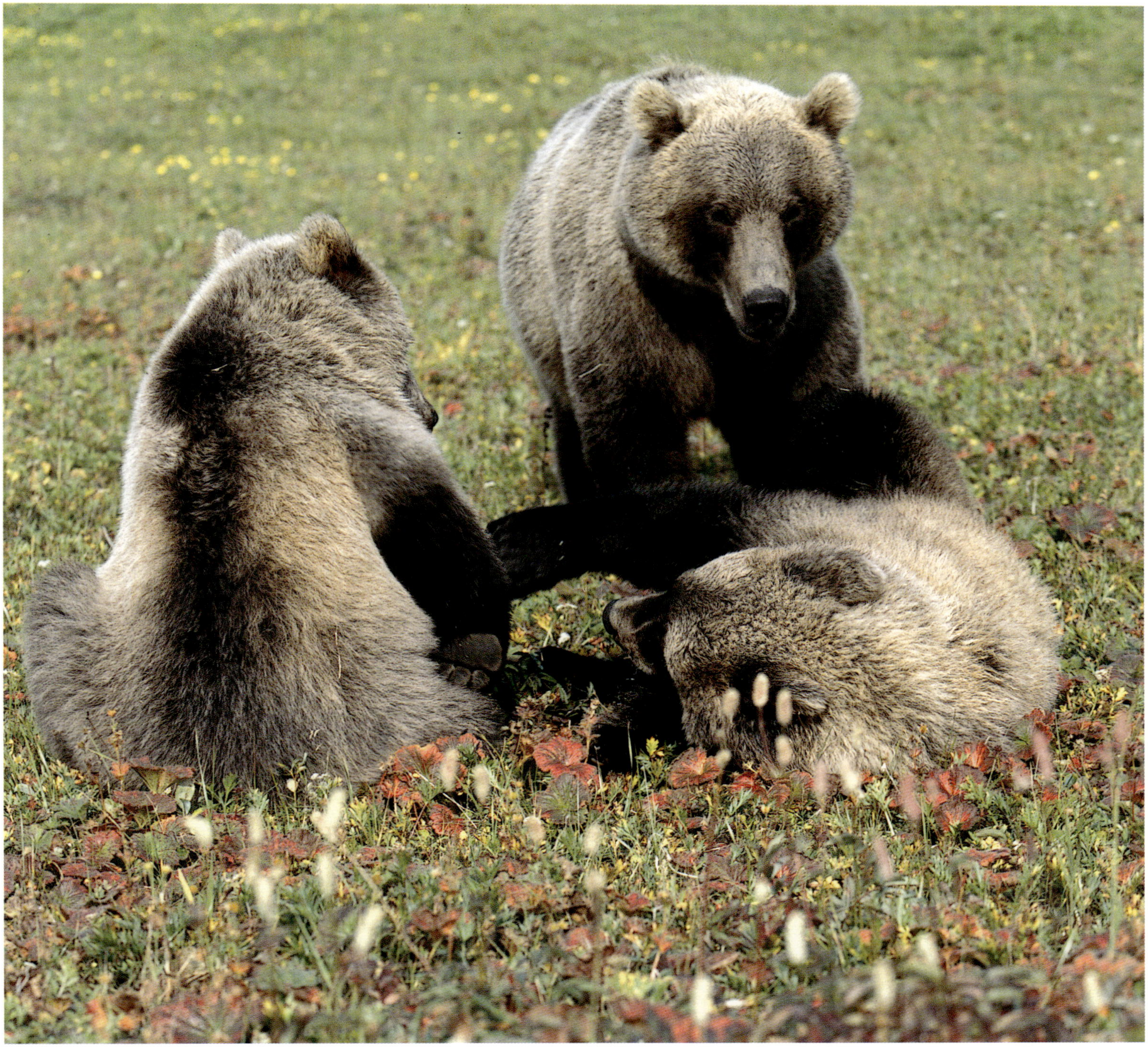

Brandy would get Lemon and Lime playing, then leave them with us to frolic.

By the summer of 2002 Biscuit stood eight feet tall, and weighed about 500 pounds.

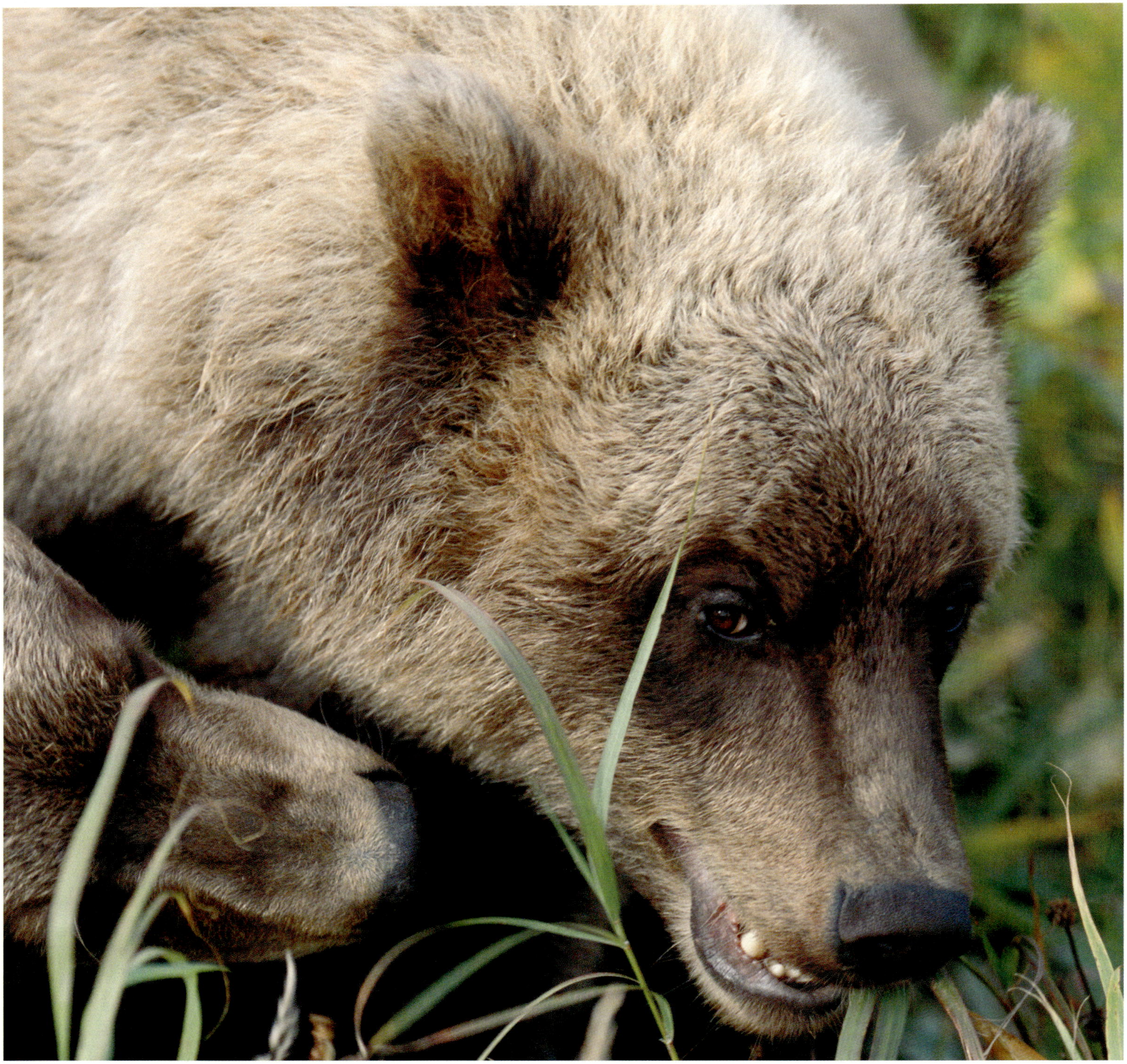

Year after year we have lived with several generations of bears who do not fear humans.
From our experiences we have grown to know the joys of being a part of their world.

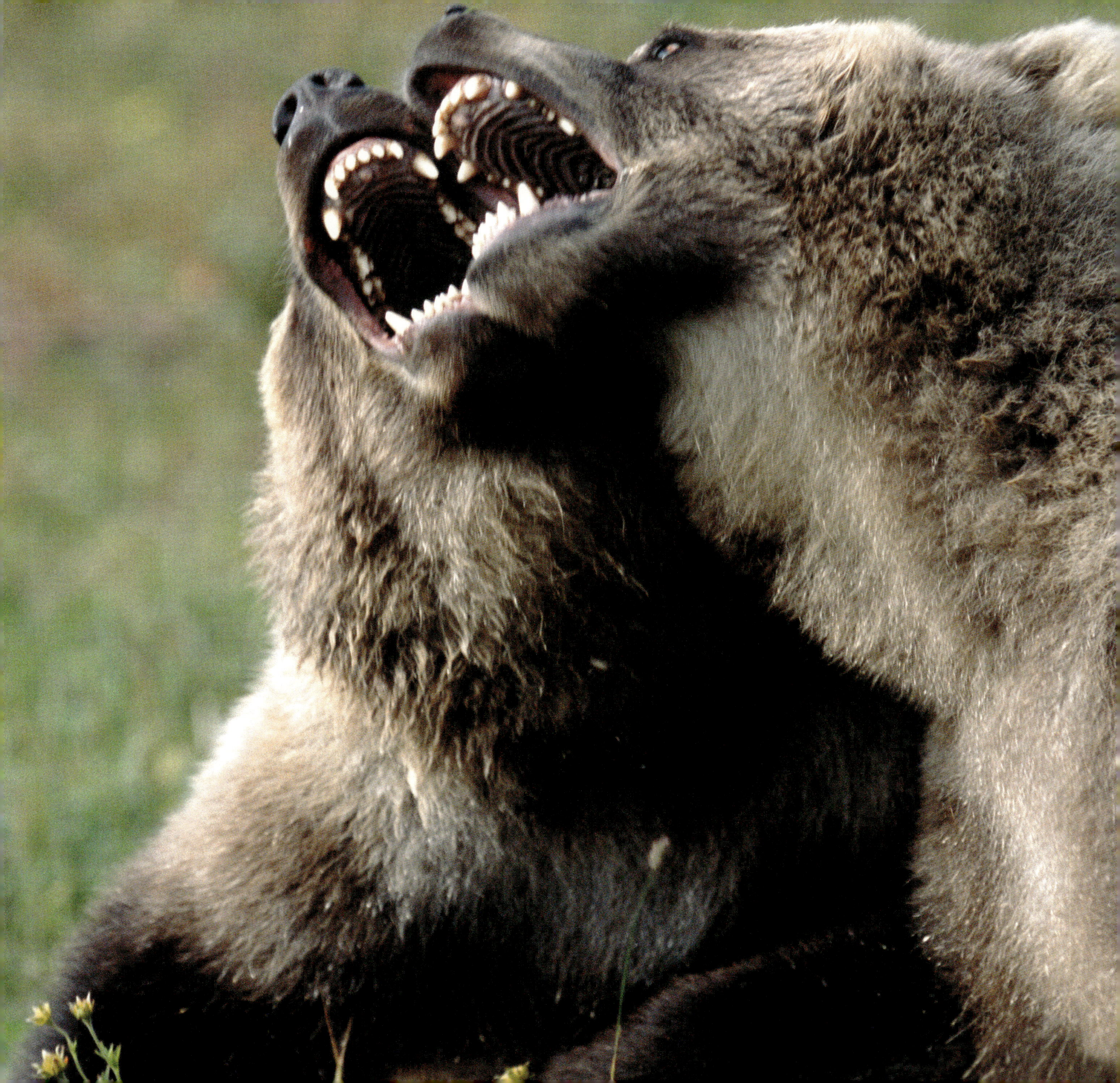

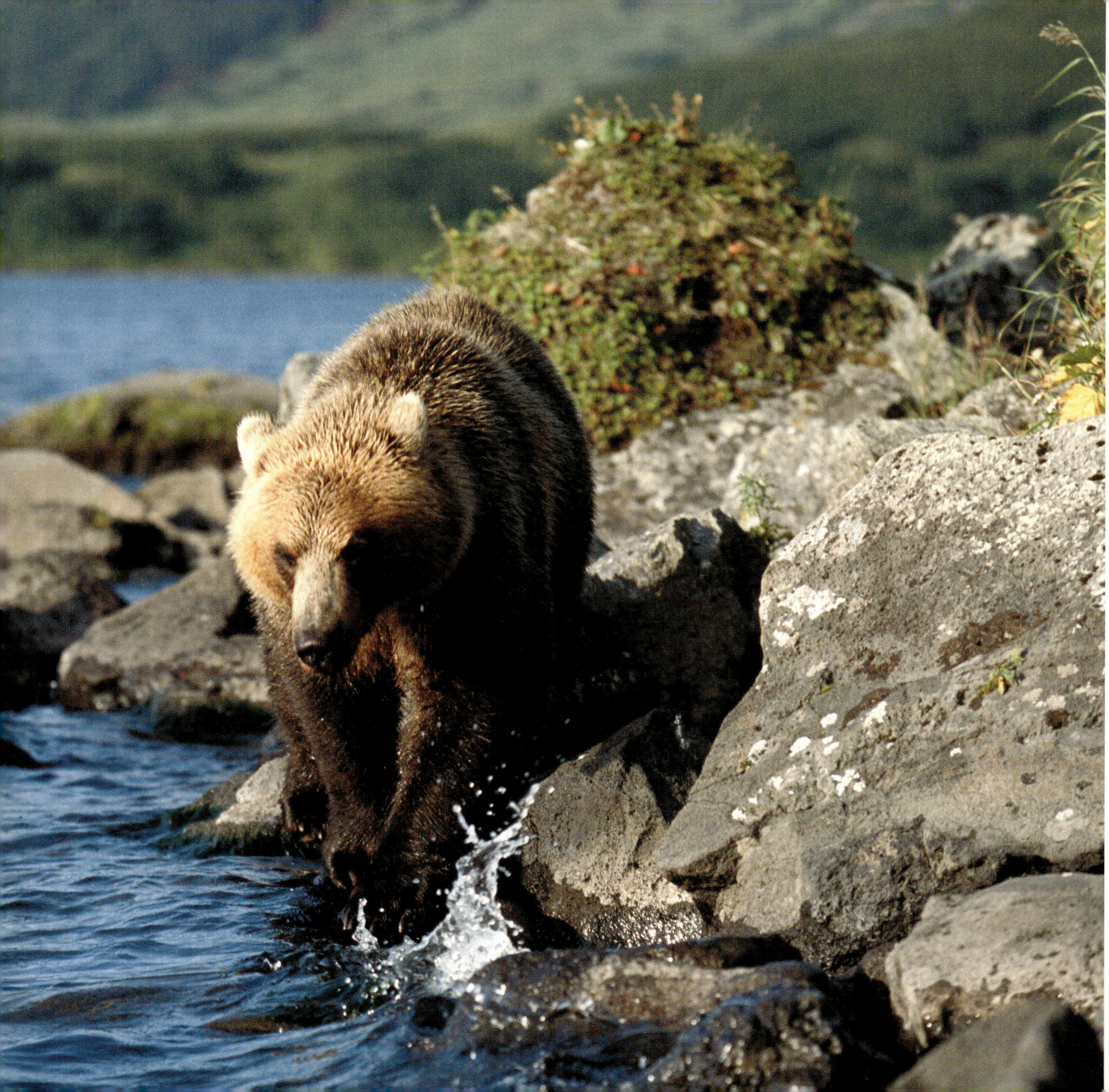

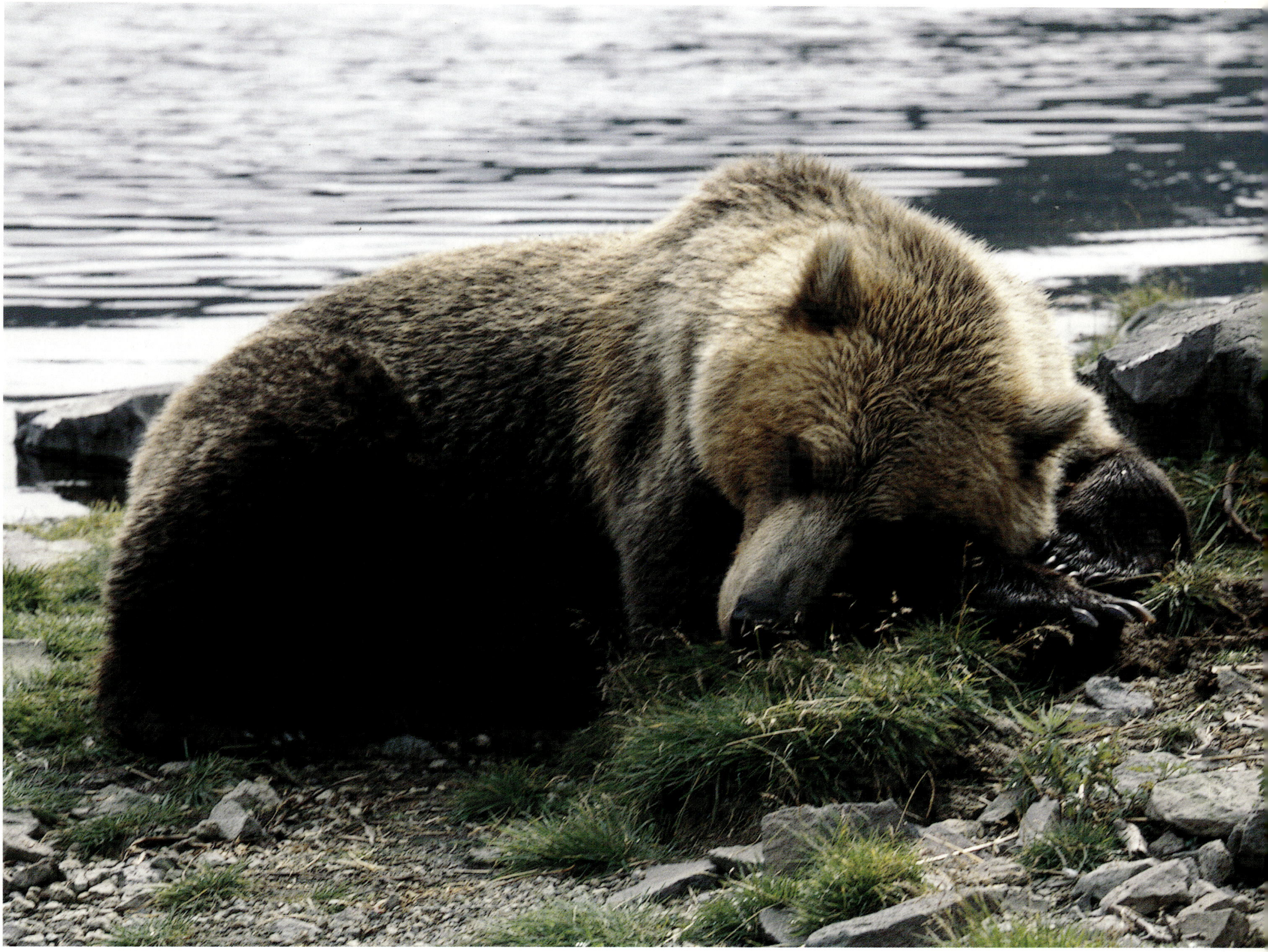

Biscuit relaxes after circumnavigating Kambalnoye Lake in search of spawning salmon.

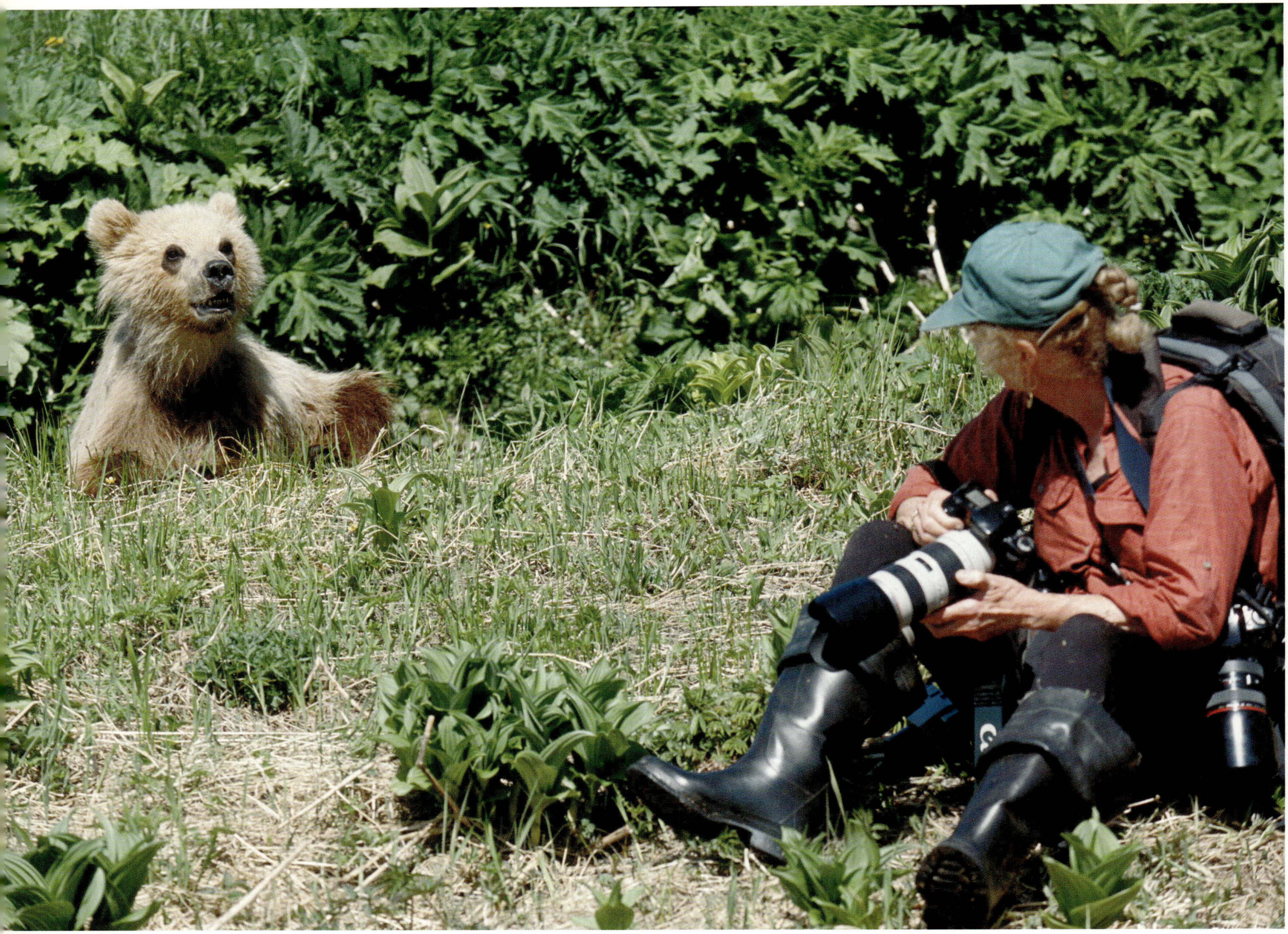

Maureen babysitting Lemon.

Lime sits still and holds her paw up at different angles. She looks like a child waiting for the teacher to call on her.

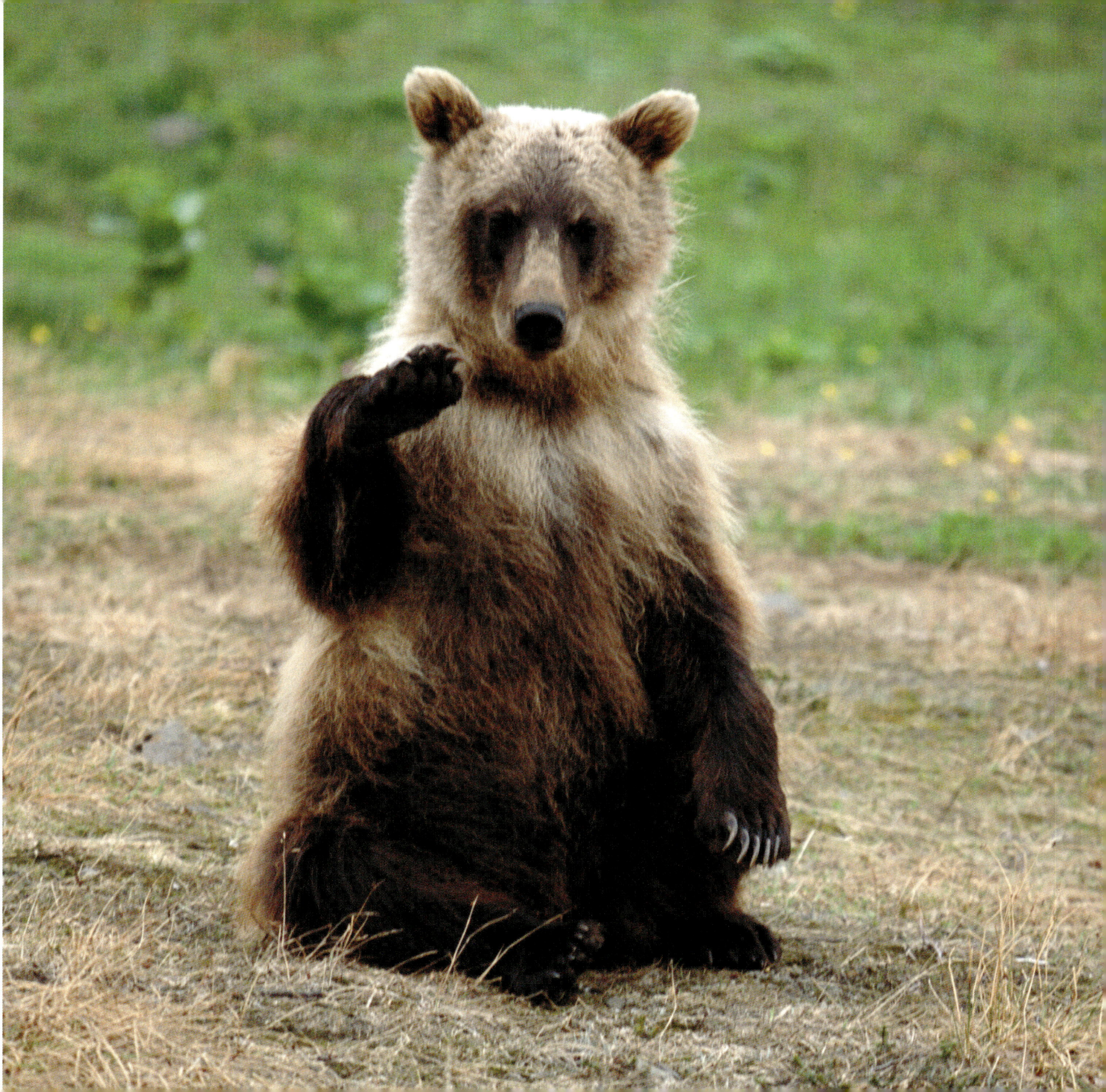

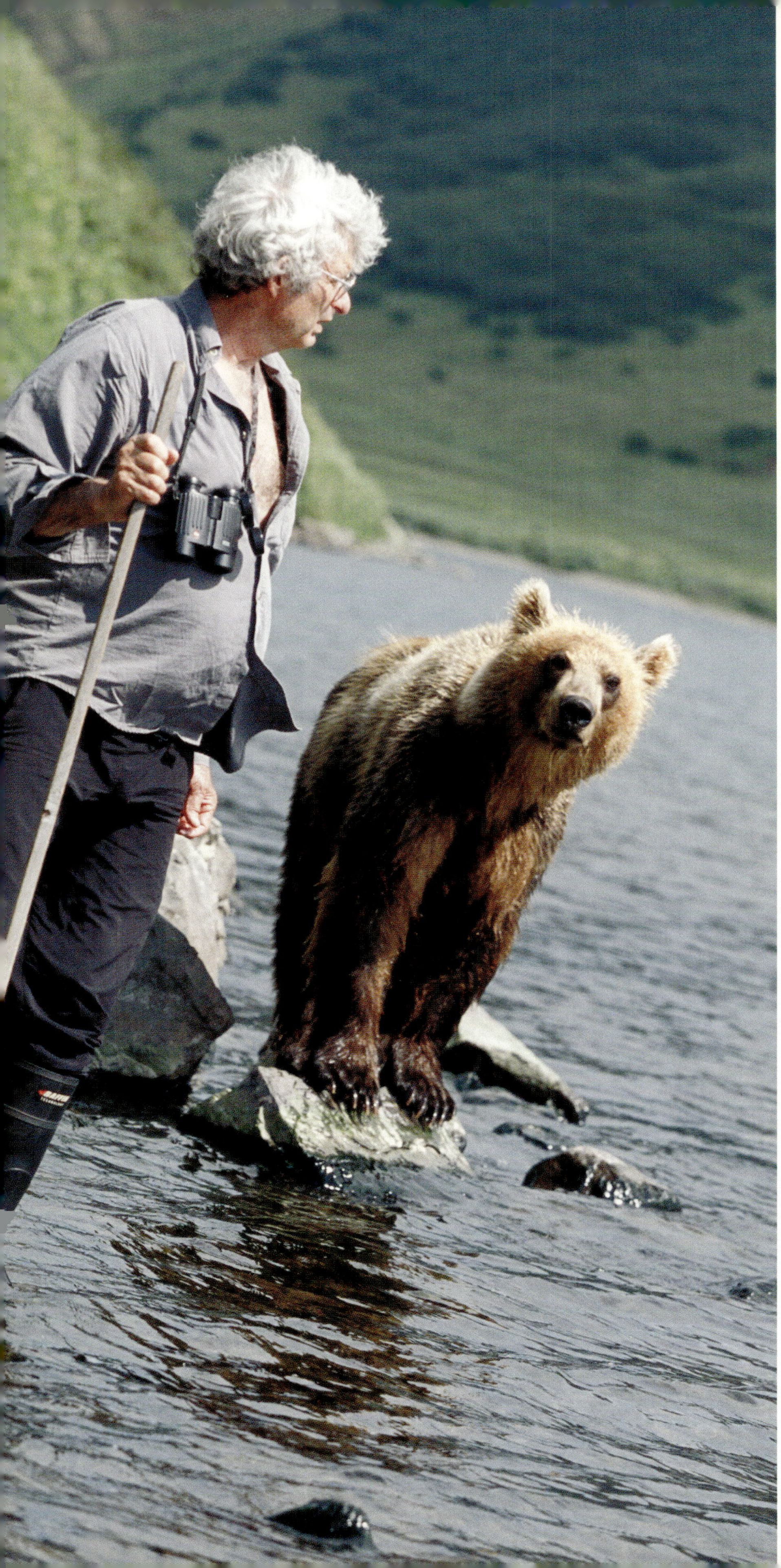

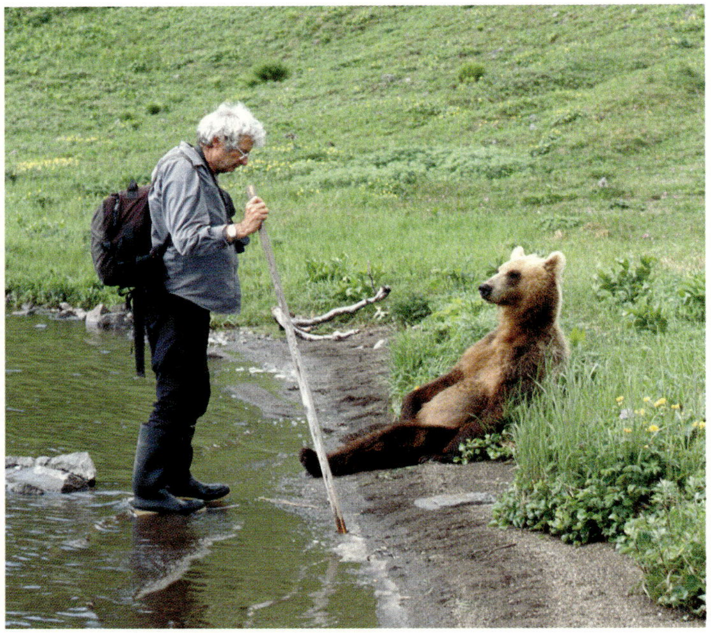

Biscuit and Charlie have a lakeside chat about trust and what it means in terms of world affairs.

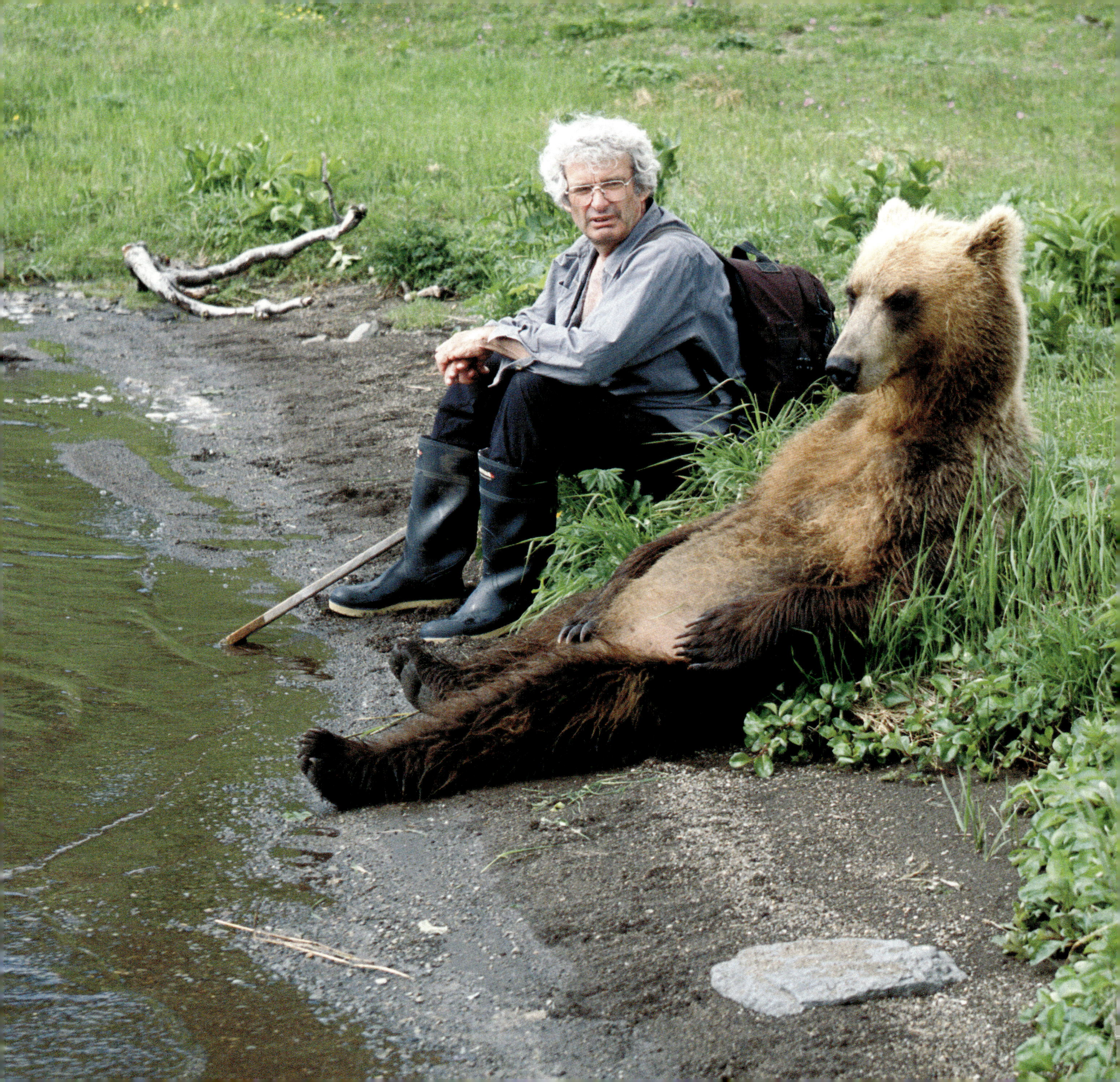

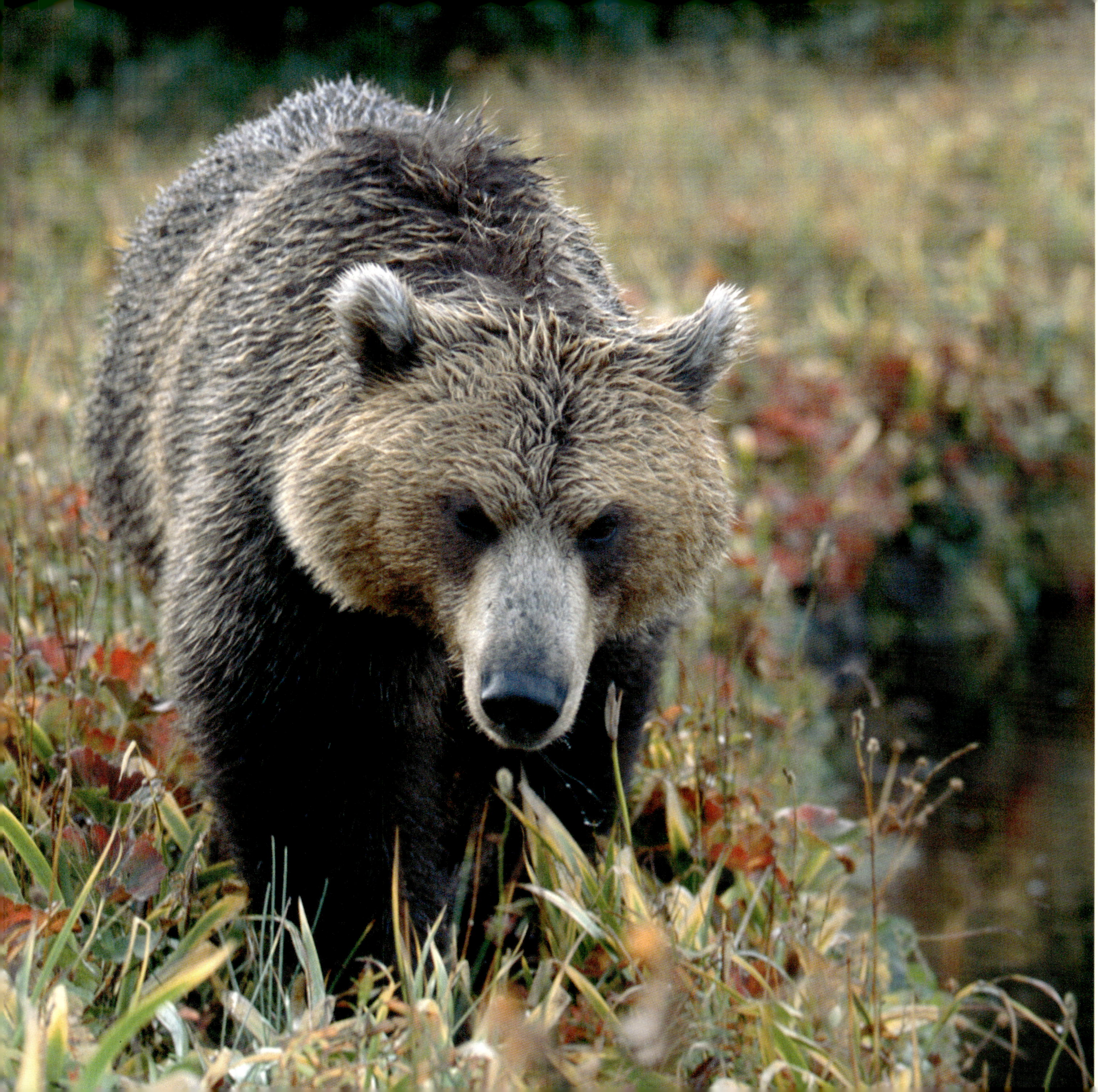

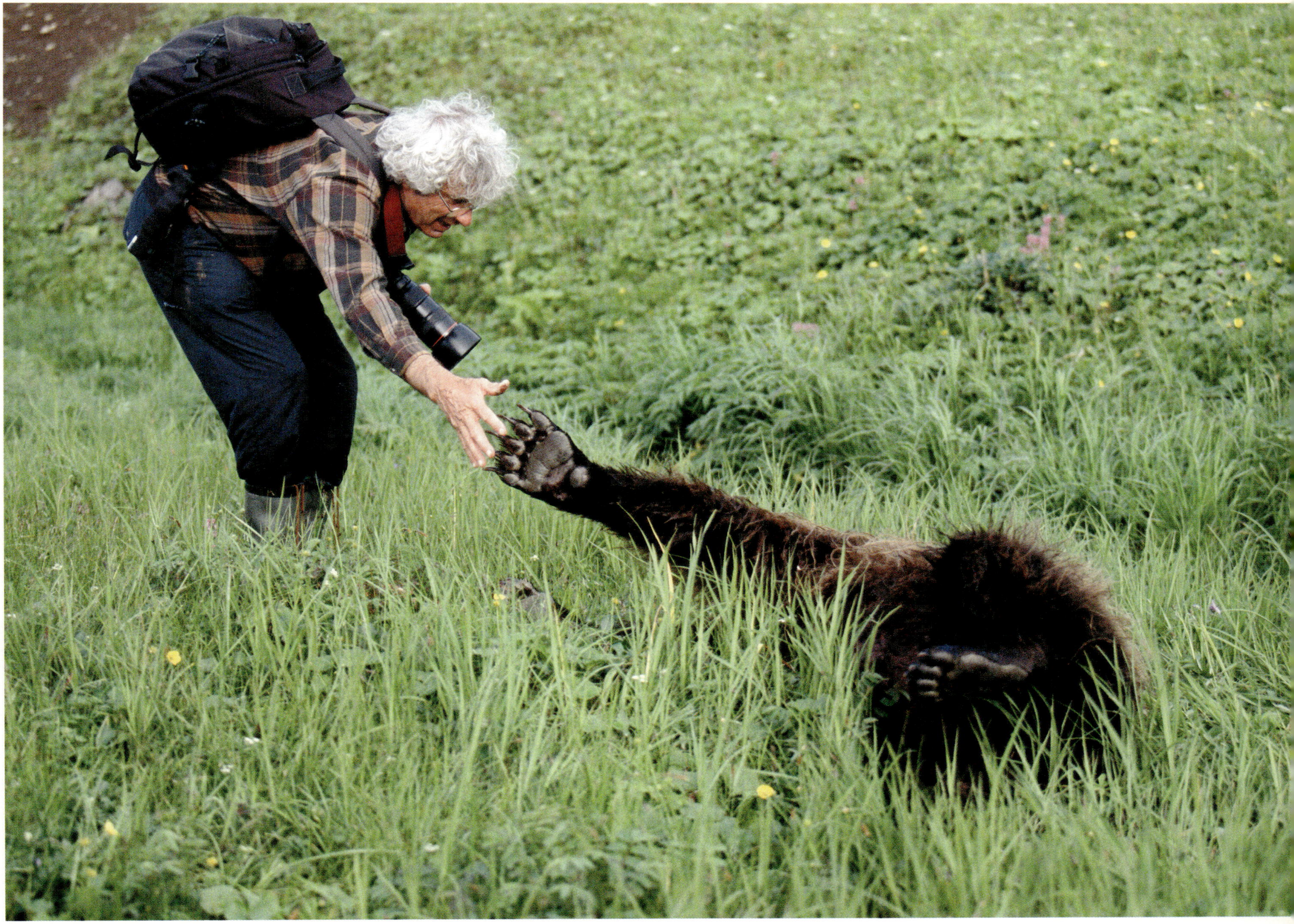

When shaking hands with an animal with a reputation as nefarious as the grizzly's, the tender finesse of the grip can be surprising.

Within three months of this photo being taken, we expect that Biscuit will have had her own cubs while snug in her den under the snow, sometime in January 2003.

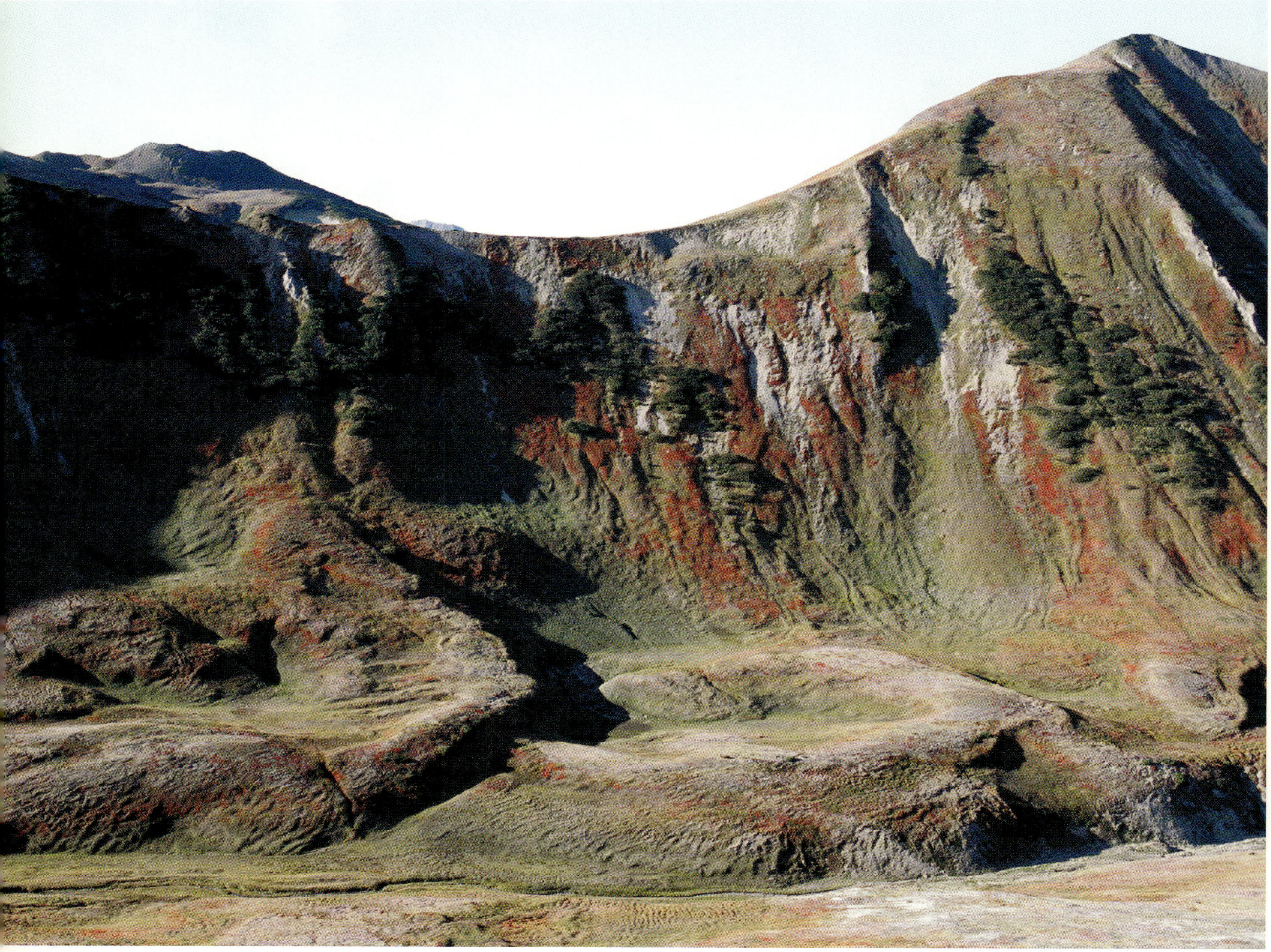

Biscuit.

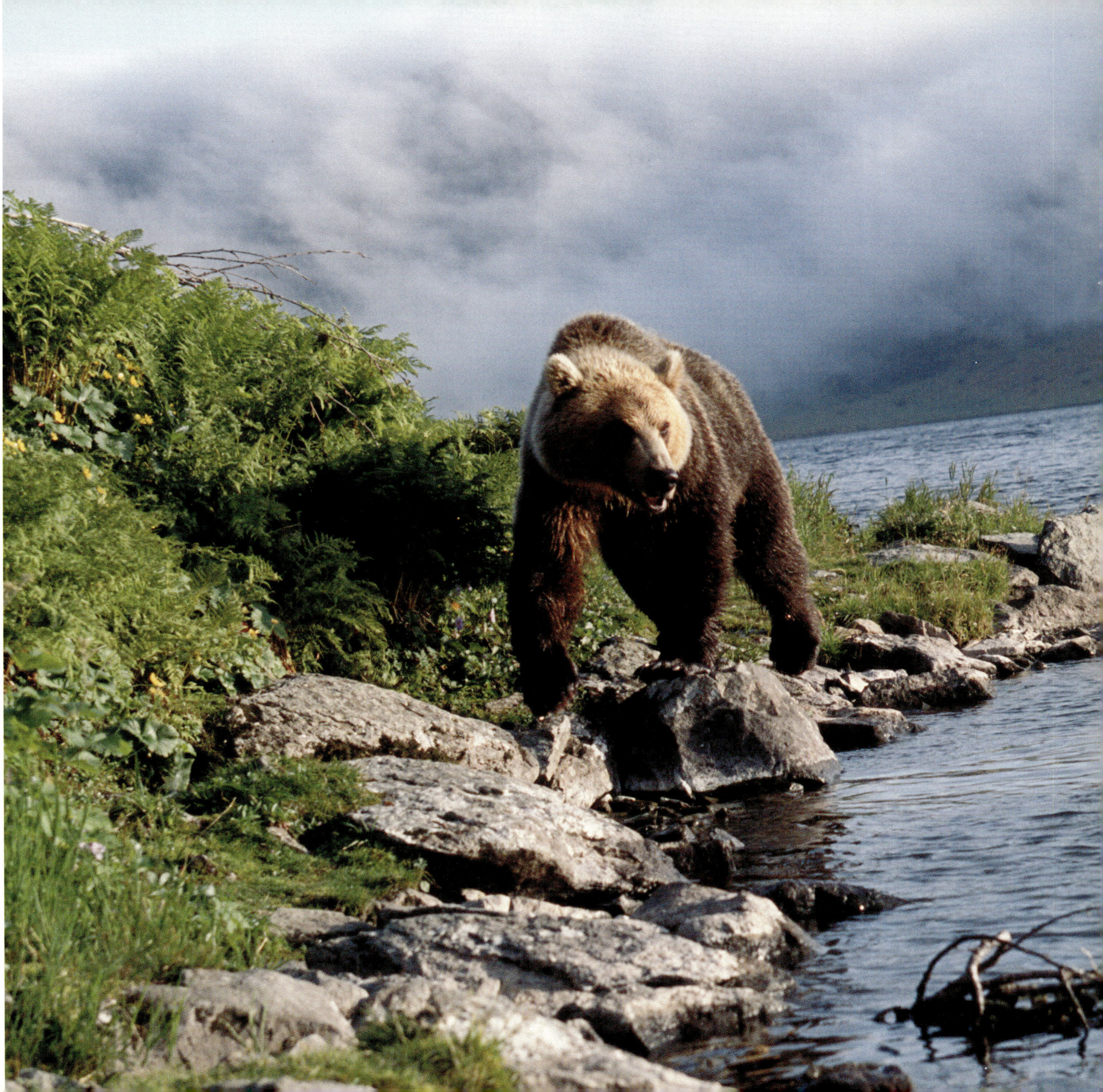

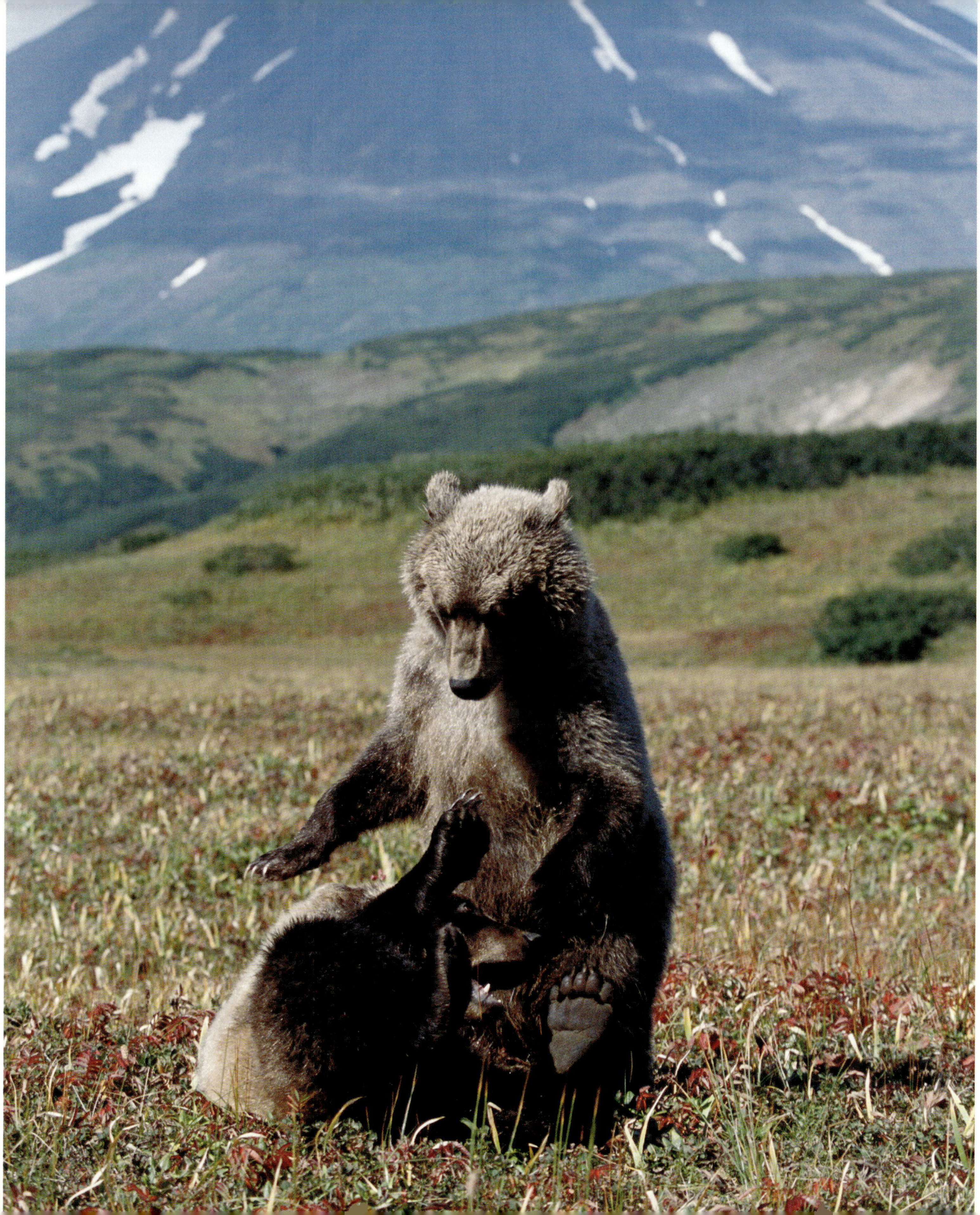

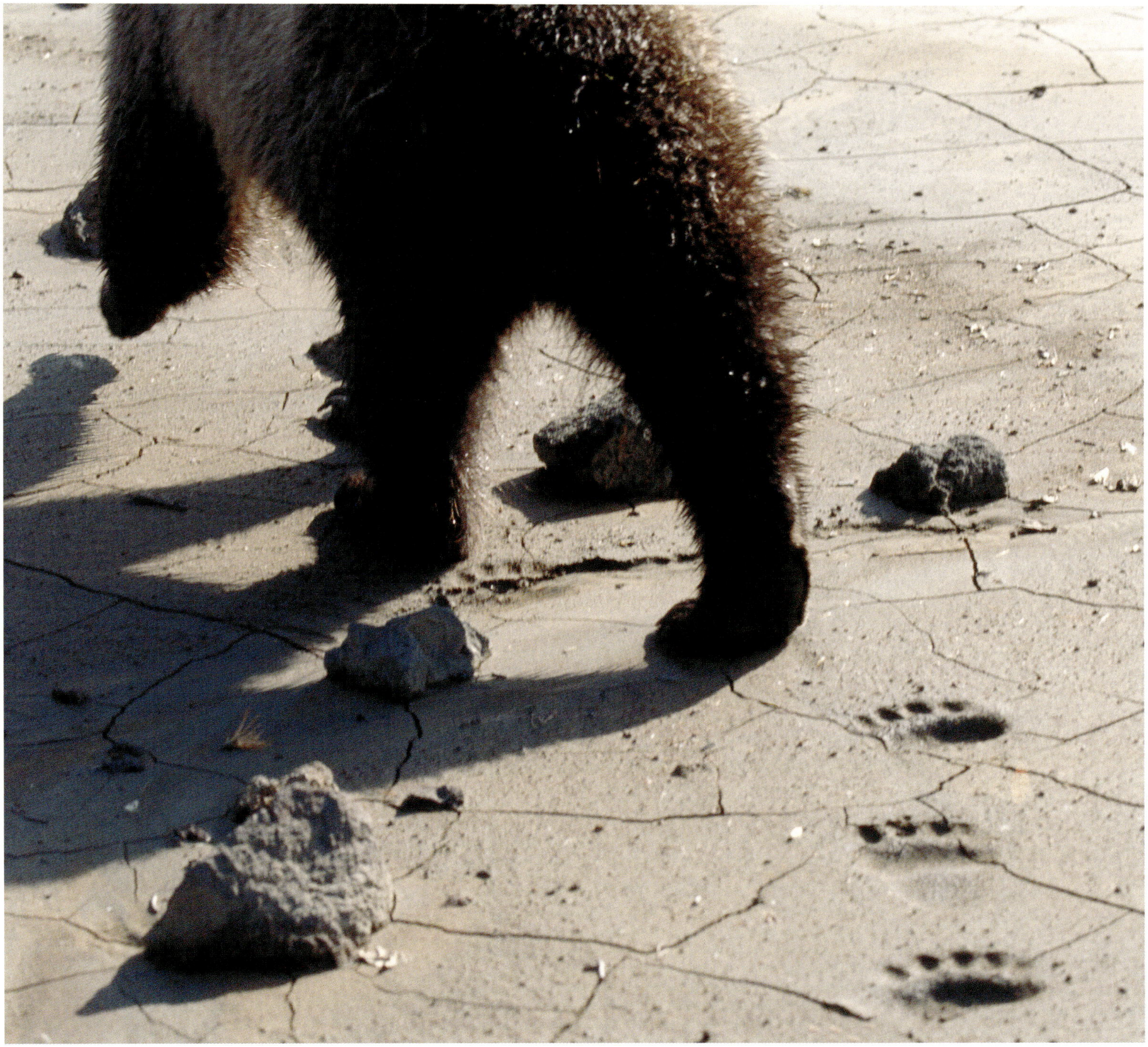

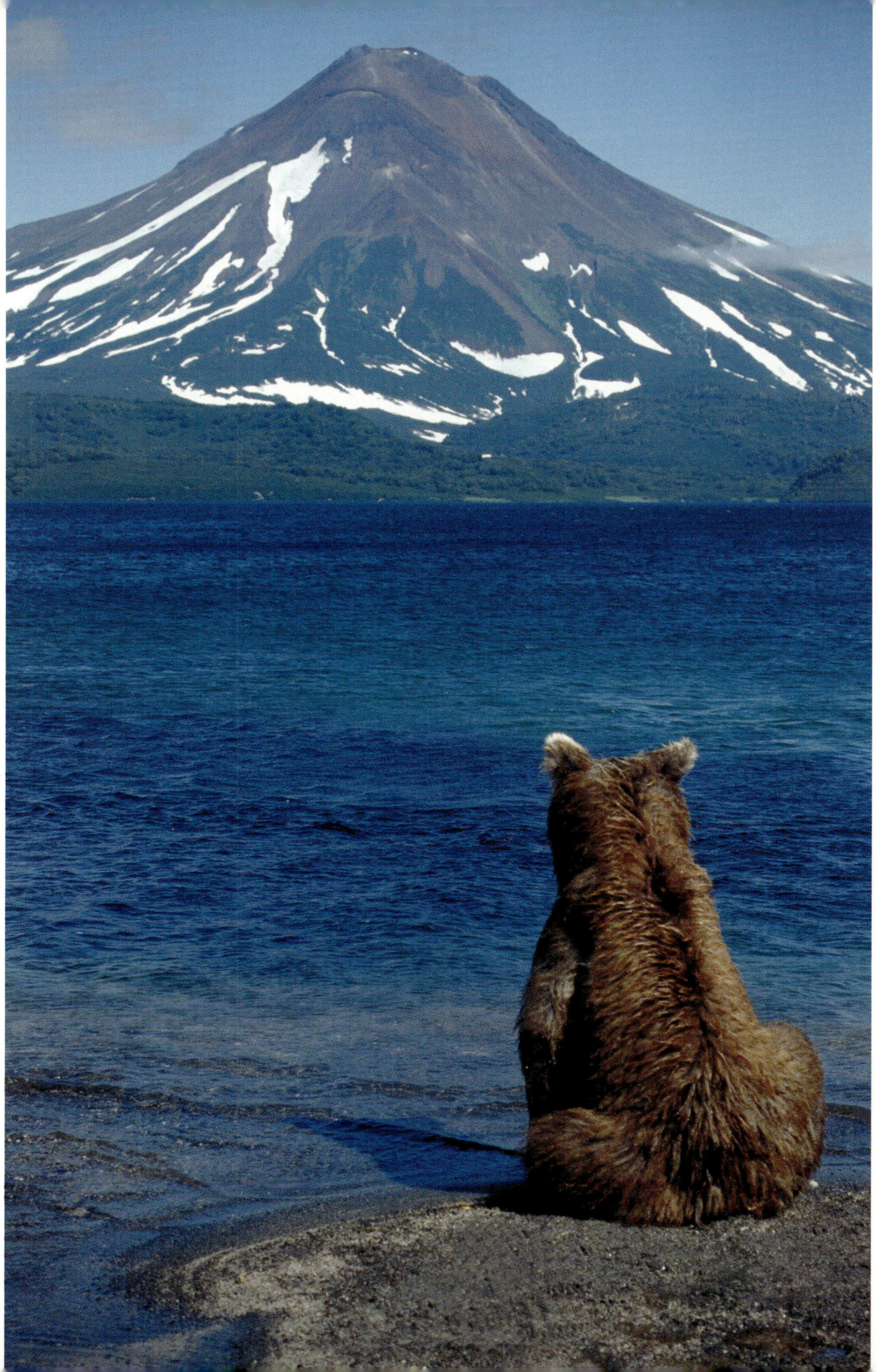

A Protocol for Co-existence between Grizzlies and Humans

• Use electric fencing to keep bears out of where people live and away from toilets, garbage, and anything else bears could eat or damage.

• Always assume that bears' activity is important to them and do your best not to interfere, especially when their need to fatten becomes urgent in late summer and fall. Staying out of bears' way is always the most important thing.

• In surprise encounters, talk to bears, calmly.

• Always carry pepper spray in bear country, to be used only at close range in dangerous encounters.

• Play dead only when you have forgotten your pepper spray, when talking to them has failed and when you know you are a couple of bounds away from being knocked down by a grizzly. (And remember, never play dead with a black bear.)

• A little harder to learn, but very enjoyable for anybody with a love of wild animals, is to appreciate the intelligence, instincts, vulnerabilities and memory of bears. If you want to go into bear country, you should be willing to learn that too.

• If you live in bear country (which can be a village or the edge of a big city), bears will periodically come calling. Don't automatically assume that this situation is dangerous. Leave the bear at peace and make sure you and your neighbours keep all attractants where bears cannot get into them. Meet as a group with your neighbours and the local officials in charge of these matters. Then, as a team, decide whether you want to attempt to live with the bears or not. There is more information available all the time on living with bears, but if you decide not to do so, bears can be encouraged to go elsewhere without having to kill or even transport them. Make sure your officials know how to do this, and, if need be, help research the necessary information.

Acknowledgements

Ideas by themselves do not ripen into achievement without funding. We have depended on foundations and corporations who believed in what we were attempting to do. Their financial support and encouragement have made our work with grizzlies possible and we continue to appreciate their much-needed assistance.

We thank the following organizations: The Schad Foundation, who have most generously supported our work from day one, Clayoquot Island Preserve, Fanwood Foundation West, Parallax Film Productions Inc., Raincoast Conservation Foundation, Craighead Environmental Research Institute, Masters Gallery Ltd., Sun Microsystems Ltd. of both Canada and the United States, Mogens F. Smed Fund of the Calgary Foundation, Smed International Ltd., Peter Bush Foundation, the Alberta Foundation for the Arts, the Canada Council, Daymen Photo Marketing Ltd., Lowe Pro U.S.A. Inc., Counter Assault, Big Rock Brewery Ltd., the Great Bear Foundation, Trail of the Great Bear Society, S. M. Blair Family Foundation, Kodak Canada Inc., Development Matters Inc., Ralph Heddin Associates Ltd., Dr. J.V. Horsely Professional Corporation, Morton H. Wynne Insurance Agency Ltd., Canada Trust Mortgage Company, Conex Management Ltd., WSG Benefit Consultants Ltd., the Lynchpin Foundation, Microsoft Corporation, Trimac Corporation, the Calgary Zoo, and a foundation that wishes to remain anonymous.

Besides the corporate donors, the following individuals were generous with their friendship, time, and money. We are grateful for assistance from Robert and Birgit Bateman, Susan Bloom, Carol A. Bowker, Tom Ellison and Jenny Broom, Roland Dixon, James Gosling, Lynne and Rick Grafton, Rod and Lois Greene, Faith Hall, Mike and Maureen Heffring, Gayadel Heimbecker, N. J. Hewitt, Dr. Margaret Horne, Pat and Rosemarie Keough, Joan A. Martin, Peter McCombs and Debbie Conrad, Russ McKinnon, Uwe Mummenhoff, John and Barbara Poole, Anne, Peter and Tim Raabe, Signa Reid, Joan and Jack Sherman, Nicki and Mogens Smed, Ellen Smith, Neil Smith, Bert Van

Bekkum, Anthony Webb, Doug Williams, Gerry Zyphers, and approximately 350 others who either contributed items or made purchases at auction fundraisers.

The support of friends has come in many forms. For nine years we have relied on dozens of people around the world to make it possible to keep going on this long, drawn-out project. We are grateful for the support of Pamela Banting, Nancy Barrios, Walter Bovich, Esther and Michael Brenner, Lance Craighead, Al Crane, Creative Travel Adventures/Ried Morrison, DLS Imaging/Jo Cookson, Wendy Dudley, Rick and Bev Durvin, Ernest Enns and Lynne Woodworth, Pat and Joe Erickson, Bristol Foster, Hal Grainer, Valerie Haig-Brown, Frank Hall, Dr. Bill Hanlon, Nancy Hauser, LeeAnne Havens, Ian Herring, Jeanne Kaufman, Pat Klinck, Helen Kovaks, Bill and Tip Leacock, Matevz Lenarcic, Nik Lopoukhine, Anne Lukey, Sid Marty, Michael Mayzel, Ian and Karen McAllister, Debbie and Tim McDonald, Tom and Elaine McFadden, Mike McIntosh, Kathleen McNally, Linda and Ed McNally, Jeannie Minchin, Pat and Baiba Morrow, Doug Murray, Sybil Palmer, Peter and Nan Poole, Matt Read, Ursula and Rick Reynolds, Andy Russell, Dick Russell, Gordon Russell, John Russell, Selena Ronnquist, Clint Scherger, Myrna Shapter, Larry and Christine Smith, Ewa Sniatycka, Reno Sommerhalder, Hopie and Bob Stevens, Tom Sullivan, David Suzuki, Dave Taylor, Jan Theunisz, Rob Walker, and David Wilkie.

Friends in Russia who have made us feel welcome and helped us to achieve our goals are Fedia Farberov, Elena Gaisina, Tatiana and Vladimir Gordienko, Allison Grant, Valery Komerov, Viktor Komerov, Anatoly Kovolenkov, Martha Madsen, Alexey Maslov and Ekaterina Lepskaya, Vladimir Mosolov, Jennya Ptichkina and her family, Igor and Irina Revenko, Irina Viter, Olga Yefimova, and my remarkable pilot friends: Evgeny, Genna, Viktor, Vladimir, and Peter.

We thank the Canadian Embassy, Moscow, former Canadian ambassador Anne Leahy, and current Canadian ambassador Rodney Irwin for assisting us in presenting our work in Moscow.

The most important outcome of Maureen's and my work in Kamchatka was to be able to tell people about it: Maureen through her art, me through my writing, and both of us through our photographs. I am indebted to several people for making the book happen. My agent, Anne McDermid, introduced me to Anne Collins, of Random House Canada, who first published *Grizzly Heart,* our book that chronicles the more detailed story of our first five years in Russia. Without Fred Stenson's writing guidance, and his marvellous organizational and editorial skills, that book would not have read nearly as well as it does.

The success of *Grizzly Heart* in Canada made it seem natural to follow up with this volume, which enables us to relate the story of our project in a different way. Anne Collins, Pam Robertson and Pamela Murray assisted us in creating this book, and Gloria Goodman in Random House's rights department deserves our thanks as well. Sue Freestone, of Hutchinson in the UK, has been a very enthusiastic supporter of this project from the moment she learned of it. In addition, we are appreciative of Nigel Lang and Dawn Saunders-Dahl for the time they have spent scanning approximately 10,000 slides and building our database.

Another way that we have kept in touch with the world about our project is via our website (found at www.cloudline.org). Thanks to Paula Oswald for taking over as our webmaster after James Gosling set up the site and skilfully managed it for three years. Thanks as well to Barb Gosling and Derek Small for their friendship and for insisting we learn about computers.